# A History of Armenian Women's Writing: 1880–1922

# A History of Armenian Women's Writing: 1880–1922

## Victoria Rowe

Cambridge Scholars Press Ltd.
London

A History of Armenian Women's Writing: 1880–1922
This book first published 2003 by


Cambridge Scholars Press

119 Station Road, Bucks, HP7 0AH, Amersham, UK
21 Desaumarez Street, Kensington Park, South Australia 5068, Australia

British Library Cataloguing in Publication Data
A catalogue record for this book is available from the British Library

ISBN 1904303234

Dedicated to the memory of
Muriel Illean Scott

# CONTENTS

# ACKNOWLEDGMENTS

I wish to acknowledge my debt to Sofia Baghumyan of Yerevan State University, a true storyteller, whose love of the Armenian language and literature was inspiring.

Thanks are due to Vartan Matiossian for advice on elements of the Armenian language, however, any idiosyncrasies are my own.

Thanks to my mother, Patricia, for our twenty-five year, ongoing conversation about women.

Special thanks to Niels Boyadjian whose belief in the value of this project was unwavering, and without whose support, this volume could never have been written.

# TRANSLITERATION OF ARMENIAN LETTERS

| | | | | | |
|---|---|---|---|---|---|
| ա | a | կ | k | ս | s |
| բ | b | հ | h | վ | v |
| գ | g | ձ | dz | տ | t |
| դ | d | ղ | gh | ր | r |
| ե | ye,e | ճ | ch | ց | ts' |
| զ | z | մ | m | ւ | v |
| է | é | յ | h, y | փ | p' |
| ը | ë | ն | n | ք | k' |
| թ | t' | շ | sh | օ | o |
| ժ | zh | ո | o | ֆ | f |
| ի | i | չ | ch' | ու | u,v |
| լ | l | պ | b | | |
| խ | kh | ջ | j | | |
| ծ | ts | ռ | rr | | |

# NOTES ON THE LITERARY TEXT AND TRANSLATION

Translations are mine unless otherwise indicated. Original dates of publication are given in my discussion and in the Appendix; dates in the note-references and the bibliography are those of the editions used. I have transliterated Armenian words according to the accompanying transliteration table; the exception to this system has been already well-established transliterations of personal and place names, i.e. Dussap instead of Tiwsab.

# INTRODUCTION

# THE AWAKENING AND ARMENIAN WOMEN

*A History of Armenian Women's Writing: 1880–1922* is a study of the formative years of the modern Armenian women's literary tradition. Although not widely known or studied, this period provides a rich and diverse legacy of women's writing in Armenian. The term women's writing, rather than women's literature, has been used in this volume to encompass the wide range of genres not usually covered by the term literature. Such writing includes novels, short stories, plays, poems, memoirs, letters, editorials and essays. The intent of this volume is to introduce the works of Armenian women writers and to offer new readings and perspectives on the (few) known women writers.

Even a cursory glance at the literary journals of the day reveals the names of many women writers, attesting to the blossoming of Armenian women's writing in the late nineteenth and early twentieth century. For example, the journal of literature and art, *Navasard*, composed by Daniel Varuzhan and H. Siruni, includes poetry and short pieces by eleven women writers, in its augural edition in 1914. These eleven women are Sibyl, Shushanik Kurghinian, Zaruhi Galémk'earian, Vittoria Aghanoor, Zabel Yesayian, Iskuhi Minasian, Haykanush Marrk, Herminé Hovian, Armenuhi Tigranian, Anayis and Mannik Berberian. Some of these women were well known in Armenian literary circles at the time, but have been largely forgotten today. The present volume focuses on six significant Armenian women writers: Srpuhi Dussap, Sibyl, Mariam Khatisian, Marie Beylerian, Shushanik Kurghinian and Zabel Yesayian, although the writings of other women writers are occasionally introduced to elucidate elements of the contemporary literary and social environment. In addition, the appendix to this volume gives biographical and literary details of fifteen women writers, including the six discussed in this volume, in order to provide a full picture of the literary environment of the period. The six aforementioned women writers have been chosen for in-depth study in this volume because each author either influenced the course of Armenian women's writing or made a contribution to the literature of the turn of the century or her writings elucidate important themes relevant to women of the day. In addition, women's writing in the eastern and western forms of the Armenian language have been included to provide a comprehensive account of developments in women's writings and to demonstrate that Western and Eastern Armenian women writers, while not displaying a uniformity of opinion and vision, nevertheless found inspiration in the activism, writings and arguments of one another and form a literary genealogy of women's writing in Armenian.

This account has two principal objectives: to situate Armenian women's writing in its sociohistorical context by paying attention to the chronological development of women's writing in the context of the *Awakening* [Zartonk] of the Armenians and secondly to present the contemporaneous intellectual debates about Armenian women's proper sphere which were so central to the content of Armenian literature of the late nineteenth and early twentieth century. These six writers were concerned with ethical questions as they related to women and Armenian society. Armenian women writers were developing a public voice in literature and part of the project of this volume is to recover that public voice. Dale Spender's suggestion in *Mothers of the Novel* that women, traditionally excluded from so many social, political and economic activities, are allowed access to the world of ideas, self-analysis and social issues through novel writing and reading, is relevant to Armenian women writers of the turn of the century. Writing novels, poetry and essays for journals enabled Armenian women writers of this period to participate in the political, intellectual and social debates of the day and as such provide a fascinating perspective into how a group of women thought and how they envisioned their own roles in particular.

Modern Armenian literature developed within the context of what was termed the *Awakening* in the nineteenth century, a period of political, social and economic upheaval, when the structures of empires were changing and reform was discussed if not implemented. Literature focused on social and political questions relevant to the Armenians living as national and religious minorities in the Ottoman and Russian Empires. Of overwhelming concern to Armenian intellectuals of this period were the themes of Armenian national identity, the origins and vitality of Armenian culture, education, the family and the role of Armenian women within this configuration.

The study of Armenian women's writing has been confined to general literary histories, which briefly discuss one or two individual women writers, without analyzing the author's works and her relationship to other Armenian women writers or male writers.[1] By writing a history of Armenian women's writing at the turn-of-the-twentieth-century I have attempted to foreground women's writing with the eventual wish that men and women's writing be bought back together in a literary history that takes into account the particularities of each literary genealogy and incorporates them into literary history on an equal footing. It is important to acknowledge Armenian women's writing developed in the context of *Awakening* and as such participated in the general trends of modern Armenian literature. This includes the development of modern, vernacular Armenian as a written language and the adoption of the novel and the short story into Armenian.

One of the main tasks of the nineteenth-century Armenian literati was the creation of a modern literary Armenian language, which could express a myriad of concepts while still being intelligible to the Armenian speaking masses. Intellectuals argued whether the vernacular Armenian language (ashkharhabar') should replace classical Armenian (grabar') as the basis of the written language. The debate over classical and vernacular Armenian was not simply a debate over language but was seen by both sides as symbolic: a debate over tradition and modernity. The church was a staunch supporter of the continued use of classical Armenian while the professionals and intellectuals, usually schooled in the new learning and sciences, supported the use of the vernacular, as a symbol of a new age, popular will and as more conducive to the interests of Armenians as a nation.[2] As a result of this linguistic debate various books of modern Armenian grammar appeared. Figures such as Krikor Odian (1834–1887) and Nahabed Rusinian (1819–1876), along with others wrote grammars of the vernacular language.[3] Armenian women too were involved in the vernacular versus classical Armenian language debate. In 1880 Dussap wrote an essay supporting the use of the vernacular as a written language. Sibyl, in collaboration with her husband, wrote a grammar of vernacular Armenian. According to a contemporary of Sibyl's, this grammar was highly popular among educated Armenians at the beginning of the twentieth century.[4] Meanwhile, Zabel Yesayian's novels, like the novels of her fellow Armenian authors, contributed to the creation of the modern western Armenian literary language by forming and using new words and styles, and by fashioning spoken language into a written form.[5] A comparison of Dussap and Sibyl's writings in the 1880s and early 1890s with later western Armenian writers, like Beylerian and Yesayian, reveals how quickly the modern, vernacular language had developed. Dussap and Sibyl's early writings, although written in the vernacular, still contain some grammatical features of classical Armenian, which are not found in the early twentieth century works of Beylerian and Yesayian and Sibyl's later writings.

In Eastern Armenia a similar controversy occurred about the use of vernacular or classical Armenian but by the 1860s the modern Eastern standard was in ascendance. The Lazarian and Nersisian schools and their printing presses facilitated the development of modern Eastern Armenian into a literary standard language.[6] Mariam Khatisian's novels, published in the 1890s, are written in an easily comprehensible and modern standard Eastern Armenian, while Shushanik Kurghinian's poetry, although written in eastern Armenian, uses many dialectical terms, perhaps for ideological reasons to mimic the speech patterns of the working class and peasantry to whom her poetry was directed.

The women writers support of the vernacular as a written language places them among the group of intellectuals concerned with modernity. Frequently these writers are simply designated as "women writers" in histories of modern Armenian literature with no attempt to integrate female writers into the intellectual debates of the time. This approach tends to obscure the ways in which women authors participated in and in some cases helped to shape the intellectual trends of the *Zartonk*.

In order to incorporate women's writing in the history of Armenian literature scholars need to re-examine periodization, genre, style and thematic concerns in ways which do not invariably position women's writing as old-fashioned, late and inferior simply because it is different from the current Armenian literary canon. For example, the periodization of romanticism and realism in Armenian literature is inevitably altered when women's writing is added to the equation. Romanticism was the first European literary school to make an appearance in nineteenth-century Armenian literature. Vahe Oshagan dates the romantic period in Armenian literature from 1855 to 1870, while James Etmekjian dates it as starting in the 1840s and continuing on after the appearance of realism in 1884.[7] Etmekjian's dates are more accurate when women's writing is integrated into the periodization. Dussap's novels, all of which were written in the romantic style, were published in 1883, 1884 and 1887. In addition, Etmekjian notes that after the advent of realism some authors wrote in a mixture of romanticism and realism.[8] This is true of Sibyl's writings, which often combine elements of romanticism and realism.

An examination of women writer's use of romanticism challenges the high valuation in the Armenian canon of realism and suggests ways some forms are conducive or not of women's imagination and creativity. The traditional Armenian literary genres were poetry and prose in the form of histories and travelogues. In the nineteenth century, novels, short stories and plays became important literary forms as European literature was translated into Armenian. In 1852 the Dedeyan brothers established a printing press in Smyrna, hired a team of translators and began to sell European novels. By 1880 approximately 200 volumes had been printed by the Dedeyan Press. Translations of Moliere, Dumas, Hugo, Sue, Racine, Goldini, Lamartine, Voltaire, Prevost, Sand and Musset were made available to western Armenian readers by the Dedeyan press.[9] As is obvious from the above titles the majority of translations were from French literature. The influence of English literature was almost negligible with only a few translations of Shakespeare and the English romantics, Lord Byron and Sir Walter Scott.[10] In Eastern Armenian literature the German and Russian traditions predominated. The European literary schools of classicism, romanticism, realism, naturalism and symbolism, were represented in Armenian poetry and prose of the nineteenth century.[11]

The literary movement known as Romanticism, made its appearance in Europe between 1770 and 1830. Romanticism has been defined in a myriad of ways attesting to its complexity and multiplicity.[12] Despite the complexity of the Romantic school certain features distinguish the Romantic text: emphasis on individualism, idealism, the primacy of the creative imagination, nature, the importance of feeling and the use of symbolic imagery.[13] Nineteenth-century Armenian authors became acquainted with European Romanticism through their reading of the European romantics. The first Western Armenian novel, *Khosrov Ev Makruhi* [Khosrov and Makruhi] (1851), was composed by Hovhanes Hisarian in the Romantic style.

Although acknowledging the thematic similarities between European and Armenian romanticism, Boghos Zekiyan notes that these movements developed under very different historical contexts and argues that unlike European romanticism which developed partly as a reaction against the rationalism of the European Enlightenment, Armenian romanticism developed alongside the national movement, speculating that it was the patriotic elements of romanticism that were appealing to Armenian writers.[14] Certainly patriotism and the betterment of society is a primary focus of Armenian romantic authors. Srpuhi Dussap's novels supporting female emancipation do so, in part, because she believed that if women were able to exercise their talents and intellect through education and employment, social conditions among Armenians would improve. An examination of Dussap's romanticism makes clear how this school could be used by Armenian women writers to add the issue of gender into Armenian literature. The French writer Jean-Jacques Rousseau (1712–1778) maintained that corruption stems from civilization, and particularly the ownership of property, which results in social inequality. His remedy was the return to nature, which he called the first social state, a communal organization based on sharing.[15] Dussap, who had probably read Rousseau, was fascinated by the notion of a more egalitarian society in the natural world. Unlike Rousseau, who emphasized women's subordination to men, Dussap hypothesized that in the natural world harmony and equality had existed between the sexes and therefore could be achieved again by following the laws of nature.

Dussap's emphasis on nature and gender equality was unique in Armenian Romanticism and caused a great deal of controversy in Armenian intellectual circles. When Dussap's first novel *Mayta* appeared in 1883 it was the first novel by an Armenian woman to address the issue of Armenian women's lack of education and decision making power. The publication of *Mayta* caused a storm of controversy. In 1885 Y. Demirdjibashian stated that no other book had caused such an uproar in Armenian literary circles as had *Mayta*. The novel was widely read, an article from 1883, said readers "consumed" *Mayta* to such an extent that it was difficult to obtain a copy of the novel.[16] The novel had supporters, including Matteos Mamurian (1830–1901), editor of *Arevlian Mamul*, who described *Mayta* as "an unique, impudent work in Armenian literature and not only in its authorship, form, style, theme and novelty, but also in its spirit and morality."[17] The novel also had many detractors, Arpiar Arpiarian (1852–1908) and Hagop Baronian (1842–1891), criticized the novel's use of romanticism.

In 1883 when *Mayta* was published realism was in ascendance in Armenian letters with supporters of realism often bitterly critical of romanticism. Dussap's pairing of gender equality in the natural world, however, provides insight into how romanticism offered some women writers the freedom to imagine alternative social realities to current social and gender constructions which were not palatable to women.

In addition, a mixture of romanticism and realism is often found in Armenian writing. Sibyl's writing consists of elements of romanticism and realism, although the author stated her preference for Romanticism in an article published in 1903 in *Masis* she wrote:

> I have always loved romantic literature, and what its authors were trying to say. I think for the majority of women, the ones I know anyway, reality is in romantic literature.[18]

In Eastern Armenia, Mariam Khatisian's novels written in the 1890s display a mixture of romantic and realist forms. I would suggest that the reason both Dussap and Sibyl preferred Romantic literature over Realism is because this style allows the authors to be inspirational and imaginative. As will be discussed in subsequent chapters, Dussap and Sibyl were concerned with identifying women's issues and offering solutions. Romanticism, with its emphasis on the imagination, allowed the authors to imagine alternatives to the current social reality. As authors who wanted to escape the restrictions of contemporary cultural conventions of femininity romanticism offered Dussap and Sibyl a literary form in which to envision a more satisfying reality for women. This is why Sibyl believed, that women in particular, preferred romanticism to realism. The author, Raffi, whose works also combine romanticism and realism, synthesised the imaginative and fantastic elements of romanticism to envision a better future for Armenians in his novel, *Khent'ë* [The Fool] (1881) with realist elements, wonderfully well.

By the 1880s, however, realism had entered the Armenian literary scene and eventually became the dominant literary school.

The advent of Armenian realism is traditionally dated from the publication of a new journal in 1884 called *Arevelk* [Orient]. The writers of *Arevelk* vehemently rejected romanticism in favour of realism. Eventually writers who supported realism came to edit both *Masis* and *Arevelk* accounting for the eventual domination of realism.[19] In 1891, yet another new journal supporting realism appeared, entitled *Hairenik* [Fatherland], it was edited by Arpiar Arpiarian, and attracted radical, young writers, like Krikor Zohrab (1861–1915) and Arshak Chobanian (1872–1954).[20]

An examination of how intellectuals defined "realism" reveals that much of the literature they admired was what is commonly termed naturalism. In an article entitled, "Our Literature," which appeared in *Masis* in 1892, Arshak Chobanian defined the job of the writer as follows:

> What do the new writers do? They walk in the streets. They look into every nook and corner. They visit the fields, the forests, and the mountains. In society, they observe everything. They note down and study events. Then they return to their rooms and write, having only their notebooks before them.[21]

Chobanian's description of the writer resembles the definition of the naturalist writer who was understood by proponents of naturalism to function as a scientist. The naturalist writer was expected to observe and record as impersonally as the scientist.[22] The influence of naturalism in the Armenian literary context is the result of the popularity of the naturalist writers, Emile Zola (1840–1902) and Guy de Maupassant (1850–1893), among western Armenian writers. The Armenian writer Krikor Zohrab, one of the influential proponents of realism and naturalism in Armenian letters, was an ardent admirer of Zola and de Maupassant and even used images and the literary structures of these two French authors in his own short stories.[23]

Women writers' participation in the realist movement had consequences for how women's issues were portrayed in literature. Zabel Yesayian, unlike Dussap and Sibyl, never wrote in the Romantic style, instead preferring realism and naturalism.

Yesayian studied literature at the Sorbonne where she was exposed to French romanticism, realism and naturalism. She stated that as a student she read George Sand, René Ghil, Maurice Marterlinck, Arthur Rimbaud, Honoré de Balzac, Gustav Flaubert, Charles Baudelaire and Henri Barbusse. She also read the American writer Edgar Allen Poe. The influence of Edgar Allen Poe in Yesayian's writing can been seen in the supernatural elements of short pieces, like *The Man* (1905). In the 1920s her son indicated that Yesayian had also read the works of Marcel Proust and Fyodor Dostoyevsky.[24]

Lilian Furst and Peter Skine argue that realism and naturalism share a vision of art as the "mimetic, objective representation of outer reality (in contrast to the imaginative, subjective transfiguration practiced by Romantics.)"[25] In Armenian women's writing the trend away from romanticism to realism and naturalism resulted in greater emphasis on depictions of "outer reality" in the works of Zabel Yesayian. Yesayian was concerned with the social oppressions, the poor, and the idea of human beings as determined by heredity and environment; themes which are hallmarks of naturalism.[26] Yesayian's experimentation with naturalism is demonstrated by her early works, *In the Waiting Room* (1903) and *When They Don't Love Anymore* (1914), in which the characters are drawn from the working class and are subject to the restrictions and temporary comforts of their environment.

The romantic emphasis on the imagination enabled Dussap, Sibyl and Mariam Khatisian to envision a social environment in which women would be emancipated from oppressive structures and unequal restrictions. In contrast, realism was the means by which Yesayian explored the impact of social oppression on women. Yesayian is generally credited with introducing the psychological analysis of characters to Armenian literature.[27] What is not acknowledged in discussions of Yesayian's psychological elements is that the vast majority of her psychological portraits depict the effects of gendered restrictions and oppressive political structures on Armenian women and society. By interrogating the use of romanticism and realism in Armenian literature we can insert women's writing into literary history in a way, which opens up the issue of gender, instead of positioning women's writing as somehow deviant and inferior.

The advent of women's writing in Armenian was widely acknowledged as new at the time, and greeted with excitement because it was viewed as a sign of societal progress. Thus from the onset women's writing was invested with symbolism. It was intertwined with modernization as women's advent into the discursive public space was seen as proof of Armenian society's level of progress. The idea of women's behaviour as determining the level of progress of a society has been discussed by Kumari Jayawardena, who states that the modern woman of the Middle East and Asia in the nineteenth century was expected to be dressed in the new style, be familiar with Western customs, to speak the appropriate European language, in order to "prove" that she was the negation of everything that was considered "backward," while still accepting that her primary role was to be in the home maintaining national culture.[28] Although women's status in society was obviously viewed in the nineteenth century as a determining factor of "civilization," in the context of European imperialism, women's writing often goes beyond the symbolic because writing, unlike basic female education, enables women to participate in and *shape* public discourse and opinion through published narratives in ways not always anticipated by the "modernization" theorists. The number of novels and journals written by women or directed at a female reading audience suggest that Armenian male and female writers saw women's roles as crucial to contemporary discussions of national identity and progress. This discussion occurring in the discursive and theoretical realm was to a certain extent implemented in institutions like the school, the charity organization and the press each of which allowed for women's participation in the fashioning of modern society.

The question of modernization, the dominance of European political and social theories, and *Awakening*, which contemporary Armenian intellectuals saw as occurring in their society had consequences for Armenian women writers, which were explored in their writings. In this volume I have sought to show how the women writers both participated in their personal lives in a redefinition of what constituted the proper role of women and to identify the contemporaneous debates about women's proper sphere as represented in their literary texts. Armenian male and female intellectuals and writers participated in the process of redefining Armenian society and women's place within society. These changes occurred in response to the advent of theories of modernity, nationalism, and contact with other modes of social organization. The greatest challenge came from contact with European ideas and education, through translation, and going to Europe for education, and foreign educational missions, like the American missions among the Armenians. The social changes occurring among Armenians, especially among Armenian women, are often dismissed as "westernization." Boghos Levon Zekiyan argues that in fact Armenians have a long history of integrating and harmonizing foreign ideas and customs in "new and often brilliant syntheses."[29] Zekiyan statement is useful when applied to the intellectual discourse of the nineteenth century. I would add that it is illuminating to examine the ideological trends of this period from the perspective of a challenging discourse. The advantage of viewing it as a challenging discourse both acknowledges the domination of western ideas due to the enormous political and economic power of the west, but at the same time enables us to see how Armenians could reshape these ideas to suit their own sense of what was necessary and beneficial to Armenian society. For a cursory reading of nineteenth-century journals reveals that even when Armenian intellectuals speak admiringly of European political structure and society, they are quick to assert the need to protect elements of Armenian culture and society deemed positive, indicating a more active process on the part of the intelligentsia than is allowed by the term "westernization," which tends to position the intellectuals as passively accepting of this foreign culture and ideology. In addition, we need a model that acknowledges the domination of imperialism but also enables us to see the strategies women employed to use the new discourses, particularly of modernity and national identity, to create at least a discursive sphere in which Armenian women's participation was legitimated.

This volume examines the theoretical constructions women writers employed to legitimate women's access to the public and national sphere in Armenian society. These include advocacy of female education, the development of the charitable association, and the women's pages of the Armenian press; as well as the re-definition of women's relations to the national sphere through the concept of the Armenian woman as mother of the nation. The latter concept has become so commonplace in Armenian discourse that it appears timeless yet as shall be discussed throughout this volume, the particulars of this notion were formulated in the nine-teenth and early twentieth centuries. One of the principal propo-nents was the author Raffi and of course the women writers dis-cussed in this volume. Put simply the notion of the Armenian woman as mother of the nation posited that women's roles as mothers had a political component by raising children to be Ar-menian and patriotic members of the nation. This notion meant that female education was justified because the Armenian woman needed to be trained in the standard Armenian language in order to teach it to her children and to learn how to care for her children in accordance with the new ideas of household management and hygiene. The concept of the mother-educator gave women the right and the responsibility to participate in discourse and devel-opments affecting the Armenian people. Intellectuals who dis-cussed the woman as mother of the nation identified it as a new concept. Raffi, Mariam Khatisian and Zabel Yessayian stated that the Armenian woman historically had been hard working and devoted to her family and the care of her children, but that this care was solely for the benefit of her individual family. What these intellectuals advocated in the nineteenth century was that the tra-ditional maternal care be extended to the nation. For this reason the national sphere was visualized as a familial space in which unrelated Armenians were reconceptualized as national mothers, fathers, brothers and sisters. This construction had many advan-tages for women's access to the teaching profession and philan-thropic work, the two careers open to Armenian at this time, be-cause women's work was legitimated on the basis of caring for the nation and its children.

Armenian women writers from 1880 to 1922 tended to be writers of fiction and social reformers. Their interest in social reform was usually actualized through education, as teachers or authors of school textbooks, and membership in charity associations, and by formulating a theoretical framework in support of women's participation in these activities in their essays and fictional texts. In the discussions of individual novels and short stories by these women writers, I have concentrated on their representation of women's roles and social issues as a way of discovering how women writers of this period analyzed the role of the Armenian woman in society, what they identified as problematic and the solutions they envisioned.

*A History of Armenian Women's Writing: 1880–1922* is a chronological account; in each chapter authors and a particular theme are discussed, starting in 1880 and ending in 1922. The date 1880 has been chosen as the beginning of this study because it was in that year that Srpuhi Dussap (1841–1901), author of the first novel by an Armenian woman, published an article on women's education, employment and social role in terms which would dominate the discussion for the next forty years. It concludes with the physical dislocations and psychological traumas of the Armenian Genocide in 1915 and the fall of the first independent Republic of Armenia in 1920. The history of Armenian literature changed after 1922, with the emergence of Armenian Diaspora literature on one hand and the creation of a Soviet Armenian literature on the other. New topics and trends appeared, which make post-1922 literature distinct from the pre-1915 tradition and outside the scope of the present volume.

Chapter one, Conditions for Women Writers explores the institutional structures facilitating the publication of women's writing, including the expansion of Armenian language education in the nineteenth century and the growth of the Armenian language press. Finally, the chapter examines the influential role of familial support for women writers.

Chapter two, Foremothers: "True Sisters" and Srpuhi Dussap discusses Armenian women writers' quest for female literary and activist models before 1880. Women writers read each other and found inspiration in the models provided by older women writers. The continuity and connections between these authors constitute an Armenian women's literary tradition. Attention has been paid to political events in the period from 1880 to 1922, which affected women's writings and consequently discussions about women's roles in society. Srpuhi Dussap's position as the matriarch of Armenian women's writing and her powerful influence on subsequent women writers is evaluated. The chapter offers new perspectives on Dussap's creation in the novel, *Siranush* (1884), of an alternative but leading vision of Armenian womanhood, and its influence on Zabel Yesayian's novel *The Last Cup* (1917).

Chapter three, Education is the Key: Mariam Khatisian and Sibyl, examines the foundation of schools for Armenian girls and boys of all social classes. Western and Eastern Armenian women writers found inspiration in the activities and writings of authors living across the border. The authors, Mariam Khatisian (1845–1914) and Sibyl (Zabel Asatur) (1868–1934) led women's charitable associations devoted to financing and providing education for Armenian girls in the Russian and Ottoman Empires. This chapter explores the advent of girls' education and women's employment in the construction of a gendered Armenian national identity in novels by these authors.

Chapter four, Women's Journals: Marie Beylerian and *Artemis*, describes the development of women's pages in Armenian journals and the publication of women's journals. The chapter focuses on one of the earliest of the journals devoted exclusively to Armenian women, the journal *Artemis* begun in 1902, and edited by the schoolteacher and activist Marie Beylerian (1880–1915). It examines Beylerian's editorials and her construction of a discourse of women's rights directed at Armenian women's particular social and political circumstances, including the notion of political exile.

Chapter five, Socialism and Revolution: The Poetry of Shushanik Kurghinian, explores the advent of socialist ideology in Transcaucasia and how this political theory was incorporated in Kurghinian's poetic representations of Armenian women and her formation of solutions to contemporary social issues.

Chapter six, Exile and Genocide: Zabel Yesayian, examines Yesayian's (1878–1942/3) exploration of migration and exile in the novel *In the Waiting Room* and offers a new reading of her novel, *My Soul in Exile* in the context of genocide and dispersion; in addition, to examining her writings on the Armenian Genocide in *The Agony of A People* (1917) and *Le rôle de la femme arménienne pendant la guerre* (1922).

The concluding chapter, Legacies and New Directions, examines the legacies of women's writing from 1880 to 1922 and briefly outlines some of the different directions Armenian women's writing took after the establishment of Armenian Diaspora communities after 1915, and the creation of the Soviet Republic of Armenia, through a discussion of the novels of Zaruhi Bahri and Louisa Aslanian, and Seza's women's journal in the Armenian Diaspora; and the poetry of Silva Kaputikian and Maro Markarian in Soviet Armenia.

At the end of the volume I have included an appendix consisting of a brief biographical and bibliographical guide of fifteen Armenian women authors' principal works, recommendations of critical studies of a particular author, and translations into English and French of her writings.

# CHAPTER ONE

# CONDITIONS FOR WOMEN WRITERS

The turn-of-the-century was a period of great creativity and opportunity for women's writing in Armenian. Women wrote short stories, novels, poems, and essays for publication in the Armenian press. There are indications that Armenian women of the princely classes did write poetry in the medieval period, for example, the poetry of Khosrovidoukht Koghnatsi, who lived in the eighth century, was discovered by scholars in the nineteenth century.[30] The name of Sahakdoukht Siunetsi, also an eighth century poet, and musician who taught classes, from behind a curtain, was known to Armenian women writers in the early twentieth century. Sibyl mentioned her in a speech promoting Armenian women's education.[31] In addition, there are medieval documents written by female scribes, attesting to women's literacy and participation in literary cultural activities.[32] Armenian women's writing of the nineteenth and twentieth centuries is distinguished by the fact writing of this period began to be written by women of various social classes and was *acknowledged* to be written by women.

In many countries' literary histories women's writing has been stigmatized as not good or of little value. Virginia Woolf speculated that many works signed anonymous were probably written by women.[33] In England the authors, Charlotte, Emily and Anne Bronte, initially published their novels under the gender-neutral names of Currer and Ellis and Acton Bell, because as Charlotte Bronte would later say, "we had a vague impression that authoresses are liable to be looked on with prejudice."[34] Russian women writers routinely used actual masculine pseudonym in order to avoid the label "woman writer."[35] The use of the author's real name suggests at least some social acceptance of the woman writer. In Armenian literature of the nineteenth-century women writers never used male pseudonyms or gender-neutral names. The reasons for this may be because in the late nineteenth and early twentieth century the Armenian intelligentsia regarded women's writing as a sign of progress and was encouraging, to a certain extent, of women's literary production. Of the six women writers discussed in detail in this volume, only two used a pseudonym and when Armenian women writers used pseudonyms, the names chosen are identifiably female. For example, Shushanik Kurghinian's early poetry was published under the name Arpenik, and Zabel Asatur used the pennames, Anahit and Miss Alice, before adopting the name, Sybil, by which she is known today. Other lesser-known writers, such as Zaruhi Galémk'earian, signed her poetry with the pseudonym, Yevterpe, and after her marriage, G. Zaruhi, while Yevp'imé Avetisian is still known primarily by her penname, Anayis. Pseudonyms appear to have been used primarily in the Armenian context to maintain the modesty of an unmarried girl, as such the use of pseudonyms by Armenian women does tell us something about contemporary attitudes to women's writing and entry into the public domain. It is marriage that tends to make the difference in the usage of pseudonyms. Sibyl, Kurghinian, Galémk'earian and Anayis began writing for publication prior to marriage and therefore used pseudonyms. After marriage, Kurghinian, used her full married name and as did Galémk'earian, who began to use a name close to her true name, "G. Zaruhi" and eventually her full name, Zaruhi Galémk'earian. Srpuhi Dussap and Mariam Khatisian never used pseudonyms but both women were already married by the time they began to publish. Zabel Yesayian did not use a pseudonym, prior to her marriage she signed her works, Zabel Hovannisian (her maiden name), but Zabel Yesayian had her father's full encouragement for her literary career, and this may have been a factor in her confidence to use her true name as an unmarried woman. Writing for publication and signing the woman's true name upsets conventions of women's modesty as it reveals the woman's name to the public and exposes her thoughts, longings and ideas to the public view. Therefore in Armenian literature, pseudonyms appear to have acted to protect the privacy and reputation of unmarried women, but did not conceal the gender of the writer. The rest of the chapter will examine the conditions, particularly the institutional structures and changing societal attitudes, which facilitated the publication of Armenian women's writing and made it acceptable in this period.

Armenian women's writing developed in the urban centres of Constantinople and Tiflis. Constantinople was the centre of the *Zartonk* [Awakening] of the Western Armenians, home to great poets, dramatists and prose writers and a myriad of literary journals. The educational opportunities and cultural contacts available to Western Armenian aspiring writers in Constantinople made that city the centre of Western Armenian intellectual and artistic life. As Rosemary Betterton has noted in the nineteenth-century European context, the modern city offered unique opportunities for aspiring artists in "education and training, as well as the possibility of economic independence and a range of cultural contacts that were less available in a provincial or rural setting."[36] Boghos Levon Zekiyan has characterized the *Zartonk* as a period of enormous social change "especially changes in habits and customs, in communication affairs and administration . . . social life and behaviour, and also in the conception of human and social values."[37] Nowhere are such changes in habits, customs and values as obvious as in Constantinople. One of the most important changes in city life relevant to the creation of a vibrant literary life was the expansion of mass education in the Armenian language. Greater educational opportunities, which were made available to male and female children of various social classes, meant that the talents and capabilities of a wide range of people were fostered, contributing to the brilliance of the city's cultural life.

Amongst the Eastern Armenians, Tiflis in the nineteenth century was the centre of the Russian administration of the Caucasus and the Armenians predominated in that city's trade, banking, bureaucracy and crafts. Eastern Armenian artists and writers were typically educated in Tiflis and a thriving press was situated there.[38] It was Constantinople, however, that produced the largest number of women writers; the majority of the women discussed in this study were born in Constantinople. Four of the authors, Dussap, Sibyl, Beylerian and Yesayian were born in Constantinople, while Khatisian was born in Tiflis and Kurhginian in Alexandropol (present-day Gyumri).

The predominance of urban born women writers in contrast to male writers of the same generation, who while largely urban, did include those born in small towns and rural areas, is due to the lack of opportunities available to rural Armenian women of the period. Unlike, their rural male counterparts, who had greater opportunities than women, to study in towns, and even occasionally received scholarships to go abroad, rural women had less access to education, beyond the primary school level, and were less likely to be sent alone, to larger cities and abroad to be educated. Zabel Yesayian, was only writer of the six discussed in this volume to receive university education, and she notes that her very liberal father hesitated over sending her to Paris alone.[39] To write well, more than basic literacy is required and to be published requires encouragement and the organizational structures to ensure this happens. This type of support was provided in the city but was not available to rural Armenian women. The inclusion of women writers in the literary scene was in large part due to the social conditions of the city, with its more "open, complex and mobile social relations," which "gave women a degree of freedom which they could not experience within the confines of a more traditional environment."[40] By the end of the nineteenth-century Armenian women in Constantinople had greater physical mobility than their rural counterparts or even their Constantinople born grandmothers had experienced. In an article written in 1903 Zabel Yesayian commented on the both the material changes and the changes in social customs and behaviour, saying that if the Armenian women of Constantinople could "change places with our grandmothers for a minute, it seems to me that we would feel different from each other, in terms of customs and progress, and we would find ourselves in an unfamiliar environment."[41] Due to the changes in mobility and attitude the Armenian women of Constantinople were involved in Armenian public life through schooling, the formation of charitable organizations, the press, salon, and theatre. Armenian women's entry into the discursive public sphere through these five institutions facilitated the development of Armenian women's writing from 1880 to 1922 and meant that women writers participated in the construction of gender and national identity and the formation of public opinion. It is clear, especially when reading their non-fiction essays, that women writers saw themselves as responsible, along with male writers and intellectuals, for defining the future direction of Armenian society and consequently in their writings the asserted the right and the duty to speak for the nation. They asserted this right and duty in their capacity as women, writers and mothers.

From its inception the Armenian educational system in the Ottoman Empire paid special attention to female education and this facilitated both women's entry into the public sphere and writing by women. In 1853, when a group of young Armenians, established a committee under the auspices of the Patriarchate to promote education among the masses, they concentrated on Armenian language teaching, the foundation of schools and the education of girls, because they believed that education would benefit the nation.[42] In 1863 with the adoption of the Armenian Constitution to govern the internal affairs of the Ottoman Armenian community, the work of the educational committee was formally established as the *National Educational Council*. It's objectives were to promote the national schools and the education of both sexes, to train and support qualified teachers, prepare textbooks and set examinations.[43] The goal of the *National Educational Council* was to educate the Armenian population in the cities and villages. A comparison of the education received by the Armenian women writers in the nineteenth century, is illustrative of the evolution of education from the privilege of the elite to a more inclusive system. The daughter of a wealthy Constantinople family, Srpuhi Dussap, received a good, private education, she was instructed in French, the natural sciences and history.[44] She is said to have mastered Greek and Italian and to have read Greek philosophy and the modern European Romantics. She studied Armenian language and literature under the tutelage of the Armenian Romantic poet Mgrdich Beshiktashlian (1828–1868).[45] Dussap's education reflects her family's social and economic status: she could afford to have private tutelage, a system of education, which traditionally had enabled members of the elite to receive education before the development of a public school system.

In addition, Dussap's primary instruction at a French school reflects the establishment of foreign missionary schools, which increased in number throughout the nineteenth century and provided some of the earliest schools for Armenian girls. Roman Catholic nuns administered a secondary school for girls in Constantinople as early as 1839, in addition to day schools for girls.[46] American Protestant sponsored education for Armenian girls increased as a result of the formation in 1868 of the Women's Board of Missions.[47]

Initially Sibyl's education followed a pattern similar to Dussap's, as she too attended a French primary school. At this school, Sibyl learned French but was not skilled in written Armenian.[48] Later Sibyl described the problems she encountered when transferring from the French school to the Armenian primary school Surp Kach' she was asked and responded as follows:

Have you read [Armenian] Christian books? No.
[Armenian] Grammar? No.
Geography? No.
History? No.[49]

As a consequence of her early French education Sibyl had to be put in a class of younger children in order to learn to read and write Armenian and to study the topics on the Armenian school's curriculum.[50]

As opportunities for education in Armenian expanded, larger numbers of children attended Armenian language schools. In 1865 there had been only nineteen female teachers in Constantinople, by 1897 there were fifty-nine female teachers and by 1908 one hundred and twenty six female teachers. Concurrently the number of female students also rose from 1400 in 1865, in contrast with 4000 male students, to even greater numbers in 1905, with 3175 male students and 2457 female students in the primary schools of the capital.[51] As is evident from the 1905 statistic the gender gap between male and female pupils was becoming more balanced. The change in the Constantinople school system is clear when comparing Zabel Yesayian's description of her formal education with her female family members' and Dussap and Sibyl's educa- tion. In contrast to her older female relatives Yesayian was liter- ate and she was educated in the Armenian schools, which prolif- erated by the 1880s when she began to attend school. In contrast to Srpuhi Dussap and Sibyl, Yesayian received her primary school education entirely in Armenian schools, first attending a private school in her neighbourhood and then the well-known *Surp Kach'* school. By 1883 when Yesayian was five years old and about to begin school, Constantinople had eleven Armenian girls' schools. In the 1880s Armenian schools faced problems of censorship as the Ottoman government routinely confiscated books on Arme- nian history and geography. In addition to the problem of censor- ship the Armenian press of the period noted many problems, es- pecially lack of standardization, in the administering of these schools.[52] Despite some difficulties, however, the schools were successful in teaching the Armenian language and instilling in a generation of students a sense of Armenian identity.[53]

The education Yesayian received at Surp Kach' consisted of instruction in history, French, Armenian, and arithmetic.[54] When Yesayian was twelve her teacher of Armenian language was the author Hrant (1859–1915), a fervent patriot, who frequently spoke of the conditions of Armenians living in the provinces and se- cretly gave the pupils books by the patriotic author Raffi (1835– 1888). Yesayian noted that reading Raffi's novels *Tavit Peke*, *Samvel* and especially *Khent'ë* [The Fool] captivated her imagi- nation, making her dream of living in provinces and helping the Armenians there.[55] In addition to stimulating Yesayian's feelings of patriotism, Hrant early recognized Yesayian's literary ability and encouraged it.[56] As a consequence, although Yesayian was not a member of a very wealthy family like Dussap, public schooling allowed her to attain an education and prepare for a literary career that would have been unavailable to her a generation earlier. Of the six women writers discussed in depth this study, Zabel Yesayian, was the only one who attended university.

In the Russian Empire, Armenian girls received a similar education to their Western Armenian counterparts as they too usually attended parochial schools for elementary school education. The *Polozhenie* (decree) of 1836 had given the Armenian Church and community in the Russian Empire the authority to operate primary schools and by the end of 1836 Armenians in the Caucasus had opened twenty-one schools.[57] At age seven, the Caucasian Armenian poet, Shushanik Kurghinian, learned to write at the local monastery where nuns taught her. After a year with the nuns, Shushanik attended the Arghutian Girls' School, where she received her elementary level education. This school had been established to educate Armenian girls in 1871. It accepted female pupils at the ages of eight or nine and had a four-year programme. It instructed girls in religion, Armenian language, Russian language, Armenian history, painting, handicrafts, mathematics, German language and penmanship. The education Kurghinian received was not enough for the mentally active girl and she is said to have supplemented her education by herself. During the reign of Tsar Alexander III (r.1881–1894) a policy of Russification was enforced and hundreds of Armenians schools were shut down.[58] Some of the consequences of this policy will be examined in chapter three in the discussion of Mariam Khatisian's novel *On a New Road* (1894), which explores the affects of this policy on female education in Tiflis. As a consequence of the policy of Russification, Shushanik Kurghinian studied at a Russian gymnasium.[59] Kurghinian desired to further her education by attending university in Moscow, but was unable to do so probably due to financial constraints.

In addition to benefiting from the nineteenth century development of female education, several of these authors were involved in the educational movement as teachers. Marie Beylerian was a professional teacher who throughout her career taught in Armenian girls' schools in Constantinople, Smyrna and Alexandria,

Egypt. Sibyl became a teacher of the Armenian language at the Yesayian and Ketronakan schools in Constantinople. In addition, she authored a series of textbooks on modern Western Armenian grammar (1877, 1899, 1902) and with her second husband Hrant Asatur, she wrote a textbook on museums, published in 1908 and 1911.

The second institution, which facilitated women's entry into the public sphere and by extension women's writing, was the charitable organization. The charitable organization allowed the active participation of Armenian women in contemporary issues and debates and stimulated women's writing. Dussap's novels are concerned with the need for female education and employment, her involvement in the *School-Loving Ladies' Association* enabled her to attempt to turn theory into reality by providing girls with education and women with employment as teachers. Indeed an examination of Dussap's *School-Loving Ladies' Association* and Sibyl's *Patriotic Armenian Women's Association*, reveals that charitable organizations granted Armenian women socially sanctioned space to engage in public work and provided the funds and necessities to open schools for girls. On a personal level women members learned how to debate, speak in public, organize meetings, write reports, raise funds and promote their objectives. Such associations also allowed women writers to meet each other. For example, Zabel Yesayian and Sibyl, who had never been friends and were actually somewhat hostile to each other, reconciled in 1909 when Zabel Yesayian joined the charitable organization, Patriotic Armenian Women's Association, founded by Sibyl.[60]

In addition to supporting education, many charitable organizations directly encouraged and supported literary endeavour by publishing literature or textbooks. For example, Mariam Khatisian's novel, *The Unfortunate Wife* (1899) was published with the assistance of the Tiflis Armenian Publishing Association [T'iflisi Hayots' Hratarakch'akan Ënkerut'iun]. Charitable associations often funded performances of plays. For example, the "Baku Armenian Theatre" company was founded through the efforts of Armenian high school students and the assistance of the "Humanitarian Society".[61]

The third institution of importance to the development of women's writing was the journal. The nineteenth-century Armenian journal was the main forum in which male and female intellectuals were able to debate and discuss new ideas concerning social and educational issues, modernization, literature and science. These institutions often complemented each other in their facilitation of women's entry into the public sphere. For example, women's writing in journals assisted women's charitable associations. In journals Armenian women expressed their views and discussed issues, including women's rights, in a public forum, read by both women and men. The press publicized the associations' activities by publishing various associations' rules and objectives, membership lists and successes. The acceptance of women's perspectives and writings in journals is attested to by the fact that by 1900 several Armenian journals included women's pages in which female contributors wrote of issues of interest to women.[62] The journals therefore gave women a public voice and a public arena for activism. The journal, unlike the salon and charitable organization, allowed women of different social classes to participate in intellectual debates. It is not surprising that Yesayian, who was from a modest household, became well known through her writings in journals; writing for a journal, unlike hosting a salon or founding a charitable organization, did not require great wealth. Lastly, the journal with its inclusion of both male and female authorial voices helped construct a discursive national space in which national brothers and sisters interacted.

The fourth institution to encourage women's writing was the salon. The Armenian salon, like its French counterpart, appears to have been organized by women.[63] The salon was one of the few spaces in the Ottoman Empire in which Armenian women and men met to discuss the pressing intellectual, political, social and literary matters of the period. Anayis wrote that her grandfather's salon was one of the first places in Constantinople where women and men could meet without being thought disreputable.[64] As the histories of Srpuhi Dussap and her mother, Nazli Vahan, demonstrate the salon enabled Armenian women to participate in contemporary intellectual debates. From an early age Srpuhi Dussap was exposed to debates concerning contemporary social questions through the activities of her mother Nazli Vahan (1814–1884), an ardent supporter of female education, and one of the founders of the St. Hripsimiants' girls' school, and a salon hostess. Srpuhi Dussap participated in the salon run by her mother where writers and intellectuals met to discuss contemporary social issues.[65] As an adult, Dussap organized and participated in the same kind of organizations her mother had founded. Following her marriage in 1869 or 1870 to the French musician Paul Dussap, she ran a salon with her husband throughout the 1870s where she hosted Armenian and French intellectuals.

In her autobiography, Zaruhi Galémk'earian, remembering the Armenian salons in Constantinople in the 1890s, wrote that they facilitated women's writing because new ideas and horizons were opened to women at these gatherings.[66] At the salons national issues, literary and artistic subjects were discussed and people exchanged ideas and read poetry.[67] Galémk'earian notes that the salons also brought together people of different ages and educational backgrounds who were united by a love of art and literature and who might not have meet otherwise.[68] This infusion of ideas and mixing of various groups of people, assisted in the creation of a vibrant literary and cultural environment. It also affirmed the right of women to speak publicly on important social, national and literary issues.

The importance of the salon in fostering women's activities and writing is attested to by Zabel Yesayian when she stated that it was at Mrs. Matakian's salon that she first made contact with the Armenian intellectuals, including Arshak Chobanian, editor of the journal *Tsaghik* [Flower] where Yesayian's early fiction and non-fiction articles were published.

The fifth institution to assist women's entry into the public sphere and the arts was the theatre. As the authors of *Modern Armenian Drama* suggest drama is an urban art, dependent on the institution of a theatre, professional actors and a sophisticated audience, conditions that were met in nineteenth century Constantinople and Tiflis.[69] Galémk'earian viewed the Armenian theatre in Constantinople as encouraging Armenian cultural development and women's participation in cultural activities.[70] Armenian women began to act on stage as early as 1856, with the performance of the amateur actress, Fenni; prior to Fenni's debut young men had played women's roles. The first professional Armenian actress was Arousiak Papazian (1841-1907), a native of Constantinople who made her debut on stage in 1861. After her marriage at the height of her popularity, Papazian's husband, refused to allow his wife to act or even attend the theatre, much to her grief.[71] The story of Papazian's prematurely shortened career, hints at the difficulties early actresses faced upon entry into the acting profession. Gradually, Armenian actresses appear to have become socially accepted. Armenian theatre groups, in addition to creating a modern Armenian theatre, are also credited with developing Turkish language theatre as well.[72] Armenian artists trained at the first professional Western Armenian theatre "Arevelian Tatron" formed the Gedikpasha theatre under Hagop Vardovian (1840–1898), known in Turkish sources as Güllü Agop, who in 1868 was given a ten-year monopoly on Turkish performances.[73] Armenian women were not limited to merely acting in the theatre as women wrote plays for the theatre too, although none of the women writers in this period achieved fame as a playwright. Nevertheless Sibyl, Zabel Yesayian and Shushanik Kurghinian wrote plays for the Armenian theatre. Sibyl's plays, *Magnet* (1909) and *The Daughter-in-Law* (1918), were performed; the former was performed on stage as part of a fundraising programme for the charitable association, *Patriotic Armenian Women's Association* [Azganvér Hayuhyats' Ënkerut'iun]. Zabel Yesayian apparently desired to write plays but in the 1930s she acknowledged that she had not yet achieved what she would like in the realm of the theatre.[74]Kurghinian's plays were never performed.

The importance of these five institutions to the development of women's writing is demonstrated by the fact that these institutions are found in much of women's fiction writing. Armenian women writers of this period, as shall be discussed in chapters three and four, portray the school, the theatre and female actresses, the literary salon, the journal and the charitable organization in their novels, in such a way as highlights these institutions facilitation of the heroine's and her author's entry into new societal roles.

Memoirs, letters and autobiographical writing provide clues as to why these women wrote, and the kinds of encouragement or discouragement they received from family, society and fellow writers. Most of these writers displayed mental quick wittedness from childhood. The young Srpuhi Dussap had attracted attention before she began writing for her facility in languages, in addition to French; she is reputed to have known Greek and Italian, and was well known for her musical talent.[75] Sibyl could recite passages of French poetry at the age of seven.[76] Yesayian, who had learned to read before attending school, was given extracurricular lessons in grabar (classical Armenian) by her teacher, before the age of ten, when she demonstrated signs of being desirous of extra learning.[77]

Despite class and educational differences all the women writers had read extensively. By the age of twelve, Dussap is said to have read Plutrarch's *Lives of Great Men*, as an adult she was well read in the classics, including Plato, Aristotle, Homer, Sophocles, Euripides, Virgil, and Dante, as well as modern Europeans such as Milton, Schiller, Byron, Lamartine and Hugo.[78] In 1863 she began studying with the Armenian Romantic poet, Mgrdich' Beshiktashlian, from whom she studied classical and modern Armenian literature. These writers usually began composing from an early age; Kurghinian began writing poetry at age twelve, as a child Yesayian read widely, made up stories and talked of becoming a writer.[79]

Many of the future writers received encouragement of their literary talents from influential teachers. Yesayian's literary talent was recognized and encouraged by her Armenian language teacher, Hrant.[80] Likewise, it is evident from a letter dated 1895, that Shushanik Kurghinian received encouragement from one of her teachers to continue writing. The teacher advised her to look to the indigenous traditions of the Armenians for literary inspiration, which she did as she continued the Armenian poetic tradition.[81]

Of great importance to the development of a successful woman writer was the attitude of her family towards women's writing. Charlotte Rosenthal's discussion of turn-of-the-century Russian women writers notes that Russian women writers of the period were frequently married to men who were in the cultural field.[82] This is fairly common among Armenian authors too. Dussap and Yesayian's husbands were a musician and a painter respectively, while Sibyl's first husband was a lawyer, and her second, an author and editor. Four of the writers, Dussap, Sibyl, Yesayian and Kurghinian were mothers. Due to the lack of biographical information about Mariam Khatisian and Marie Beylerian, it is not known if these women had children. The women writers' status as wives and mothers appears to have been a reassuring model for aspiring women writers. Galémk'earian later stated that as a young woman she visited Sibyl's house and was impressed to see that a woman could be a good housewife and mother, while pursuing a literary career and charitable work. Galémk'earian's statement makes sense when placed in the context of late nineteenth-century society in which young women writers, such as Galémk'earian and Anayis, were told not to write and concentrate on being good mothers.[83]

The majority of successful women writers of this period attest to their family's positive attitude towards women's creative expression. The less successful writers, such as Zaruhi Galémk'earian and Anayis, discuss being discouraged by family to write and told to concentrate on marriage and motherhood and perhaps this discouragement was a factor in their lack of success in writing. In the preface to her first novel, *Mayta*, Srpuhi Dussap acknowledged the influence of her mother's progressive ideas on her intellectual development: "I was inspired by my mother's progressive ideas which stood out like a beacon in the conservative Armenian world. There is nothing as strong as a mother's encouragement." Dussap continued by acknowledging her husband's support of her advocacy of women's emancipation and her writing.[84]

Zabel Yesayian also attested to the importance of familial support in encouraging her literary career. In Yesayian's autobiography, *Gardens of Silihtar*, learning is portrayed as part of the domain of men as writing and reading are activities associated with male relatives. Yesayian states that her father and his male relatives had attended secondary schools.[85] Her own experience of learning to read is connected to her relationship with her father:

> While the water for tea boiled my father opened the daily newspaper *Arevelk* and read. I sat on his lap covered by his fur robe. In that warm nest I passed many happy hours as my eyes followed the letters on the paper. Sometimes I would put a finger on a letter and ask my father what it was and he would interrupt his reading to answer. Often my mother or one of my aunts would scold me: 'Leave your father alone. Don't bother him.' But my father would signal with his hand that he was fine and would hug me tighter, answering my questions with great patience. Suddenly one day I was reading! At first my father could not believe I was truly reading. He pointed out letters on various pages of the journal and in a stammering voice I read them aloud.[86]

Yesayian always attributed her father's continuing and steadfast support as instrumental in her successful pursuit of a literary career. Her female relatives also provide Yesayian with talents, which assisted in her development as a writer. It is they who are described as the source of the stories Yesayian listened to enthralled.[87] Her grandmother, although illiterate, is said to have spoken "pure Armenian" thereby endowing Yesayian with a rich and varied vocabulary.[88] Oral storytelling had a long history among Armenians, Movses Khorenatsi had identified two sorts, the zruyts (stories) and the araspel (legends).[89] The epic, David of Sassoun, had been passed down through oral tales, until it was written down in the nineteenth century. It is through this long tradition of oral story telling that Yesayian's female relatives also assisted in her development as a writer.

In the case of Sibyl, although we are not told anything about her family's reaction to her writing, it is clear that they supported her founding of the *Patriotic Armenian Women's Association*, since it was her paternal aunt who went to the Ottoman authorities in order to receive permission to establish the organization, this demonstrates that her family supported Sibyl in playing the active, public role, which would eventually provide material for her writing.[90]

Finally, a significant factor in the creation of a woman writer is self-confidence. In order to become a successful writer, a woman had to believe that she had the talent and the right to write and be published. As Zabel Yesayian said about her desire to overcome obstacles facing her as a women:

> It is true that I am often forced to struggle against prejudices, but that struggle is spontaneous, strong and always victorious because I have never retreated from my position.[91]

Women's writing in Armenian is intimately connected to debates about women's place in modern society. Each of the six women writers discussed in this volume participated in the debates about women's roles in the public sphere, her position as mother-educator, and particularly women's role in Armenian national identity. The following chapters will discuss themes found in each author's literary texts in order to recover the turn of the century discussions of Armenian women's role in society and the nation.

# Chapter Two

# Foremothers, "True Sisters" and Srpuhi Dussap

When nineteenth-century and early twentieth-century Armenian women sat down with pen in hand to write they looked to female models to guide them in determining what were suitable subjects for women writers. The public expression of a woman's thoughts, feelings, fantasies and desires, revealed in her published writings, threatened to compromise accepted notions of women's femininity and modesty, which was largely based on silence and enclosure in the home and family. This was true of Armenian and European women writers of the nineteenth and twentieth centuries. Virginia Woolf succinctly articulated the problem when she stated that a young woman letting her imagination freely range stops when she thinks of the body, and of passion, "Men, her reason told her, would be shocked. The consciousness of what men will say of a woman who speaks the truth about her passions had roused her from her artist's state of unconsciousness. She could write no more."[92] In Armenian circles too writing by women carried the taint of immorality. This is evident in Sibyl's play *The Daughter-in-Law*, in which the writing of novels by the heroine is construed by her mother-in-law to indicate that her daughter-in-law will try to act out her written imaginings in extramarital affairs.[93] To write was a risqué act, which upset definitions of femininity as silent virtue, therefore in order to overcome injunctions of silence, women looked for examples of other women who had entered public space.

Armenian women writers looked to history for examples of active, patriotic Armenian women in order to provide models for women's advent into new public roles in the fields of education, social work, political activity, and writing. This period's writing by women has sometimes been accused of being westernized, however, it should more accurately be described as hybrid. As Zekiyan argues in a discussion about modern Armenian culture, what he terms "syntheses," has a long history among Armenians: "Armenians did not copy their models, rather they integrated and harmonized them in new and often brilliant syntheses."[94] Armenian women writers, like their male counterparts, looked to European writing, by men usually, and to a lesser extent to women writers, as a model of how to write in the new form of the novel. Numerous translations and publications of European books by Armenian presses attest to the popularity of European fiction as a literary model.[95] What is usually overlooked in discussions on the question of influences on Armenian women writers is a genealogy of Armenian women's history and writing. Armenian women had two empowering genealogies to draw upon, a genealogy of women's social and political activism and a genealogy of writing.

A genealogy of Armenian women's activism was a pressing need as Armenian women authors looked for models of how to combine writing and social and political activism. Every notable Armenian woman writer from 1880 to 1922 sought to combine writing with patriotic activity designed to alleviate the social and economic hardships of the Armenians of the Russian and Ottoman Empires. Each of the Armenian women writers discussed in this study, was involved in social and political activism in some form, by leading national charitable organizations, opening schools for Armenian children, teaching, caring for orphaned children and/ or as a member of a political party.

The reprinting of the historian Eghishe's *History of Vardan and the Armenian War* facilitated the task of finding a genealogy of Armenian women's activism. In general, nineteenth-century writers saw parallels in the story of Vardan Mamikonian and the Armenian people's struggle against the powerful Persian Empire in 451 A.D. and in their own situation as a conquered people living in the Ottoman Empire. The allure of the history of Vardan Mamikonian is demonstrated by the poems and dramas written about him in the nineteenth century, including L. Alishan's (1820–1901) poem, *Nightingale of Avarayr*, and Raphael Patkanian's (1830–1892) *The Death of the Valiant Vardan Mamikonian*.[96] The history of Vardan Mamikonian was also included in school textbooks, contributing to its popularity.[97]

The story of the Armenian revolt in 450/1 A.D. is described in two Armenian sources, the histories of Eghishe and Ghazar Parpetsi. Eghishe's account became the most popular with Armenian women writers, because as Robert Thomson notes, while both authors comment on the bravery shown by Armenian women of the time, Eghishe spends several pages extolling the virtues of Armenian women.[98] The inclusion of Armenian women's bravery and heroism in Eghishe's portrayal of the Armenian resistance became a powerful symbol of the positive role Armenian women could play in the public and patriotic realms.

In a speech delivered in 1909 to raise funds for the education of orphaned children, writer and social activist, Sibyl evoked the women of Vardan Mamikonian's time as an inspiration for Armenians in the aftermath of the Cilician massacres, as well as a justification for concentrating on educating orphans rather than simply providing humanitarian aid. She stated:

> Centuries ago, in the time of Vardan's troubles, the wives of martyred princes didn't lounge about on cushions, crying, in their fine palaces. In spite of all of their troubles and sorrows, they lavished great care [on children] and the children weren't allowed to remain uneducated. Particularly remembered is the story of Hmaiak Mamikonian's wife, who with mourning veil upon her head, personally went knocking on the doors of the hovels of the poor and persuaded the illiterate parents to send their children to school and became the head of education activity.[99]

The historical accuracy of Sibyl's speech is not as important as her use of the story as a method of presenting Armenian women's activities as having an Armenian historical precedent and

not based on foreign practice. Sibyl and Yesayian call contemporary Armenian women the "true sisters" of the women of Vardan
Mamikonian's time and employ the imagery of those fifth century women in times of national crisis to applaud and stimulate
women's resistance. The writer Zabel Yesayian would later employ the imagery of the Vardan Mamikonian women to praise
Armenian women's resistance to the deportations of the Armenian Genocide of 1915.[100] Indeed there are striking similarities
between Yesayian's description of Armenian women's resistance
to deportation and their suffering and Eghishe's portrayal of fifth
century Armenian women's stoicism in the face of hardship. The
tracing of descent from fifth century Armenian women functioned
as a source of empowerment for Armenian women writers, as it
provided legitimate, indigenous models of Armenian practice, in
contrast to many of the customs of the immediate past which were
viewed as having been corrupted by Turkish, Islamic practice.[101]

Armenian women writers of the early twentieth century continued to look for models of women's activism and found it in the
contemporary period in the person of Srpuhi Dussap (1841–1901).
Largely forgotten today or dismissed as a "romantic" writer, Srpuhi
Dussap was the most prominent Armenian women writer of the
nineteenth century. She was a powerful influence on subsequent
Armenian women writers and her theories about women, modern
society and the public sphere dominated the debate on Armenian
women's role in society until 1922.

Srpuhi Dussap was born in 1841 in Orta Kuegh on the European shore of Constantinople, to a wealthy Armenian family. When
she was a year old her father died and Dussap was raised by her
mother, Nazli Vahan (1814–1884), who was an ardent supporter
of female education, founding the St. Hripsimiants girls' school
in 1859 and the *Charitable Women's Association* [Aghkatakhnam
Tiknants Ënkerutiun] in 1864. Nazli Vahan was also a patron of
the Galfaian orphanage and the Narekian and Hamazgiats' schools.
Nazli Vahan ensured that her daughter was well educated and
from an early age Srpuhi Dussap was exposed to debates concerning contemporary social questions through the activities of
her mother. Srpuhi Dussap was a member of the *Charitable*

*Women's Association* founded by Nazli Vahan. She may also have participated in the salon run by her mother where writers and intellectuals met to discuss contemporary social issues.[102] As an adult, Dussap organized and participated in the same kind of organizations her mother had founded. Following her marriage in 1869 or 1870 to the French musician, Paul Dussap, Srpuhi ran a salon with her husband throughout the 1870s where she entertained Armenian and French intellectuals who discussed literary and social matters. In the 1870s Dussap had two children, Dorine and Edgar, whose education she actively supervised. In 1879 she became an ardent member and eventually head of the *School Lovers Armenian Women's Association* [Dbrots'aser Hayuhyats' Ënkerutiun], which was devoted to the training of Armenian women as teachers for Armenian girls' schools outside of Constantinople.[103]

After the appearance of her final novel, *Araksia or The Governess* (1887), Dussap continued her activities in benevolent organizations, particularly those devoted to education. In 1889 she travelled to Paris with her daughter Dorine for medical treatment. Upon their return to Constantinople in 1891 Dorine died at 18 years old. Following her daughter's death Dussap published no new works although she did continue to keep a journal and hold literary salons at her house in Constantinople until her death on January 16, 1901.

Srpuhi Dussap's bold introduction of the question of women's emancipation into Armenian literature began in 1880 with the publication of three articles: *Women's Education* (1880), *The Principle of Women's Employment* (1881) and *A Few Words About Women's Unemployment* (1881). These articles reveal Dussap's concern with female education, and employment and the potential for creating social change; these themes were an important part of her fictional oeuvre and would dominate the debate about Armenian women's role for the next forty years if not beyond.[104] In the 1883 publication of her first novel, *Mayta*, Dussap began to systematically portray the psychological, social and economic affects of women's economic dependence on men and to theorize solutions. *Mayta* gained immediate attention among the Armenian intelligentsia as the first novel written by an Armenian woman and because of its daring, feminist content. *Mayta* was lauded by some critics and condemned by others, the most notable of the latter being the author, Krikor Zohrab (1861–1915).[105] In *Mayta* Srpuhi Dussap challenged the dominant concept of "natural" male superiority and argued that women needed to emancipate themselves from their inferior social position through society's recognition of women's intellectual capacity and by providing access to education and employment. She refined her theories of women's emancipation in two subsequent novels, *Siranush* (1884) and *Araksia or The Governess* (1887).

The world of Dussap's novels was the urban world of Constantinople. The novels reflect an urban, middle-to-upper class sensibility and are representative of the fact that in the Western Armenian context the earliest discussions of the position of women in Armenian society took place among the female and male intellectuals of Constantinople and these literary texts reflect the social and educational status of the authors and audiences. Literacy among Armenians of this period tended to be low in urban and rural areas. In 1851 an article in the journal *Banaser* complained that ninety percent of the Armenian population was illiterate and only two percent of the population was in school in Constantinople.[106] Although the numbers of literate people was greater by the 1880s and 1900s the audience for these literary works was still restricted to a small elite in the capital and larger towns.

There was some contemporary criticism of the urban character of the novels of Dussap, for example A. Arpiarian, writer and literary critic, stated in a critical allusion to Dussap's urban novels: "The Armenian woman is on Armenian soil, whoever wants to defend her cause must first study her life by living with her."[107] The irony of a man telling an Armenian woman that she knows nothing of Armenian women is conspicuous, however, Arpiarian's criticism reflects a prominent vision among the intelligentsia that the true locus of Armenian identity lay in the peasantry living in Armenia. By the nineteenth century, however, Constantinople was the economic, political and cultural centre of the Western Armenian community with a well-established Armenian population.[108] Although never denying the importance of the Armenian population in Armenia, many female and male authors believed that the issues facing urban Armenian women had relevance in terms of the future structure of Armenian society. Despite the novels' restricted readership, they were relevant to young urban Armenian women of the 1880s and 1890s. In her autobiography Yesayian noted that in her youth, many of her female friends lamented the fact that they had little freedom; they "wanted to be educated, to participate in ordinary life, go out with male friends, meet, travel, etc." They regarded Yesayian as fortunate because she had an "enlightened father." Her friends did not know how to change their circumstances and often became depressed and together they "began to read the works of Mme. Dussap and in the feminist author's works we tried to find a solution to our disturbing questions."[109] Yesayian's description illustrates that the problems and issues outlined in Dussap's novel were viewed by contemporary young women to have relevance in their own personal lives. Many of the issues women authors discussed, for example arranged marriage, parental authority, and lack of economic opportunity concerned Armenian women of all classes and localities. The urban and upper-class milieu of Dussap's works and life seem to have made Dussap's feminist theory possible. Commenting upon Srpuhi Dussap's influence many years later, Zaruhi Galémk'earian, wrote that Dussap had the "liveliest mind of all the women writers" but her ideas on women were considered so radical that they could only have been expressed by a woman of Dussap's wealth and social status. Galémk'earian stated that a woman of a middle class background would have been severely condemned by society if she had attempted to write the type of novels Dussap produced.[110]

Srpuhi Dussap's immediate legacy to Armenian literature was her introduction of a powerful female voice into the exclusively male Armenian literary and intellectual establishment of Constantinople. She insured that women's issues would not be ignored or debated without women's participation in the debates. The acceptance of women's issues as a relevant topic is attested by the fact that by 1900, twenty years after Dussap's first article, several

Armenian journals, for example *Tsaghik* and *Arakatz*, included women's pages in which female contributors wrote of issues affecting women. The development of the Armenian women's press is addressed in greater detail in chapter four.

Dussap's most valuable legacy was the affect she had upon young Armenian women who aspired to write. Following her meeting with Dussap in 1899, Sibyl wrote that as a young woman she had dreamed of becoming another Srpuhi Dussap. In particular she admired: "her renown, intelligence, learning and literary career [which] filled my imagination . . ."[111]

Zabel Yesayian attested to Dussap's influence on her in a scene in her autobiography in which the young Zabel and Arshakuhi Teodik[112] visited Dussap, seeking and receiving her approval for embarking upon a literary career:

> When Madame Dussap heard that I had decided on a literary career, she warned me that for a woman to be a writer there were more thorns than laurels on that road. Our communities, she added, regarded it as insufferable that a woman should enter the public sphere and take her place there. In order to overcome that obstacle, one ought to rise far above mediocrity. "A man may be a mediocre writer, but not a woman," she said. Madame Dussap made a deep impression on us. On our way home, we talked enthusiastically, and Arshakuhi confided that she too wanted to be a writer. We both agreed that in order to rise above mediocrity, we would continue our higher education in Europe.[113]

Dussap's position as a literary foremother, is evident not only in her activities on behalf of women's education and her example as an erudite, witty writer, but in her theories of Armenian women and modern society which, influenced the writings of generations of women writers. The teacher and editor of the journal, *Artemis*, Marie Beylerian, stated: "The loss of Mrs. Srpuhi Dussap to Armenian letters and especially for the issue of women's rights is an irreplaceable one."[114] The accounts of Dussap's positive legacy by Sibyl, Zabel Yesayian and Marie Beylerian, attest to the validity of Joanna Russ' argument that women benefit from having female literary models:

Models as guides to action and as indications of possibility are important to all artists–indeed to all people–but to aspiring women artists they are doubly valuable. In the face of continual and massive discouragement, women need models not only to see what ways the literary imagination has been at work on being female, but also as assurances that they can produce art without inevitably being second rate or running mad or doing without love.[115]

The remainder of the chapter will examine Dussap's exploration of "being female" and particularly her theories of women's emancipation, romantic love and the influence of modernity. In addition, the influence of her theories on subsequent women writers is assessed. An examination of central themes, characters and social theories in these novels elucidates the principal concepts of women's rights, roles and relationship to modern identity in Armenian women's writing and how these ideas developed and altered over time.

Problematizing the relationship of modernity to Armenian society's construction of gender and class was the central concern of Srpuhi Dussap's novels. Her three novels pose the questions, "what is modernity and what is its relationship to tradition? How should modern women and men behave?" The answers to these questions, which Dussap provided in the novels, were meant to guide Armenian society in the process of creating a modern, but at the same time, just, society.

The question of modernity runs not only throughout Dussap's novels, but much of Armenian literature of this period. As Lila Abu-Lughod notes in her study of women in the Middle East, modernity was the dominant discourse of the nineteenth and early twentieth centuries, because the "rhetoric of reformers and literate women themselves was full of references to "the new"–with calls for "women's awakening" and "the new woman" reverberating through the magazines, books, and speeches of the era."[116] As the very name of this period, *Zartonk*, [Awakening] in Armenian suggests, Armenian intellectuals too were deeply influenced by the notion of newness and the idea of waking up after a long slumber. This "awakening" included Armenian society in general, and positioned women as central to this process. In 1859 Stepan Voskan wrote that women should be more than bedfellows or wives since patriotism towards the Armenian nation "beats in their hearts." He argued that patriotism or lack thereof in women was of the uttermost importance since women have the ability to wield great influence:

> The homeland is in the heart of women, and when that heart is found to be empty (as is the case in many Armenian ladies . . . ) it is impossible for patriotism, true patriotism to blossom, and for the multitude to stand firm under freedom's banner. Women, with their soft hands are preparing that firm independence, which is the mark of a human being and with these moral weapons they shatter the roots of bondage. Finally in many instances faith is spread to many places and in many nations by women's influence.[117]

Abu-Lughod suggests that what is confusing about what she terms, the "remaking of women" in the nineteenth century and first half of the twentieth century, is the advocacy of both women's participation in the public world and at the same time the emphasis on the enormous importance and responsibility of women's domestic role.[118] In Armenian intellectual discourses of this period, Armenian women were positioned in a similar dichotomy. Armenian women entered new public realms, as members of charitable organizations, as journalists, and as schoolteachers, at the same time as their domestic roles were accorded greater political significance. Armenian women were imagined as the teachers and protectors of Armenian culture within the framework of the family. A statement made by the author and advocate of female education, Raffi (1835–1888), makes this clear when he wrote in response to a young Armenian peasant girl's statement that she did not need to know how to read:

> No, I will take this aberration out of your innocent head, poor girl; you need to read more than the cleric and the priest; you have to educate a new generation, you have to level the path of our

brilliant future. You have to learn to read, then you will no longer
be poor and wretched, and your children will pass their days happy
and in comfort.[119]

Raffi's notion, shared by many advocates of female education,
envisions the Armenian woman as, what I call the mother-educator,
of the "new" generation. The task of mothering was no longer
simply the physical act of bearing of children, nor was the bring-
ing up of children, simply a private matter confined to family,
women's role as mother became linked to nation-building. Raffi
was perhaps the single most influential male writer on this period's reconceptualization of women's roles. Most Western and
Eastern Armenian women writers make reference to reading
Raffi's novels and essays. In an essay published in 1879, Raffi
discussed the Armenian woman, dividing his discussion of women
into various categories: the rural woman and the urban artisanal
class woman. Raffi's approach to women and their different lifestyles, as well as his acknowledgment of various hardships women
experience, was one of the earliest studies of contemporary Armenian women's lives and issues. The 1879 essay entitled *Armenian Woman* made the study of the contemporary Armenian
women a legitimate field of study and his novels; especially his
vision of Armenian society in the late twenty-first century in *The
Fool* (1881) offers a positive model of women's abilities and potential social role. In the vision at the end of *The Fool* Raffi portrays an ideal world for the Armenian population in which they
are economically productive and largely self-sufficient, practicing
efficient and communal farming techniques. The inhabitants in
this vision have good schools, a hospital, and a press office and
representative government. In the protagonist's comparison of the
past with this "future" he notes that of all the negative practices
the population has shed, they have retained one positive element
from the past and that is the usage of the modern Armenian language. In this vision of the ideal future, Raffi was careful to include the Armenian woman. The descriptions of the schools portray the village children, both male and female attending a coedu-
cational school, while in his description of higher level educa-

tion-both at the school of rural economics, the high school, and the university, the author deliberately included female pupils. It is the contrast of the character of Lala, who in the year 1877 had to be dressed as a boy to avoid abduction and rape, and died tragically after the destruction of the village, that Raffi's vision of Armenian women's role is most striking. In the envisioned future, Lala is free to be a woman; she greets the male visitor without fear, and talks naturally. Lala has had an article she wrote published in a newspaper; she is graduating from high school, and is planning to attend university where she will study medicine.[120] It was due to Raffi's construction of the contemporary woman as a legitimate figure of study and his positive assessment of her social and political potential that accounts for his enormous influence on women writers. The aforementioned quote by Raffi makes explicit Abu-Lughod's contention that nationalism is not simply a political movement but "a cultural or discursive project in which ideals of womanhood and notions of the modern were key elements"[121]since for Raffi the mother-educator is the key figure in forging a "brilliant future" for the nation. Raffi's view, shared by many Armenian intellectuals, firmly allied Armenian women's domestic role to national development.

Inherent in discussions of the New Woman is the colonial discourse of the inferior position of women in the "Orient," contrasted with the western woman, who was constructed as occupying a "superior" position. Even when this designation was rejected in the Middle East, the issue of gender still functioned as key marker of difference between Middle Eastern and European society, in Joanna de Groot's words: "thus bonding gender to ethnic/national characteristics or identities in their cultural discourse."[122] This same process is evident in Armenian discussions of women. When reform-minded intellectuals, such as Stepan Voskan, Matteos Mamurian and Krikor Chilirigirian, compared the status of Armenian and European women, they talked of Armenian women as having a unique national identity and like the women writers, saw the brave women of Vardan Mamikonian's period as an indigenous Armenian model, while at the same time advocating greater rights for Armenian women.

Sibyl went even farther in bonding gender to ethnic/national identity when she argued in a speech in 1909 as follows:

> Do you see the Armenian woman as worthy only of pity? She isn't. She is going to earn her bread through her own efforts. The Armenian woman is as intelligent and hardworking as the American woman, the Englishwoman, the Frenchwoman. In fact she is more modest, courageous and especially stronger than they are, but she must be educated as they are educated.[123]

In this speech Sibyl constructs Armenian women as having traits of "modesty, courage and strength" which are seen as both national, all Armenian women have them, according to Sibyl, and gendered as they are attributed to women. Her emphasis on Armenian women's superiority to Western women in terms of modesty was a fairly standard concept among the Christian and Muslim intelligentsia of the Middle East and in this text it serves to differentiate Armenian women from Western women, while asserting special and positive national qualities for Armenian women. At the same time, however, she introduces the contentious issue of Armenian women's employment, which as we shall see, was not wholly endorsed by the Armenian intelligentsia and therefore hints that the attribution of unique gender, national characteristics to women could sometimes be mobilized to overcome conventional gender restrictions.

Understanding womanhood and the modern as key elements in the development of Armenian nationalism, enables us to situate Armenian women's writing and the authors themselves as central to the process of Armenian national development and creators of forms of national cultural identity. Armenian women who wrote about contemporary Armenian society, about the new roles for Armenian women in marriage and in education, about relations between Armenian women and men, were not simply responding to larger cultural developments or talking about purely personal issues, they were active theorists of the role of Armenian women in national development and in the new world that appeared to be developing. This is not to say that women were wholly free of the constraints that limited women's power on the basis of arguments of "women's nature." A reading of Armenian women's novels and short stories, however, reveals that they sought to shape their roles to a greater degree than has previously been acknowledged.

Dussap's novel *Mayta* began to address women's role in modern society, but it is in her second novel *Siranush* that Dussap constructed a more fully developed theory and argument of modernity. In *Siranush* Dussap explored the issue of modernity and gender through the prism of romantic love.

Romantic love, with its suggestion of (female) sexuality, was a taboo topic in Armenian society. In women's novels romantic love and marriage are central, the fact that women writers chose to discuss and defend such a risqué subject indicates that they were aware of creating something new and rejecting traditional roles for women.

In part the centrality of marriage is due to the sociological fact that the majority of Armenian women in this period expected to marry, and marry through arrangement. Memoirs by Armenian women born at the end of the nineteenth century confirm that a woman was expected to accept the husband chosen by her parents.[124] The traditional arranged marriage among Armenians was based on a conceptualization of marriage as an alliance between families, rather than an alliance between individuals.[125] Although this did not always preclude individual preference, the family made the final decision.[126] The fact that such marriages were commonly against the preferences of the bride is shown by folk songs, such as the following one sung by a reluctant bride and her mother:

> *Mother*: Bride, don't cry, don't cry, your eyes will hurt. May he who married you so young, may his household topple.
> *Girl*: Why should I not cry, Mother? You fooled me. You didn't give me to the one I loved; you have made my heart yearn.
> *Mother*: He is young and poor; he has no house, no position, nothing.
> *Girl*: His condition is good; what should I do with a house? If it were only a nest, if you had given me to my loved one, I would have been satisfied with my loved one.[127]

Urban centres were not so very different from rural areas in the custom of arranging marriage. Yesayian's description of attitudes to love matches during the 1880s and 1890s enables us to see how radical the rejection of arranged marriage in the novel *Siranush*, published in 1884, appeared to a reading audience and explains the fervour caused by Dussap's novels. Writing of the social mores of her family and neighbours in the Constantinople of the 1880s and 1890s, Yesayian reveals:

> These were the customs of the capital Constantinople. Young people who perhaps spoke to each other, exchanged looks and with feelings of mutual love wanted to marry, but did not have wealth or sufficient means, were regarded as shameful. In my teenage years I heard of families who "had married for love" spoken of with disapproval.[128]

In novels, the concept of romantic love enabled women writers to offer alternatives to the traditional custom of arranged marriage although not to the institution of marriage. In Armenian women's writing marriage was considered normative and desirable. What was new in this discourse was that the writers articulated a vision of equality and companionship, commonly called companionate marriage, between the partners based on romantic love, which they hoped would enable women to attain happiness and a sense of independent self in order to benefit women and society.

Romantic love and companionate marriage, as understood by Srpuhi Dussap and subsequent authors, was a political ideology, which enabled women power in the home, while at the same time constructing the domestic as part of the public sphere. Marriage and the upbringing of children, construed as women's responsibility, were political acts in this period because they were linked to the preservation of Armenian culture and the development of modern Armenian identity and not viewed as purely personal, family acts.[129] *Siranush* is often simply called the story of an arranged marriage but I argue in this chapter that it is the story of the transition from one mode of marriage and of a particular social and political structure, based on preservation of the class structure and Ottoman political structures, and a "modern" view of marriage as part of a larger social process, which was more democratic, as it broke down class and gender hierarchies, thereby allowing women greater power in the family.

In Dussap's texts love is constructed as a moral force superseding societal laws, which are viewed as based on vile motives such as greed, envy and domination. Susan and Clyde Hendrick's work on romantic love state that historically the concept of love as defined in Plato is the desire for the possession of the good or the beautiful and resulted in the striving towards goodness, causing self reflection which stimulated the development of the idea of selfhood.[130] For Dussap romantic love is connected to goodness and self-development, and capable of undermining existing power structures. Because romantic love is a personal emotion, the moral authority of love is located in the soul or self of the individual female character and authority is not located outside of the self but within it. The frequent use of the term *hogi* (self, soul) which is a gender neutral term indicates that Dussap and subsequent authors were also anxious to construct the moral authority of love as available to all human beings regardless of gender, unlike societal laws which gave the male authority over the female. The authors did not portray love as hedonistic abandonment, however, if real authority lies in the loving soul, that soul must also be a moral one. It is in the creation of the new ethical woman and man and the criticism of traditional morality that we see how Srpuhi Dussap envisioned the ideal modern person and ultimately the ideal modern world.

The plot of the novel, *Siranush*, centres around the heroine, Siranush, who falls in love with Yervand, the son of a poor artisan; because she is the daughter of a wealthy amira[131] she is not permitted by her father to marry Yervand and instead is married to Mr. Darehian who like Siranush's father is a wealthy amira. Siranush and Yervand's doomed love is contrasted by the author with the happy love affair of Siranush's friend and Yervand's sister, Zaruhi, and her lover, Hrant, who because they share similar values and understandings of the place of the individual in society, have a happy and harmonious marriage. In contrast, Siranush and Darehian's marriage is a failure because each character is representative of opposing and conflicting modern and traditional values and social and political structures. At the beginning of the novel *Siranush*, Dussap describes the contemporary Armenian ruling elite as being divided into three competing groups, the amira, bureaucratic officials and the intellectuals:

> Eventually the bureaucratic official gained prominence over the amira and this resulted in a new elite, based on the state bureaucracy, which competed for influence with the wealthy merchant class. The third class, the intellectual class, competed for existence with the other two classes. This was a struggle over position, gold, and enlightenment.[132]

Dussap characterizes the bureaucratic class as dependent, the amira as independent and the intellectuals as progressive, adding, however, that while the intellectual class had some strength it was not as powerful as the other two groups.[133] Dussap's description of the different aspects of the ruling classes reflects the political situation of the elites of Constantinople in the nineteenth century. From 1810 to 1845 through their control of the Armenian patriarch, who was the spiritual and civic leader of the Armenians of the Ottoman Empire, the amira dominated the Armenian millet. The amira were frequently generous patrons of schools, hospitals and churches within the Armenian community, and thus facilitated the cultural revival of the nineteenth-century. The source of their wealth and prestige in the Armenian millet, however, was dependent upon their role as intermediaries between the Ottoman state and the Armenian millet. They were frequently seen by their contemporaries as not protecting the Armenian population in order to retain their position within the state.[134] A challenge to their power occurred in 1838 when liberal Armenians and members of the guilds had demanded a voice in the government of the community. The result of this conflict was the proclamation in 1860 of the Armenian National Constitution, which governed the internal affairs of the Armenian community. The new representative government was composed of lay and religious members, which curtailed some of the power of the clergy and the amiras.[135]

In *Siranush* Dussap reveals how this political conflict is manifested on a personal gendered level. She depicts the conflict between the amira class, represented by Siranush's father and husband, and the new intellectual class, represented by Siranush, as a family conflict between father and daughter, husband and wife. Siranush's education and way of thinking, which makes her part of the intellectual class, is contrasted with the figure of Siranush's father, Mr. Haynurr. Mr. Haynurr is the son of a wealthy amira family; he is portrayed as uncultured, and as not valuing anyone who does not have wealth or at least a position in the bureaucracy.[136] Her future husband is described in a manner that is reminiscent of Dussap's portrayal of Siranush's father. He too is from a wealthy family, a high-ranking official who "possesses a pride which is the product of having inherited wealth." He is also known to behave "immorally" by consorting with prostitutes, but despite this is considered by Siranush's father, and other wealthy families, to be a good match for their inexperienced daughters because of his wealth.[137] The connection between Siranush's father and husband is also made clear by the fact that both are referred to as Mr. Haynurrr and Mr. Darehian respectively, and never by their first names, unlike the other characters in the novel, who are drawn from the intellectual and artisan classes. Their roles and titles indicate that Mr. Haynurr and Mr. Darehian are the patriarchs and the upholders of traditional modes of political structures and of male authority in the novel.

The differences between Siranush and Mr. Haynurr and Mr. Darehian serve to illustrate the differences between the intellectuals and the amiras, Dussap, who never lost sight of the category of gender and its relationship with class, demonstrated that what also divided Siranush from Mr. Haynurr and Mr. Darehian was the position of women in the amira class. As the daughter and wife of amiras, Siranush could be considered part of the amira class and yet she is not; Dussap firmly allies her to the intellectual class. By demonstrating the alienation and powerlessness, which both Siranush and her mother experience the author questioned the extent to which women belong to any social class when they do not have the same power in it as men. The inequality of women is made clear by Dussap in the conflict over Mr. Haynurr's decision to marry Siranush to Mr. Darehian. Without asking for either Siranush's or his wife's consent, Mr. Haynurr agrees to Darehian's proposal. At this point Dussap interjects into the text in a mocking tone:

> After all isn't he the father? Doesn't he have absolute authority over his child's fate, particularly in this sort of illustrious case?[138]

When Haynurr finally informs his wife of his decision, he is surprised to discover that she is not pleased, arguing that the groom's debauched lifestyle is not in harmony with her daughter's tender feelings:

> Mr. Haynurr roars: "Our daughter will live in luxury and greatness, she will be the reigning queen of her house and in the face of all this you want to raise obstacles based on this elevated individual's youthful behaviour? Men are free and no one can meddle with their lives."
>
> Mrs. Haynurr replies: "Yes, they are free, while they have no wife, while there is no fear of wounding a tender heart. But from the day a holy, pure soul becomes their life's companion, a soul who searches for her happiness in love and in mutual love, I say, from that day onward men cease to be free. From that day marital duties should weigh upon men as they do upon women and they must give up unfair ease and concentrate their desires and dreams in the marital state."
>
> "For centuries men have enjoyed their freedom," her inflamed husband responds, "and have lived happily with their wives."
>
> "You are incorrect, familial harmony is achieved only when men reject adultery, when they are decent and faithful to their wives. Look also at us, how everything has changed. When Armenians maintained their honour, when women were jealous of their honour and lived loyally according to their class, what calm prevailed in family life, what virtue, what peace! But be-

cause men began to raise the flag of [their sexual] freedom in marital life, inner bliss was destroyed and lawlessness reigned absolutely."

"Women's contemporary demand for equality is a new disease which has affected the well being of the family. When a woman lives in wealth and glory what more can she desire?"

"She can desire a faithful heart, a heart which will be a companion to her joy and grief."[139]

The dialogue between Siranush's parents reveals Dussap's understanding of the conflict between the modern and the traditional. Siranush's mother argues in favour of marriage based on mutual love and respect while Mr. Haynurr represents customary expectations of male and female behaviour in marriage among members of the amira class, and particularly the subordination of women within that system. In this world, men are allowed sexual license both before and after marriage while women are not. In return for their compliance women are supported financially and expected to be content. The connection between female acquiescence and male financial power is made clear in the novel when after her marriage Siranush returns home one evening to discover her husband and his mistress in her house, Siranush is very angry and demands that the woman leave immediately. The next morning Darehian attempts to give Siranush a valuable diamond ring as a form of compensation. Siranush rejects the ring, saying:

> You men think that woman is your plaything who is there when you want her and can be cast aside when you don't want her, and then taken up again when that is your will. You are wrong; women have hearts and honour. She continues, "Darehian you will never occupy a place in my heart, I wanted to respect you as my life's companion and to make you happy. But you are a man who doesn't know how to respect his wife, and instead rubs her face in the mud.[140]

By rejecting the ring and refusing to acquiesce to Darehian's behaviour, Siranush rejects the traditional balance of power between the sexes in marriage. The tragedy of *Siranush* is that while

Siranush and her mother argue against the idea of marriage as an economic transaction, favouring the idea of marriage as a union of companionship, their protests remain unheeded. Mr.Haynurr is unmoved by his wife's opposition to the marriage with Darehian and as a consequence bullies her to such a degree that Siranush feels compelled to marry Darehian in order to protect her mother from her father.[141] After her marriage Siranush's situation worsens, she is virtually a prisoner in her home, spied upon by servants and subject to her husband's jealousies while he is free to visit his mistress.[142] Siranush and her mother are not compliant; they verbally protest, but because they are women they do not have access to the wealth and public position, which are the origins of amira power and status. Women are regarded in society as possessions of men to be exchanged between amira families through marriage. As such they are powerless and cannot ameliorate their circumstances despite ostensibly belonging to the powerful amira class.

Dussap did not attempt to conceal her contempt for the amira class, specifically its customs and mores that she identified as harmful to women. In her preface to *Siranush* Dussap criticized the amira:

> [they] live in a sordid [moral] atmosphere and at the same time demand to be loved and respected by their wives. Love! Respect! What an astonishing ambition, a foolish dream. To be loved it is necessary to love and to respect.[143]

In contrast to the traditional amira's devaluation of women, Dussap saw the intellectual class as being the locus of progress and the hope of women's emancipation. Unlike the amira Dussap portrays class the intellectual class as being fluid. In her novels admittance into the intellectual class was not achieved through the possession of wealth or social standing but through the intellect, the world of art, commitment to progress and the modern and was not restricted to men alone. The new standards of the intellectual class had the potential to undermine the traditional amira evaluation of human worth. In the novel when Yervand decides to go to Rome to further develop his talent in painting, he does so because he wants to improve his social position in order to be considered worthy of marrying Siranush in the eyes of her father. He believes that his success in art will elevate him to her social level because "intelligence is the highest equality."[144] The belief that intelligence is the highest equalizer had the potential to subvert the old structure, which was based on hierarchy determined by wealth, social, position and gender. The intellectual class's emphasis on knowledge as the basis of merit and value rather than gender and birth was potentially inclusive of women. Dussap shows that Siranush and her mother could not participate in decision making as members of the amira class because that class did not allow women access to the wealth and employment which formed the basis of value in amira society, the same is not true of her portrayal of the intellectual class. Dussap depicted Siranush as a member of the intellectual class through her description of Siranush's education and interests:

> To study was a beloved dream of Siranush's, particularly the study of ancient and modern national [Armenian] history and the literature of other nations too. She loved to study the causes of national progress and decline, and she wisely noted that the intellectuals gave people life, while vice and ignorance brought only death.[145]

In Dussap's portrayal of Siranush she created a young woman who reads, studies history and literature, and desires to improve the condition of her people. This portrait demonstrates Dussap's hope for the support of the intellectual class in the issue of women's emancipation. As an intelligent young woman with intellectual interests Siranush could and clearly desires to participate in the movement for national progress. The fact that she is prevented from doing so in the novel is the result of her weak position as a woman within her upper-class family, which retains its position because of the traditional Ottoman political structure.

It is the character of Zaruhi, not Siranush, who is more fully able to actualize the benefits offered her by membership in the intellectual class and reveals Dussap's vision of the ideal modern relationship between women and men. A daughter of the artisan class, upon her parents' death, Zaruhi was adopted by Siranush's mother. Although Zaruhi and Siranush received the same education their fates are quite different due to their social standing. In the novel Zaruhi is able to use her education and work after marriage because she is not a member of a class, which enforces female idleness. After her marriage Dussap depicts Zaruhi as able to utilize her education by teaching and doing translation work.[146] Zaruhi and Hrant's marriage is portrayed as equal and therefore harmonious.

Dussap was not naïve, however, she knew that some elements of the intellectual class would reject women's participation in the public sphere, which they saw as their domain. Her preface to *Siranush* acknowledged the opposition she herself had experienced from some male intellectuals:

> When *Mayta* appeared many males were excessively upset and also scandalized. Why such upset? Why that outrage? If my pronouncements are legitimate then I am serving the cause of justice and instead of fear and anger I should inspire gratitude.[147]

The opposition Dussap experienced did not make her lose hope in the intellectual class as the group most likely to support women's emancipation, she advocated that women and their male supporters continue to actively promote women's emancipation. Indeed Dussap viewed this as a duty stating: "They will criticize me for these declarations but what is audacious to them is to me a duty. To see evil and to hide it, fearfully striking at it, certainly does not reveal the spirit's courage."[148] Dussap's three novels are impassioned but reasoned pleas for Armenian women's emancipation and unhindered participation in the work of the intellectual class.

In her novels, Dussap posited that women's emancipation could be achieved only by abandoning traditional gender constructions in favour of an inclusive system, which allowed women to exercise their talents in areas traditionally restricted to them. As shown above she viewed the intellectual class with its rejection of traditional power structures as the class most likely to support women's inclusion in new social, political and economic roles and in participating in discussions of the future of Armenian society. She utilized the theme of romantic love to formulate her concept of the need for a new basis for the relations between women and men. Although Dussap was an ardent supporter of women's education and paid employment, she perceived romantic love as an important basis of women's emancipation because the majority of women in her society married and it was this personal relationship between women and men which had the greatest impact on women's lives. For Dussap the expression of romantic love was a means of altering the traditional institution of marriage and women's place within this system and to facilitate women's participation in the modern public sphere. That Dussap was particularly interested in Armenian women's entry into public life is demonstrated by her statement to the young Zabel Yesayian that Armenian women would encounter difficulty from men in entering the public sphere but that they should still attempt it.[149]

Inherent in Dussap's representation of modernity is a vision of the Armenian new woman. Dussap carefully constructed this figure in her two novels, *Siranush* and *Araksia or the Governess*. An important aspect of Dussap's vision of the modern was the re-evaluation of accepted customs and norms governing male and female relations. According to traditional mores Siranush's love for a man before marriage was scandalous and immoral behaviour in a woman, Dussap challenged this conviction by contending that true corruption was treating women as if they were possessions to be passed from one man to another without regard for the woman's desires or feelings. In the following scene Siranush has confessed to her husband that she has always loved Yervand and only consented to marry him (her husband) because she feared for her mother's well being:

> Darehian said: "Your behaviour is unconscionable."
> Siranush replied: "But you never bothered to inquire if my heart was free or if I could love you, you were content with my father's consent. You wanted my person and you got my person, but

you don't have the right to complain if I kept my heart for another and I will keep it until the end of my life."[150]

Siranush's answer to Darehian's accusations of immorality demonstrates the new social morality Dussap was trying to create. She identified the true locus of conflict as being one of patriarchal thought which allowed women no feelings and thoughts independent of what men desired them to have rather than women's subversion of traditional customs as conservatives would argue. It is because of this established custom, that when Darehian felt attracted to Siranush he could simply ask her father for permission to marry her, without considering if he was desirable to her, without wondering if she had committed herself to another man, and without knowing much about her character or thoughts since he had only spoken with her once. Siranush's aforementioned reply defied the unspoken assumptions of patriarchal thought, by repudiating the notion that men have a right to expect behaviour from women when it does not take into account women's thoughts and feelings. Through Siranush's statement that, "you don't have the right to complain if I kept my heart for another," Dussap asserted women's right to have control over their emotions and thoughts irrespective of patriarchal rites of ownership which legitimized the passing of women from fathers to husbands, demanding chastity and loyalty to both. Dussap made it clear that the fault in this situation is not Siranush's for forming a bond with another man prior to marriage as traditional mores would posit, but that the fault is Darehian's and society's because both her husband and society did not regard Siranush as a rational human being who had the right to make decisions about her own life. In this novel old forms of morality are disregarded, while the modern morality of love prevails. Nor was modern morality restricted to women alone, Dussap extends her social criticism to challenge the traditional acceptance of male sexual freedom. Darehian attempts to justify the different standards of male and female sexual freedom, saying:

> Don't you know that man is free and that upon him the stain doesn't
> show, while it stains the woman in a way, which cannot be
> erased?[151]

Throughout the novel Dussap argues that women and men should share the same ethical principles in sexuality. She demonstrates that while men may not bear physical signs of sexual activity, their morality is reflected in their daily behaviour. It is due to Darehian's suspicious attitude that Siranush cannot love him. The author clearly shows that it is his suspicious attitude, which is a result of his association with prostitutes, that causes him to view all women as being like prostitutes, his suspicion is constructed as a sign of his moral decay despite his claim that "the stain doesn't show" upon the man.

Dussap attempted to inspire Armenian women with a vision of a comfortable space for women in the modern world by describing an alternative representation of femininity. It is a process Dussap believed Armenian women needed to be involved in, in order to ensure positive roles for women. For this reason Dussap created as a model a woman who has her own particular sense of self and honour. In traditional Armenian society what constituted personal honour [pativ] was gendered. A man's honour was shown by his ability to earn money and command his household, while a woman's honour was demonstrated by her chastity before marriage and faithfulness to her husband after marriage.[152] Although Dussap supported the notion that women should be chaste, she abhorred the fact that men were not subject to the same restrictions of chastity and frequently caused a woman's disgrace:

> She thought that women's honour had become a sacred issue in
> society, such that one stain became the subject of accusations,
> criticisms and judgments, and many times women's conduct and
> thoughts were misrepresented and dishonourable aims were
> presumed. Without scruple and with ease they struck a blow against
> women's honour without the male perpetuators being subjected
> to punishment.[153]

But Dussap went beyond simply deploring the fact that men and women were not subject to the same restrictions concerning sexual behaviour. She constructed a new vision of women's honour, which had nothing to do with sexuality. In her construction women's honour was related to a woman's personal sense of self and right behaviour, which is not enforced but freely acted upon. This is demonstrated by the following scene when Darehian tells Siranush that she must never meet with Yervand again and adds:

> ". . . if you act against my will you will never receive forgiveness from me."
> Siranush answered: "I will never ask for forgiveness, my honour and blameless conduct don't need pardon."
> "But who will guarantee me that you won't act against my will?"
> "I will."[154]

Siranush's statement that she alone will be responsible for her own behaviour indicates Dussap's contention that women are rational beings. Dussap's rational woman was a new character in Armenian literature. Dussap's construction of the New Armenian women's rational capacity was further developed in her third novel *Araksia or the Governess* in which the main character is described as follows:

> Araksia studied Armenian and then French but she particularly loved ancient and modern philosophy. She *compared, she examined, she thought* and finally that reading helped her, and instead of blindly following established customs, thoughts and prejudices, she formed within herself a powerful determination and influenced others. She showed people the path where they must proceed; she wanted to have the freedom to think and to work. With that same freedom, however, she wanted the dignity to be able to stand up as a virtuous woman and to despise society's trifles, which censured the girl from thinking, speaking and sacredly loving freedom. She wanted this because humanity is born to enjoy freedom and love.[155] [italics mine]

Dussap constructs the new educated women as a leader who can guide others on the path towards true progress as evinced by the line, "[Araksia] showed people the path where they must proceed." In her final sentence: "to despise society's trifles which censured the girl, thinking, speaking and sacredly loving freedom, because humanity is born to enjoy freedom and love" she asserts women's right to think and freedom as a basic human right.

In her third and final novel Dussap created her ideal educated woman in the character of Araksia. Araksia is thoughtful, intelligent and continually subverts social conventions in a polite but firm manner. Dussap describes her as someone who "wants to keep the rights given by nature, she wants to be a useful person, without being presented as a societal ornament." Although Araksia does not always agree with her mother she manages to "remain true to her own path" without hurting her mother.[156] Araksia thus embodies what is positive in traditional custom in that she demonstrates filial respect for her mother but at the same time remains loyal to her own principles. Showing filial respect yet remaining true to their own principles is a characteristic of all Dussap's heroines, suggesting that the author viewed respect for family members as an important custom but one which should not compromise the individual's ethical principles.

Like Siranush, Araksia has an ethical sensibility, which is quite different from societal norms of proper behaviour represented in the novel. When her mother argues against Araksia's finding employment on the grounds that she will tarnish the family name because society will know of the family's poverty, Araksia argues that to be poor is not shameful and she would rather work than starve. When her unconvinced mother insists that a wealthy relative will assist the family Araksia construes receiving charity instead of earning one's own money as the true source of shame, saying:

> Mother what does it matter what others know, when we know that we are the objects of charity? How can our conscience and our honour bear this?[157]

It is because of her reading of philosophy and her mind's reason that Araksia has a strong sense of her personal honour, which is different from common societal notions of honour. Araksia's sense of herself as a separate and distinct person is further developed when she finally does enter into the working world.

Dussap's portrayal of Siranush and Araksia portrays both women as highly intellectual and concerned with Armenian national development. The study of philosophy has an important function in Dussap's texts as it is understood to teach women to interpret and question tradition and to recognize that established customs are not natural but socially constructed.

In Dussap's novels personal development and social progress is always intertwined. In her own life Dussap practiced this by running an educational organization, the *School-Loving Ladies' Association*, devoted to training Armenian women as teachers, to teach Armenian children outside of Constantinople, where there was a need for teachers and schools. She envisioned a compatible and harmonious process of Armenian women's and society's progress.

The problem as outlined in *Siranush* is that a modern woman such as Siranush can be ruined by traditional attitudes to women. Siranush is forced to marry without love and her resultant grief and final death are depicted as caused by outmoded custom and patriarchal obedience. Likewise, Araksia, who has an inclination for mathematics, must work as a governess because education and employment in mathematics is not open to women. Although Dussap viewed modernity and the emerging intellectual class as opening more opportunities for women's participation in activities outside of the traditional spheres, she portrayed these new entities as weak and unable to combat traditional, patriarchal customs.

The influence of Dussap's discussion of women's roles, modernity and romantic love is demonstrated by numerous novels, including Sibyl's *A Girl's Heart* (1891) and particularly, Zabel Yesayian's *The Last Cup* (1917). Dussap's novel *Siranush* depicted a woman caught between traditional and modern mores and offered romantic love as a solution to the problem of women's position in marriage, in contrast Zabel Yesayian's novel *The Last Cup* published thirty-three years later portrayed a world in which many of the traditional restraints had disappeared without a corresponding improvement in the position of women within the institution of marriage. Yesayian's novel *The Last Cup* in many ways reads as a response to Dussap's *Siranush*. The similarities and differences between these two novels reveal the ways in which the question of modernity and romantic love evolved in the context of changes in societal attitudes and the worsening circumstances of the Armenians of the Ottoman Empire.

The comparison between Dussap and Yesayian's literary representations of women's problems in society is quite deliberate. Most critics of Armenian literature, such as Hagop Oshagan, who prefer Yesayian's work to Dussap's, have emphasized Yesayian's debt to French literature and realism, while ignoring Dussap's influence.[158] Although it is true that Yesayian's literary style in particular owes much to French literature and realism, and that Yesayian's characters in contrast to Dussap's more one-dimensional characters, reveal complex and varied psychologies, the content of many of Yesayian's works, and especially her concern with the position of women in Armenian society, was influenced by the novels of Srpuhi Dussap. In the autobiography of her formative years Yesayian mentioned by name only two writers who had a great impact on her during adolescence: they are the Armenian romantic poet Bedros Tourian (1851–1872) and Srpuhi Dussap.[159] Elsewhere Yesayian publicly acknowledged her respect for Srpuhi Dussap.[160] The particular influence of *Siranush* on *The Last Cup* is evident in Yesayian's discussion of love as a solution for women's problems in marriage and through her portrayal in the novel of the ideal male lover.

*The Last Cup* is written in the form of a letter from the heroine, Atriné, to her lover, Arshak Serobian. It describes, with particular emphasis on her feelings and thoughts, Atriné's courtship and marriage to Mik'ayel Hovsep'ian, and her meeting with Arshak and their resulting affair. Through these relationships Yesayian explores how issues such as women's legal and social subordination and the oppression of the Armenians of the Ottoman Empire affected Armenian women's ability to shape the discourse of modernity and womanhood and by extension, Armenian national development. The date of publication of the novel is 1917, however, from reference to events in the dramatic action of the novel, the story appears to take place around 1914 or even early 1915, before the arrests and deportations of Armenians in April of that year. The novel is not about the Armenian Genocide, but rather portrays the period immediately prior to the Genocide, including the sense of unease and oppression experienced by Armenians in Constantinople in that period, who are described thus: "The entire nation betrayed fear, waiting from one minute to the next for frightening events." The story, set in the context of oppression and violence against Armenians, influenced how Yesayian discussed the issues of Armenian womanhood and national identity, and accounts for many of the differences between Yesayian's and Dussap's novels.

In Yesayian's portrayal of Atriné's life some of the traditional customs, which Dussap had identified as the cause of women's problems in *Siranush* have been eliminated by the author. Unlike Siranush, Atriné's father does not force her into marriage; instead, she is free to choose her husband.[161] The manner in which Yesayian portrays the courtship and marriage of Atriné and Mik'ayel, however, reveals a disturbing distribution of power, which makes Atriné's apparent freedom illusionary.

Yesayian's portrayal of Mik'ayel and Atriné's courtship is replete with images of hunting, trapped prey and a suggestion of masochism, which underscores the balance of power between women and men in society. Although Yesayian calls Mik'ayel a "true man" because he is honest in a world where people live according to societal demands rather than the inclinations of their natures, if the imagery used in connection with him is analyzed it is apparent that Mik'ayel is an oppressive presence in the novel. Describing Mik'ayel's desire to marry her Atriné states:

> To be free from his pursuit [hetapndum] I was prepared to fall into any marriage and I tried several times, every time a new suitor appeared I pretended that my attention was on the new person.

Mik'ayel's face would take on an expression of greater sad severity, his pained and reproachful glance would fall heavily upon me
with an expression almost of hostility, and with that dominating
gaze I would feel that I was trapped prey [tkar vors] that I was
already in his hands, despite my feeble attempts to avoid him and
these feelings caused fear in me or even anger but also a type of
sharp and painful delight.[162]

The use of the words *pursuit* and *trapped prey* evoke images
of Mik'ayel as a hunter and Atriné as the prey, revealing a world
in which love is constructed as oppressive. Atriné's experience of
fear and anger, but also a type of painful pleasure reveals how
women have been conditioned by society to venerate male
aggression despite the fear and anger it causes. In a society, which
legitimizes men's pursuit of women, women's power to defend
herself is shown to be severely limited. Atriné's power to use
love for her own benefit, as the following passage shows, is inadequate:

Love in him was strong, and I felt *power*. . . with great patience
and trouble he bore my ever changing and whimsical regard, sometimes he remained *hunting* in my face for a smile, a polite smile,
then he left immediately as if frightened that my disposition would
change, I could alter that moment of happiness. How he loved me
and how I shuddered, thinking about that love and reflecting that
I could bow down before that fearful power.[163] [italics mine]

Although the passage seems to indicate that Atriné had power
because Mik'ayel loved her as illustrated by the statement "Love
in him was strong, and I felt power," the limitations of the power
of women's allure is made clear in this passage by the final sentence. Atriné conceived of Mik'ayel's love for her as a force outside of herself, not something she could control.  His love was
something that compelled  her to "bow down before that fearful
power." Due to the force of that "fearful power" Atriné marries
Mik'ayel and the images of hunting intensify as Atriné continues
to elude Mik'ayel's control:

> After ten years of marriage he still loved me with the same ardour, the same passion, what can I say? He continued to *pursue* me because, despite the fact that we never discussed it, he felt that my soul eluded him, that a part of me, the best and essential part of me, wasn't united with him.[164] [italics' mine]

The model of love depicted in the relationship between Atriné and Mik'ayel is ultimately portrayed as a failure by Yesayian because it is based upon the narrow concept of men as active and aggressive in pursuit of women, who were then positioned as passive and submissive in this construct, a construction which could not facilitate companionship and understanding between women and men. As stated earlier, one of the aims of Armenian women's writing of this period was the reconstruction of marriage as a form of partnership. Dussap and Yesayian clearly believed that wives and husbands' roles should be complementary and equal, with each partner achieving emotional fulfillment from the marriage. The union between Atriné and Mik'ayel, which is based on dominance, fails to satisfy either character's emotional needs and therefore is represented as a disaster.

In *The Last Cup* Yesayian made it clear that the issue of women's experience of love and marriage was related to the social and political structure of Armenian society. Yesayian indicated that the reason the flawed courtship of Atriné and Mik'ayel resulted in marriage was due to the prevailing social construction of Armenian society, which she viewed as being weak and clinging to outmoded custom out of fear. Throughout the text Yesayian uses images of sleep to describe Armenian society and Atriné's state of being throughout her life until her meeting with her lover Arshak. What distinguishes Atriné from the society around her is her to desire to awaken from slumber and free herself from the social conventions she instinctively understands as detrimental to individual freedom and happiness. She says of her soul "[it] wanted to awaken, to reveal itself and live with all its power."[165]

In this novel Yesayian is concerned with the forces of oppression. Atriné is unable to live as a free and independent individual because social conventions support male aggression and female passivity, which results in the suppression of the female self. Societal rules and laws, for example the father's right to custody of children at the expense of the mother, are identified by the author as obstacles to the development of female subjectivity.

In *The Last Cup* the legal and social subordination of the Armenian woman is mirrored by the legal and social subordination of the Armenians in the Ottoman Empire. Gender inequality is part of a system of hierarchies by which people are divided into groups with varying degrees of power based on categories such as gender, class and race or ethnicity. In the Ottoman Empire Armenians as a group suffered oppression based on religious and national identity. Armenian women writers understood that in order to ameliorate their own condition the position of Armenians as a group had to improve. Yesayian looked to political solutions to improve the position of the Armenians in the Ottoman Empire. The Armenians of the Ottoman Empire, like the women of Yesayian's novels, were subject to events and laws outside of their control.

Encoded in the novel's argument against social convention is Yesayian's critique of the oppression of Armenians in the Ottoman Empire. At the beginning of *The Last Cup* the author declared that this story is a break with tradition, that instead of the usual literary practice she will write differently, "What do I care about tradition, about literary method?"[166] This declaration signifies that much of the novel is concerned with the breakdown of structures of authority, which include literary method, women's "proper" roles, and finally political authority. Yesayian elaborated her theory that the soul of each individual should not be subject to societal laws, which she saw as being false:

> . . . every *man and every woman* is not acquainted with her/his soul, clearly they don't know their own desires and individual laws, and therefore they are blind to themselves, and intolerant and strict towards others. People don't know that in them there is a limitless and constantly changing thing, with its separate and unknown rules, which are different from humanity's forced rules.

It's an endless sea whose shores we cannot even see and whose storms and calm we carry within us and enjoy without knowing why or how.

But particularly never, never forget the fact that there is no government upon our souls and that it acts for reasons that are outside of our will and thus we must not criticize each other, instead we must be infinitely and honestly forgiving of each other.[167]

This statement is a call by the author for freedom from oppression of two kinds, the oppression of gender hierarchy, signified by her specific mention of *"every man* and *woman,"* and from political oppression in the words "there is no *government* of the soul."

In *The Last Cup* Yesayian illustrated the conflict of gender and ethnic subordination through Atriné's relationship with an unnamed Turkish officer. In this relationship, which is brief and never fully develops, imbalance of power destroys the potential for love as it did in the relationship with Mik'ayel. Whereas the imbalance of power between Atriné and Mik'ayel was based on gender conventions and hierarchy, in her portrayal of Atriné and the Turkish officer Yesayian demonstrates that the imbalance of power in this relationship is based on both gender and national and political domination.

A relationship between Atriné and the Turkish officer cannot develop because each character represents irreconcilable divisions based on the social and historical interaction of Turks and Armenians.

In the following scene Atriné is walking alone in the hills on the outskirts of Constantinople. The ensuing encounter between Atriné and the Turkish officer depicts the vulnerability of Atriné's position as both a woman and an Armenian:

I was alone . . . A feeling of fear gripped me, everywhere was deserted, the hills, valleys, in front of me and behind, it was all empty of human life, a strange silence reigned.[168]

In this environment:

Various thoughts, fear and anger, past events, future crimes, victorious hopes, and a particular fanaticism of unequal struggles, all passed through my mind with alarm.[169]

She is frightened, but too proud to admit her fear. In this frightened, alone state, she sees the Turkish officer she has known since childhood:

> Suddenly I saw him on the other side of the hill mounted on a black horse. Why didn't I immediately leave? Why did I stand there alone upon the hill until the pleasant evening wind blew the veil from my head, why?
> I felt him coming towards me, with great speed the horse's hooves shook the incline and the ground and pounded towards me.[170]

In this passage Yesayian depicted a scene both frightening and familiar to an Armenian audience. She suggested danger by describing Atriné alone in the wilderness, vulnerable, a Turkish horseman riding towards her with the suggestion of untamed sexuality. This image conjures up the rape and abduction of Armenian women by Turks, which was a feature of the massacres and Genocide committed against the Armenians.[171] That this was a period of political instability is alluded to in the text by a reference to the massacres of the Armenian population of Cilicia in 1909.[172] When the Turkish rider reaches Atriné, however, the text moves away from suggestions of danger to portray mutual erotic attraction:

> When he reached my side he immediately dismounted the horse and with great respect and in the manner of their custom he greeted me. He had newly returned from his unsuccessful expedition, a tired and hopeless man's thoughtful sadness was written upon his face. His eyes, wide with affection and admiration, enveloped me. My glance turned from him and fixed on a vague point, my blood was pounding in my head and I felt throbbing in my temples.
> "In these troubled times, you're not afraid to be alone in this solitude?"

"No, I'm not afraid of anything." Despite myself my voice was my enemy and it seemed to me that there was a sound of foreign accents.

"But it was very reckless, your actions . . . " He fell silent and bewildered. My lowered eyes saw that his hand shook on the whip.

"I saw you from afar," he said like a song with a tender and harmonious voice, "I couldn't see you clearly but I felt it was you . . . And my heart and my horse galloped to you . . . "

A wave of warm blood rose to my cheeks, my forehead . . . I felt a furious blushing and bravely I raised my head and courageously fixed my eyes upon him . . .

"You can't imagine," he said quickly, "how beautiful you are at this moment, a disturbing beauty . . . "[173]

How can I explain my precipitous feelings? It was as if his nervous fingers were touching my heart and I felt a sharp pain, a sort of grief. It disturbed me, I couldn't comprehend whether I was pleased or displeased . . . I had lost sense of reality as if with one great blow reality had fled through my soul's doors. It caused a dizzy sensation in me like that caused by wine, he continued talking but only certain phrases reached my ears . . . The horse suddenly neighed several times and the wind became gusty, covering my face with my undulating veil."[174]

The dominant imagery in this scene evokes sexual attraction in the man's words, in Atriné's physical reactions, in the image of Atriné's veil, covering and uncovering her face, and even in the horse's neighing, (the word used, vrnchel, meaning literally "to neigh," and according to a dictionary from 1879 has the slang meaning "to lust after.").[175]

As the text explores the possibility of love in three male-female relationships, the relationship between the Turkish man and the Armenian woman is emphatically rejected because of the political domination of the Turks over the Armenians, and specifically its gendered form of rape and abduction of Armenian women, overshadows individual inclinations. Atriné expresses this feeling:

> Sometimes with favour and even tenderness I reflected upon that
> intangible and durable presence [the Turkish officer's presence],
> but often I saw him as an enemy.[176]

Because this novel was published in 1917, literary critics have
found *The Last Cup* difficult to understand, they have looked for
references to the Armenian Genocide, in ways similar to Yesayian's
novel, *Among the Ruins*, which chronicled the massacres of Armenians in Cilicia in 1909. Although not overtly about the Armenian Genocide, I find the references to sexuality as invariably
masochistic or associated with images of rape, and the persistent
imagery of sleep and death in the novel, to be indicative that this
text was written while the Armenian Genocide was occurring and
that it is through this psychological exploration that Yesayian began
to look at the consequences of the Genocide. This theme will be
explored further in chapter six.

In *The Last Cup* Yesayian presented only one relationship in
which male-female equality is achieved because neither Atriné
nor her lover, Arshak, dominates each other, however, this relationship is not portrayed as overtly sexual. Yesayian's emphasis
on Arshak's moral qualities and artistic sensibility resembles
Dussap's description in *Siranush* of the moral qualities and artistic sensibility of Siranush's lover Yervand. Yesayian's portrayal
of love as an equal union of souls resembles Dussap's concept of
romantic love:

> ... two souls, two separate worlds ... [meet] who knows by what
> mysterious and divine force, breaking down all obstacles, all
> oppressions and fog, they are able to meet and find two drops of
> light that are the same and light each other.[177]

Both authors thought that a prerequisite for the type of love,
which would ensure equality and harmony between women and
men, a new type of woman and man had to be formed. The new
man had to be one who was artistic, since art signifies both culture and sensitivity in these novels, and one who was not a slave
to patriarchal customs like Mik'ayel and his jealousy or Darehian

and his extramarital affairs. Yesayian's portrayal of artistic, and indeed many other qualities, as inherent to both women and men reveals the way in which she, and Dussap collapsed some of the boundaries of the feminine and masculine by emphasizing shared characteristics inherent in human beings regardless of gender.

The characters of Atriné and Arshak are portrayed as sharing many of the same thoughts and concerns, which is meant to show how they are the equals of each other. When they contemplate leaving their spouses for each other, they recognize that they have the same problems:

> My eyes met your eyes. You also are married and have children whom you love very much. Your loving but troubled gaze met my thoughts.[178]

In the course of the text Arshak never tries to dominate Atriné or persuade her to act in accordance with his wishes. When Atriné decides that she has to return to her children, although described as "grief-stricken" Arshak accepts her choice.[179]

Implicit in Dussap and Yesayian's creation of new women and new men is the creation of a new standard of behaviour. Yesayian's sense of ethical behaviour was somewhat different from Dussap's as she allowed Atriné to have an extramarital affair (something Dussap did not allow Siranush), while still representing Atriné as a decent, honest woman. In Yesayian's text Atriné and Arshak are ethical because they are true to their feelings rather than empty and corrupt social conventions. Indeed in Yesayian's text love is constructed as a force, which breaks down barriers, both traditional barriers of morality and empty social conventions:

> No one and nothing can ravish my soul, in which love, like an eagle triumphantly soars. In my happiness I feel so complete, so free, that which I'm not brave enough to reveal, it's as if I have thrown out humanity's rules and fate.[180]

Love is freedom for women in this text because it assists in the process of self-development. The society around Atriné, however, does not acknowledge Atriné's individual freedom and punishes her by allowing Mik'ayel to take her children away. Although Yesayian was concerned with the question of female subjectivity as Dussap had been, she was also concerned with portraying the obstacles, which hindered self-development. This difference is due to changes in the position of Armenians in the Ottoman Empire and divergent concepts of the role of literary. For Dussap literary works were meant to be inspirational to women, while Yesayian's works focused on identifying the complex structures of oppression, which hindered women's and Armenians' emancipation.

Despite the differences between Dussap's inspirational novels and Yesayian's realist novels, an examination of *Siranush*, and *The Last Cup* reveals some striking similarities between the authors' visions of romantic love, women's position in society and the emancipation issue. Implicit in the constructions of romantic love in these novels is the idea that love is a powerful force with the ability to break down social, but not political, structures of authority viewed by the authors as oppressive to women. In place of oppressive structures the authors constructed romantic love as a transformative force, which would create a harmonious, equal relationship between lovers to ensure marital harmony. Romantic love based on companionship, similar values and thoughts between the lovers, was understood as an alternative to the situation of possible incompatibilities between partners in arranged marriages. Romantic love was viewed as a means of allowing women access to the world outside of the home because the authors believed that romantic love would create trust and loyalty between lovers, which would eliminate feelings of jealousy and the need for female confinement in the home. For this reason the concept of trust and like-mindedness between the lovers was emphasized in the texts. In order to create a social environment of trust in women the authors constructed a vision of a New Woman who was at once rational, feminine and ethical. The new ethical stance constructed by the authors was based on current ideas on the modern. Self-knowledge and true morality was believed to exist within the individual's soul. These alternative sources of authority, were liberating to Armenian women writers as it enabled them to locate authority outside of custom and current legal restrictions, and instead locate authority in the individual woman and man. As we shall see the importance placed on the individual did not preclude a sense of group identity and responsibility towards the Armenian nation. In the following chapter the individual's commitment to the Armenian community is explored through a discussion of charitable organizations and the foundation of schools by several prominent Armenian women writers.

The tenacity of patriarchal custom, however, continues to be visible in the texts. In Dussap and Yesayian's writings while the main characters, Siranush and Yervand, Atriné and Arshak, embody the ideal of equality based on romantic love, neither author portrayed these relationships as coming to fruition with a successful ending. Instead the relationships end in separation because custom, paternal authority, and law overpower romantic love. The failure of romantic love to attain success in the texts suggests that the authors believed that the ideal of an equal relationship between women and men was not achievable in the circumstances of contemporary society.

In an essay on Srpuhi Dussap in *The History of Modern Armenian Literature* the author states that although Dussap was accurate in her critique of women's lack of rights and in her description of prevailing social norms, she revealed "sentimental ethical deficiency when she proposed that the question of unequal rights and freedoms can be resolved by women's individual determination."[181] This statement misses the point of much of Dussap's, and the other women authors', emphasis on the individual woman. The authors believed that in order for women to participate in new roles and enter new domains women had to develop a sense of the female self which was distinct from the patterns and traditions of Armenian femininity of the immediate past, but not the distant past, which through the women associated with Vardan Mamikonian, served as an authentic model of Armenian behaviour. The authors' focus on Armenian women of various social classes and circumstances created a variety of images of Armenian womanhood, which challenged the representation of the urban

Armenian woman as simply frivolous and the rural Armenian woman as passive. Armenian women's writing challenged social constructs of femininity through a process of examination, rejection and reinterpretation of traditional customs in order to offer a new vision of Armenian femininity and the self through the creation of the New Armenian Woman. The authors' conviction that change in women's status cannot occur without a corresponding change in society's conception of what constituted proper female and male behaviour demonstrates awareness that gender roles are social constructs and must be altered before other kinds of change can occur. Instead of being a weakness, Dussap and Yesayian's portrayals of the limitations of individual struggle are an early call for societal support in redefining women's place in Armenian society.

# CHAPTER THREE

# EDUCATION IS THE KEY: SIBYL AND MARIAM KHATISIAN

The nineteenth century was a period in which Armenian women's roles were in a state of flux as marriage and motherhood were theorized in relation to new political concepts of the nation and national identity. This meant that a new understanding of public and familial space was formulated. In this discourse the nation was reconstituted as a home with national father, mothers, brothers and sisters. Although such concepts are not confined solely to the Armenians, the Armenian intelligentsia of the nineteenth century, heartily embraced this concept and added elements to it in order to conform to Armenian circumstances. The viewing of the national public space as familial space enabled Armenian women to enter the national public sphere as mothers and sisters. This had an enormous impact on the concept of women's roles and on the transformation of the public sphere. The key elements in the new conception of the national mother and sister are found in contemporary discussions of female education and employment. The concept of the Armenian woman as mother-educator of the nation was not just a way of including women, it was a concept central to Armenian political discourse. As Kumari Jayawardena's research in the late nineteenth- and early twentieth-century Middle East and Asia has shown, emancipation through education, including female education, was viewed by intellectuals as a precursor to national emancipation in countries, which were subject to foreign political and economic colonization. Jayawardena states:

> Faced with societies that were sufficiently developed and power-
> ful enough to subjugate them, and with the need to modernize
> their own societies, many reformers of Asia seized on the appar-
> ent freedom of women in Western societies as the key to the
> advancement of the West, and argued that 'Oriental backward-
> ness' was partly due to women's low status.[182]

According to Jayawardena, the belief that modernization and strength on the European model could be achieved only through changing traditional social organization, especially the upbringing and education of future generations, resulted in an emphasis by the intelligentsia on preparing women for motherhood through education. A similar process can be identified in the history of Armenian education.

The 1863 Armenian Constitution, which governed the internal affairs of the Armenian millet in the Ottoman Empire, was an attempt by the Armenian community to reform its governing structures and open up governing to a more diverse group, including laymen and members of the artisanal class. One of the key issues the Armenian Constitution regulated was education. The 1863 Armenian Constitution formally established the National Educational Council and outlined its objectives in Article 45:

> The Educational Council consists of seven well-educated laymen.
> Its object is the general inspection of the education of the nation.
> Its duties are to promote good order in the national schools, to
> help the Societies that have for their object the promotion of the
> education of both sexes, to improve the condition of teachers and
> to care for their future, to raise well-qualified teachers and to
> encourage the preparation of good text-books.[183]

The nineteenth-century Armenian intelligentsia viewed education as the key to strengthening the Armenian nation by teaching and preserving the Armenian language and cultural traditions, and in improving the living conditions of the Armenian people through knowledge of sciences, especially health care and hygiene. Armenian intellectuals embraced the concept of female education as a necessity in the development of a strong, modern, Armenian nation because of the influence mothers have upon their offspring. When reformers accorded women's influence to be of great significance over child and national development they sought to ensure that maternal influence would conform to what they defined as modern and patriotic. This vision was taught to girls through education. Private schools opened by Armenian philanthropists emphasized the correlation of education and motherhood. An account written by Tikranuhi Apkariants' describing the foundation of an Armenian girl's school in the town of Nor Jugha in Iran makes clear the connection between national development and female education among Armenians. Apkariants states that female education began in Nor Jugha in 1858 with the establishment of a girls' school at the local convent. The school was established through the funds of Manuk Hordananian, whose purpose, Apkariants explains, was to:

> Dispel the centuries old darkness of his country and make it attain a higher level. In his opinion, educating mothers would give the nation rational members.[184]

According to Pamela Young's research on Armenian education in the Ottoman Empire, education for girls emphasized friendships and communication, as part of lessons on social customs. Textbooks on social customs centred on women's roles within the domestic sphere and taught girls to be polite, quiet, set a good example for younger siblings, learn handicrafts and make the home a pleasant place. Boys were instructed to be thankful for this work, as it would guarantee the future beautiful girls and mothers.[185]

The extent to which literate, urban Armenian women embraced the notion of female education and the centrality of women's role to national identity and development is shown by the numerous articles they wrote in support of female education, motherhood as crucial to nation-building, and advocacy of public roles for Armenian women. This emancipation movement was not restricted

to Armenian women in the Ottoman Empire but flourished among
Armenian women in Russia, Iran and India. This chapter will examine the careers and writings of two Armenian women, based in
Constantinople and Tiflis respectively, Sibyl (1868–1934) and
Mariam Khatisian (1845–1914). As participants in the education
movement, as founders of influential charitable organizations and
writers of novels, which take on the theme of women's roles in
modern society, Sibyl and Khatisian were participants in the fashioning of national, familial space and creators of theories of women
and nationality.

Afsaneh Najmabadi's suggestion that in turn-of-the-century
Iran, girls' schools were where young women learned how to constitute themselves as citizens and the establishment of women's
associations was an expression of citizenship, is relevant to the
history of Armenian women's education and charitable work.[186]
Sibyl's and Khatisian's work in female education and charitable
associations are expressions of female political participation in
the Armenian context. The majority of early Armenian women
writers were teachers and founders and/or members of charitable
educational associations before they began to write. Participation
in education and charitable associations gave women entry into
the public, political sphere, which enabled them to begin to theorize about women's political participation and public role.  In
novels, women writers set about transforming the public sphere
to include the values associated with the family sphere, particularly, women's nurturing and maternal role. That women novelists were producing theory in addition to fiction is quite clear.
Indeed much of Armenian literature of this period has an ideological and didactic function. The representation of women's lives
in fiction, particularly in a period when women's roles were subject to scrutiny and debate, is not simply a reflection of reality or
experience, it is an attempt to construct and define women's place
in the contemporary world. This chapter looks at two women who
were active in charitable educational associations and their ideological constructions of women's public role through the novelistic creation of the employed Armenian woman, a figure, which I

have termed "the professional Armenian woman." The chapter examines the construction of this figure, the function of Armenian patriotism in her creation, the obstacles identified by the authors in the path to women's entry into the professions, and finally the desired objective of this figure.

### Sibyl and the Patriotic Armenian Women's Association

In the late nineteenth-century, well-educated Armenian women of Constantinople and Smyrna organized women's benevolent associations devoted to the promotion of female education in the Armenian provinces. The foundation of charitable associations and the participation of young women in organizations devoted to social welfare is how Armenian women entered the public sphere. The concept of the public sphere, as defined by Jürgen Habermas, is the space in which the common good is debated and promoted, and where public opinion is formed based on free exchange of ideas and not on status or tradition. Many scholars, including Anne K. Mellor and others, have argued that Habermas' statement that women did not participate in the public sphere except as readers is incorrect. Mellor sites English women's participation as writers, educators, philanthropists and social reformers, as indicators of their full participation in the discursive public sphere and in the formation of public opinion. Mellor also argues that women's words and ideas were disseminated orally as well as in print through debating societies and speeches.[187] There is a similar development in Armenian women's writing and participation in philanthropy. In these spaces women sought to use their influence in the creation of theory and to insert values traditionally associated with women into the public sphere as nurturers of the nation.

The benevolent associations had two important functions in the lives of Armenian women and girls, they granted Armenian women a socially sanctioned space to engage in public work and they provided the funds and necessities to open schools for Armenian girls. The largest two women's associations in the Ottoman Empire were *Dbrots'aser Tiknants' Ënkerut'iun* [School-Loving Ladies' Association] and *Azkanver Hayuhyats' Ënkerut'iun* [Patriotic Armenian Women's Association], were founded in 1879, the latter by Sibyl. The former was devoted to training female teachers to teach in the Armenian provinces, while the objective of the latter was to open schools for Armenian girls in the provinces.[188] The two organizations were separate but had a cooperative relationship as teachers from *the School-Loving Ladies' Association* sometimes taught at schools supported by *Patriotic Armenian Women's Association.*

The *Azkanver Hayuhyats' Ënkerut'iun* (AHË) was founded on April 11, 1879, by a seventeen year old graduate of Scutari Chemaran, Zabel Khandjian, and eight of her (female) classmates. Zabel Khandjian more commonly known by the pen name, Sibyl, under which she subsequently published poetry, plays and articles in the periodic press, was a devoted advocate of female education. After founding AHË Sibyl worked as a teacher in the provinces for eight years. In 1879 Sibyl was supported in the creation of AHË by her mother and aunt, Srpuhi Alanakian, who received permission from the Ottoman government to establish the association.[189] Throughout its existence AHË was plagued by governmental repression, it was forced to close in 1894 at the beginning of the Hamidian massacres and remained closed until 1908 when Sibyl re-established the association following the declaration of the Ottoman Constitution. The newly revived *Azkanvér Hayuhyats' Ënkerut'iun* continued its activities until 1915.[190]

In its years of operation AHË was successful in opening schools and attracting members. It is said to have opened thirty-five schools in its first five years of existence.[191] By AHË's second meeting it had gained a great deal of attention and as a consequence one hundred and fifty young women and matrons from all districts of Constantinople attended the meeting. According to a speech later given by Sibyl the women who joined AHË tended to be educated young women from upper- and middle-class Constantinople families. These young women desired to be engaged in socially productive work but had found that there were few channels open

to them to do so.[192] Membership in AHË enabled women to engage in voluntary work in order to aid women they termed "their
provincial sisters."[193] Funds for opening schools in the provinces
were raised by selling tickets to lectures and social events organized by AH in Constantinople.[194] This latter fact helped train Armenian women in the skills particular to the public domain. In
her work on English feminists from 1885 to 1914 historian Lucy
Bland notes that philanthropic associations gave women important practical skills such as public speaking, committee chairing,
and the writing of reports.[195] A similar type of training is observ-
able in Armenian women's benevolent organizations. The activities Sibyl and other members performed on behalf of *Azganvér
Hayuhyats' Ënkerut'iun* [Patriotic Armenian Women's Associa-
tion] include fundraising, selling tickets, giving lectures in order
to procure funds for her Association and organizing schools in
the provinces.[196] These activities taught association members the
skills necessary for functioning in the public world.

AHË's policy of teaching the Armenian language was part of
its mandate to instil girls' with a sense of national identity. As
AHË member Arshakuhi Teodik succinctly expressed it during
her visit to Cilicia in 1909: "We open schools so that they [Arme-
nian girls] will love their language and their race."[197]

AHË members responded to calls by intellectuals to create a
strong nation by enlisting Armenian women's support and attempt-
ing to build a system of mutual cooperation between rural and
urban Armenian women through the establishment of girls' schools
in the provinces. One of the goals of the modern Armenian educational system was to create a shared sense of national identity.
As Pamela Young's research has shown the use of standardized
textbooks ensured a common basis of knowledge in rural and urban
Armenian schools. In addition the study of history, the Armenian
language and nature, all combined to "strengthen student awareness of their nation."[198] AHË desired its members to work in the
public sphere, alongside men, and saw its work as extending
maternal care outside of the individual family to the Armenian
nation which was conceptualized in familial terms, as shown by

the common usage of the term "provincial sister" or "provincial brother" [kavarrats'i kuyr/yeghpayr] by AHË members.

Sibyl's description of why she founded AHË, in a letter to her friend, Arshakuhi Teodik, reveals the importance of national solidarity and development on Sibyl and thus on one of the most important women's charitable organizations of the period. Sibyl explained that she had decided to establish AHË for the benefit of provincial Armenians after hearing of provincial conditions from a family servant named Hagop Agha. When Hagop Agha returned to Constantinople from a visit to his birthplace of Khghi, Sibyl stated that she asked him about the local conditions in his town to which he replied:

> In my town it is very dirty, there is hardly any bread to eat, there is no work for the men, the women don't have any idea about human health and hygiene, they do not know how to read, write, add or sew. There are no doctors; no pharmacies and the ill frequently die without proper care. Children do not go to school and do not have any books.

Sibyl wrote to Arshakuhi Teodik that his words:

> . . . haunted my imagination; before my eyes the image of the procession of brave children, barefoot, unwashed, tangled hair, wan, pale and abandoned would not fade. Often I had written of the flowering shores of the Euphrates and of Shavarshan's fragrant lilies in my awkward beginner's verse, but I had never reflected upon the misery of the living people.[199]

It was, in part, to redress her lack of knowledge of and connection with rural Armenians that Sibyl established AHË. The creation of a sense of responsibility by urban Armenians for rural Armenians was one of the intellectual themes of the period as demonstrated by S. Kapamajian's school textbook, *Nor Patmut'iun* (1900), which asked students to describe the conditions in the provinces. The expected answer given in the textbook is:

"the conditions in the provinces are very sad because there is limited education, however, the hope is that the *Miatsial Engerutiun, Azkanver Hayuhyatz*, and the *Tbrotsaser Dignants* would bring reforms to the local schools and give a new impulse to national education."[200]

There was a widespread feeling that the elite of Constantinople was unconcerned with the plight of rural Armenians and that this attitude needed to be changed. Sibyl's daughter, Atriné Tonelian, later stated that Sibyl believed it was her duty to ensure that the wealthy elite of Constantinople assisted AHË's efforts to establish and finance schools for girls in the provinces.[201] Intellectuals came to believe that only through mutual cooperation among all Armenians could the Armenian nation progress. Women like Sibyl and other members of AHË thought that in order for national progress to occur, the talents and strengths of Armenians, female and male, rural and urban, had to be used. At a speech in Constantinople to raise money to finance schools in Cilicia, Sibyl concluded:

> We have taken a vow, whatever they say and do against us, we are not going to digress one iota from our objectives. Until our last breath we are going to work for our provincial sisters. We are going to raise them, we are going to give them a worthy position. We are going to train our future generations to serve their sisters and in turn they will learn to love their urban sisters. It is through mutual responsibility towards each other, that the sacred constitutional system will be realized—Liberty, Equality, Fraternity and Justice.[202]

Based on the evidence of this speech it is clear that Sibyl saw AHË's activities as having political consequences shown by her statement that together women can create a just political system and her usage of the terms, liberty [azatut'iun], equality [havasarut'iun], and fraternity [yeghbayrut'iun], which reflect the political language, liberté, égalité, fraternité, of the French Revolution. Sibyl's statement that the participation of women, both rural and urban, is necessary to create a just political system is a radical one and goes beyond merely viewing Armenian women's activities as complementary to national development, instead it positions women with men, as central to Armenian political and national development.

If female education was designed to create a mother-educator of the nation, the establishment of benevolent organizations and their assistance in disseminating education to girls and their training of Armenian women in skills useful in the public sphere, created the figure of the new professional woman. The professional woman was deemed necessary because her participation in the public sphere was seen as a necessary ingredient in the addition of values of family and care to the process of national development. A speech delivered by Sibyl in 1909 demonstrates how the author conceived of the theme of female education as a means of creating an active role for Armenian women in the public sphere and in national development:

> [Those who] argue that the Armenian woman should be given bread instead of education, here, officially from this rostrum, I answer them for once and for all: even more than bread the Armenian woman needs education, she is the fatherland's heart and soul, on her we are going to build our patrimonial house and nothing will be able to stop her.
>
> Do you see the Armenian woman as worthy only of pity? She isn't. She is going to earn her bread through her own efforts. The Armenian women is as intelligent and hardworking as the American woman, the Englishwoman, the Frenchwoman. In fact she is more modest, courageous and especially stronger than they are, but she must be educated as they are educated.[203]

In this portion of the speech Sibyl utilizes the language of patriotism when she states that Armenian women are the foundation upon which the nation is going to be built. Her statement that the Armenian woman's intelligence and industry is equal to that of the European or American woman is a declaration of equality with the women of the powerful countries of Europe and America, countries called "civilized" in the Armenian press of the time.[204] In her conceptualization of women, and she clearly states that it is both urban and rural Armenian women she is thinking of, they are active participants in the struggle for developing the Armenian nation. Her declaration that Armenian woman does not need charity in the form of food but rather the training to earn her own living, constructs Armenian women as powerful and active and introduces the more unacceptable theme of employment. Female education was acceptable because it was viewed as preparing women to be better mothers, while female employment was often viewed as destroying the family. In the same speech in order to overcome objections to women's public role, Sibyl legitimizes Armenian women's political participation by citing strong women in Armenian history:

> 1200 years ago the Armenian took great interest in women's education. It may come as a surprise when I say that Stepan Siunetsi's sister, Sahakatukhd, established a music school in eighth-century Armenia; today such schools, which are the mark of a civilized nation, do not exist.
>
> History has also given us the name of the lady Shushan Pahlavuni who established schools in villages in the remotest regions of Armenia.
>
> And in the eleventh century the daughter of King Ashot I, Mariam, the mother of Prince Siuniats', had a great love for literature and passionately loved the Armenian language. She didn't like the translation of the Gospel of John and had it translated again . . . In the twentieth century are we going to abandon the women of Armenia to carry dirt and be a servant to farmers?[205]

A common tactic among Middle Eastern and Asian reformers of the nineteenth century was to position women as guardians of ancient, national culture while still being modern. Kumari Jayawardena notes that: "To seek legitimacy for this position many reformers idealized the civilization of a distant past, speaking of the need to regain the lost freedom that women were once said to have possessed in their societies."[206] Sibyl's speech uses similar devices when she presents the audience with a series of women in history who supported education or were learned themselves. Her references to women from Armenian history construct female education not as foreign but rather as essentially Armenian. Although Jayawardena views references to the ancient past as supporting women's "traditional subordination within the family," Sibyl's use of history has a liberating potential not acknowledged by Jayawardena. Armenian intellectuals of the nineteenth century, such as Mik'ayel Portukalian, encouraged Armenians to look to the heroes of Armenian history as models.[207] In the absence of an independent state, Armenian intellectuals based much of what it meant to be Armenian on the practices of historic independent Armenia. Sibyl's justification of female education on the basis of historic practice was a potentially powerful argument as it connects women's emancipation with Armenia's emancipation suggesting the two concepts can exist only when both are achieved. Sibyl juxtaposes eighth-century Armenia with twentieth-century Armenia implying through the use of the word "civilized," in contrast to the image of carrying "dirt," that the past was more progressive than the present. This argument drew upon the nineteenth- and early twentieth-century intellectual and political concern with achieving progress. In this speech Sibyl portrays female education as assisting Armenian women in participating as full members in the shaping national identity by recapturing their national heritage and by implication contributing to national development.

### Mariam Khatisian and the Tiflis Armenian Women's Benevolent Association

Like their counterparts under Ottoman rule, Russian-Armenians formed charitable associations and paid special attention to female education. The nineteenth century was one of great political and socio-economic change for the Armenians of the Russian Empire. The annexation of the Crimea in 1783, of eastern Georgia in 1800–1801, and the khanate of Yerevan in 1828 brought tens of thousands of Armenians into the Russian Empire. It is generally believed that Russian state policy at this time aided the economic growth and political power of Armenian merchants at the expense of former and competing elites, such as the Georgian nobility.

The Russian government granted Armenians tax exemptions and a degree of self-rule in their communities and placed them under the religious authority of Etchmiadzin. Among its powers the Catholicosate was given the authority to censor Armenian books throughout the empire, to open and run religious schools, and punish wayward parishioners. The Polozhenie (Decree) of 1836, regularized the Tsarist government's role in church affairs while sanctioning church authority over religious schools.[208] Armenian merchants and tradesmen dominated the urban centres of Transcaucasia. In 1823 the Nersesian Chemaran in Tiflis was opened and became the premier school for Armenians in Transcaucasia. Other schools opened in churches and homes and were usually taught by a single dedicated teacher. By the end of 1836 Caucasian Armenians had 21 church schools.[209]

One of the influential proponents of female education in Russian territory was Mariam Khatisian. Mariam Khatisian (neé Marisian) was born in 1845 and died February 9, 1914, in Tiflis. She served as president of the Caucasus (or Tiflis) Armenian Women's Benevolent Association [T'iflisi Hayuhyats' Baregortzakan Ënkerut'iun] from 1882 until 1907. Sibyl's *Armenian Women's Patriotic Association* was enormously influential, not only in terms of providing education to Armenian girls in the Ottoman provinces, but in serving as a model for Armenian women beyond the borders of the Ottoman state. In 1879 the AHË sent a letter to the Tiflis Armenian community asking for donations for the Association's works. A group of Tiflis women did send funds and at the same time resolved to establish a similar women's association in Tiflis. The *Tiflis Armenian Women's Benevolent Association* was established on March 7, 1882, at Gayanian Girls' School. The forty-five matrons and young ladies who were present become the Association's first members. At that time the governing council was elected, consisting of Mrs. Maria Khosrovian, Yekaterina Yevangulian, Lidia Tamamshian, Mariam Khatisian, Srbuhi Yeritsian, Nina Ghambarian and Miss Mania Hakhverdian.[210]

According to its regulations the *Tiflis Armenian Women's Benevolent Association*'s goal was to assist in the enlightenment of

the female sex by a) opening and financially maintaining schools
for girls and b) to assist by every available means girls' parochial
schools and to assist those women who desire to become school
teachers at parochial schools.[211] In goals and objectives the Tiflis
organization closely resembled the work undertaken by the AHË
and other benevolent associations founded in Constantinople. As
Houri Berberian has noted Armenian women's organizations,
across national borders, had very similar objectives and engaged
in similar activities, such as establishing schools and providing
students with clothes, books and paper necessary for school.[212] As
in the Ottoman Empire, philanthropy enabled women's participation in the public sphere, as well as extending maternal care to the
Armenian children in need of education.

The activities performed by charitable organizations, in particular, education and health care, in most countries have been
state-building activities. For example, at the same time as Sibyl
and Khatisian were establishing charitable organizations devoted
to education and social welfare (meaning care of the poor,
including hospitals and medical care) among Armenians in the
Russian and Ottoman lands, women's charitable organizations in
Iran and Argentina, were establishing educational systems and
hospitals which would be incorporated eventually into governmental ministries of education, social welfare and health.[213] Because the Armenians were minorities in the Ottoman and Russian
Empires, their charitable organizations would not become governmental ministries, nevertheless Armenian women's activities
in these areas show that the women were performing potential
state-building activities.

Sibyl's and Khatisian's charitable activities demonstrate the
author's access to the national public sphere, while their novels
represent their efforts to form public opinion to accept diversifi-
cation of Armenian women's roles in society. The remainder of
this chapter will examine Sibyl and Khatisian's representation of
the new professional Armenian woman, her ideals, her politics,
her relationship to the notion of the mother-educator, and the
obstacles facing her.

## Sibyl: A Girl's Heart

Sibyl was primarily a poet and short story writer, who also wrote several plays and one novel, *A Girl's Heart*, published by the journal *Arevelk* in 1891, which was then reprinted as a separate book in that same year. The focus of Sibyl's fiction was an analysis of love, marriage and women's entry into the public sphere. Sibyl presents the reader with paradoxes. On the one hand she stated that women's true calling was to be exclusively a wife and mother, yet at the same time her writings portray the injustice women experience in the name of convention and portray some of the earliest representation in Armenian literature of the professional woman. Srpuhi Dussap's last novel *Araksia or the Governess* had appeared only four years before Sibyl's novel *A Girl's Heart*. The influence of Dussap's novels on *A Girl's Heart* is evident in the emphasis on love as a moral signifier and the portrayal of the lover as an artist. *A Girl's Heart*, while still situated in the upper-class milieu reminiscent of Dussap's Constantinople, begins to add more diverse social elements as the characters include members of the middle- and working classes. In addition, in the latter half of the novel, the action shifts from Constantinople to the town of Pilechik'. What is new in the novel *A Girl's Heart* is the portrayal of female characters who are involved in women's organizations and work in Armenian schools.

An examination of Sibyl's fictional oeuvre reveals that she was concerned with the question of the morality and ethical behaviour of the modern Armenian woman. She was sensitive to the fact that traditional constructions of Armenian femininity were based on silence and devotion to the home. The manifestation of this was the custom of the Armenian bride entering her husband's family, and not being able to speak to anyone until the birth of her first child.[214] Devotion to the home was seen as being practiced by women's sewing, cooking and care of children. Although Sibyl's heroines are never expected to practice the custom of silence in the family, (this custom appears not to have been part of Constantinople custom), modesty and good reputation are of the utmost importance. One of the problems Sibyl's heroines face is that as writers (and many are portrayed as writers) and members of benevolent associations, their activities appear to threaten notions of female modesty, either because their names are published or because they are bold enough to publicly comment on male-female relations. Unlike Srpuhi Dussap or Zabel Yesayian, both of whom appear to have been able to ignore social convention, the latter even stated that she had always defended whatever she believed in despite social opposition,[215] Sibyl, of the Western Armenian women writers, appears most conscious of the social injunctions against women entry into the public sphere. When the novel, *A Girl's Heart*, was first published it was published under the pseudonym, Miss Alice, and is suggestive of Sibyl's discomfort with public exposure. The female characters in *A Girl's Heart* reflect Sibyl's ambivalence towards the new options opening up to Armenian women, and their interaction with women's role in the family. Sibyl tells her readers in this novel that women's primary goal in life is love and marriage and that the only life for women is family life, and the only calling motherhood.[216] In fact, in 1895 Sibyl restated the idea that love was life for women in a letter to her (future) second husband Hrant Asatur, written expressing some reluctance to become involved with him, as she was then a widow with a child, and no longer a romantic girl.[217] Despite her stated belief that love was central to women's lives, Sibyl had a long career as a teacher and writer, and in her novel, *A Girl's Heart*, the reader can discern the birth of the professional woman in Armenian letters. Despite the author's evident anxiety about feminine modesty, at the same time Sibyl's writing manifests a desperate courage in her commitment to women's entry into Armenian letters and certainly in her support of women's social activism in the form of benevolent associations and women's entry into the teaching profession. The basic outline of the plot of *A Girl's Heart* is of a failed love affair in which an innocent girl loves a young man who ultimately betrays her. The interest of this novel lies in its characterization of, and the relationship between, the heroine, Bubul, and her governess, Sofie and the problems encountered by professional women. One of the ways in which

Sibyl tried to overcome social injunctions against women's activity in the public sphere, was by constructing in literature the figure of an Armenian woman who enters the public sphere as a writer, or benevolent association member or teacher, while maintaining high ethical standards.

Bubul, the first of Sibyl's ethical, new women, is characterized by her creativity, freedom from hypocrisy and her love and care of her family. Bubul has grown up under the care of her adopted father, Mr. Aleksandr Geghamof, a Russian-Armenian, who has settled in Constantinople. He has encouraged Bubul's natural development. Initially, he engaged a German woman as Bubul's governess but wanting the young girl to have an Armenian education and upbringing, he hires a "serious and modest" Armenian girl, Sofie Gumarian, as her governess. Sibyl comments that:

> Geghamof isn't one of those fathers who stifle the teacher's efforts for the development of his daughter. He wanted an independent education, which complied with all demands. He understood that free speech and honest behaviour was the basis for a great and honest character. He smiled lovingly when that pretty little girl, with flashing eyes, protested against anything that appeared unjust and ugly to her.[218]

Because of her upbringing and education Bubul is free from hypocrisy and many of the social restraints common of young women. Consequently, Bubul is free to develop her natural talents and instincts. She becomes an accomplished musician and painter. Her governess, Sofie, encourages her talents and persuades Mr. Geghamof to hire special tutors for Bubul. Loving art, Bubul and Sofie, who are accepted into Constantinople high society as the wealthy Mr. Geghamof's natural daughters, where they are very admired, are not content with admiration, and desire to do something, therefore they establish a young ladies' organization devoted to the arts, "The Art-Lover's Young Ladies' Association."[219]

In addition, to being creative and natural, Bubul is also faithful to herself and those she loves. Her faithfulness to her own feelings and beliefs are shown in the novel by her problems and attitudes to her fiancé, Tigran Geghamof. Bubul was engaged to Tigran Geghamof, her adopted father's son, when she was a child. As children they were good friends, however, Tigran is sent to Germany for his higher education, and when he returns to Constantinople he is extremely cold to his family, he feels no real affection for them and ridicules Bubul's art, her membership in *The Art-Lover's Young Ladies' Association*, and all her beliefs. In the novel the question of women's roles, and particularly women's entry into the public sphere, is explored through the conflict between Tigran and Bubul. Bubul's entry into the public sphere occurs when she writes a play for the benefit of *The Art-Lover's Young Ladies' Association*, which is performed by Armenian actresses and actors in the garden of the Geghamof house with Constantinople high society in attendance. The reception of the play by the audience suggests some anxiety about women's public social presence and her daring to engage in social commentary. We are told that the play is about women's role in marriage and that it addresses women's lack of freedom and also adultery. Initially the audience does not know who the author is, although everyone guesses it is Bubul. It is said that Bubul did not want authorship known before the performance because: "she didn't want to be plagued by false or honest congratulations, which would irritate the young author, when the success of the play wasn't certain."[220] After the play the women congratulate her, saying: "that it would raise "our sex" if your name was on the play."[221] After everyone leaves, however, a very different reaction to the play and Bubul's writing of it, is described. Sibyl comments: "Of course some people, especially married women, thought it was improper that an unmarried girl should have such certain views about love and expound them in public."[222] Sibyl states: "In different circumstances and conditions, envy could have destroyed Bubul's esteem, but her position was high enough and [her] life decided. She had the right and even the duty to reflect upon and speak about married life, since she was engaged and would shortly be married."[223] In this passage Sibyl indicates that it is only women who are protected by wealth and position, and already engaged or married, who may dare discuss women and love in public, but even then not without some compromise of the woman's honour, because as Sibyl comments, "A woman who is master of great talent, dazzled everyone, but no one believed that she could demonstrate proper wifely modesty."[224]

When Tigran returns from Germany and hears of Bubul's play, he disapproves of her actions on the grounds of traditional morality, saying:

> Plays, poems, dances, are all empty, frivolous things, and they cannot bring any pride to Bubul or to me, I desire to receive praise for her modesty.[225]

Throughout the novel Tigran continues to criticize women who are educated and who dare to enter the public sphere in any fashion. When the Geghamofs host a dinner party, Tigran describes the guests as they arrive in a sarcastic fashion to his uncle who has recently arrived from Russia:

> "There is Constantinople's most happy girl," Tigran said after her retreating back, "She has twenty thousand voski and there are many hopefuls but men don't like her because she is one of the art lovers. Do you know what it is to be an educated girl in Constantinople? It's a guarantee to remain unmarried.

As Bubul continues to introduce guests to the General, every time a member of the Fine Arts Association was presented, or a literary and artist person, Tigran mocks her:

> Our Mozartess, our Mme de Stael, Vilie du Lille, here is our nation's Flaubert.[226]

At breakfast the next morning, when Bubul states that she likes to think that the party last night was enjoyable and will live in people's minds, that it may even become part of people's stories in future, and at least will provide pleasant memories, Tigran declares all this is nonsense and unimportant. He says that stories have no existence, that women's hearts are false, that dances are games for children and expresses surprise that any adult wanted to come to the party.[227]

Tigran is the voice of opposition to women's access to the public sphere in the novel. His conceptualization of honour is based on his future wife's adherence to conventional modes of behaviour, in this case her "modesty." Because Tigran responds sarcastically to everything Bubul says, she quickly realizes that a union between them is impossible. Bubul longs for, if not love, at least the camaraderie that existed between them in childhood, but this never occurs, and Bubul despairs wondering how she can marry a man who does not value anything she values. The reason Bubul hesitates to tell Tigran that she does not want to marry him is because she fears hurting her adopted father, Mr. Geghamof. She feels terribly guilty and wretched over this. Sibyl constructs this as a sign of Bubul's noble and tender feelings, which she characterizes as a special and necessary quality of an Armenian girl:

> . . . a new school novelist will laugh at these lines and a Parisian woman would perhaps call Bubul "silly" for her wretchedness. But a well brought up Armenian girl of a certain type will sympathize with Miss Geghamof. When a progressive and high-minded Armenian girl of this sort is unlucky enough to make a mistake because of her inexperience, she will atone for it for her entire life.[228]

Sibyl's construction of this attributions as unique to the Armenian girl, demonstrates de Groot's contention, that gender functioned as a means of underscoring difference between Middle Eastern and European society, by bonding gender to ethnic/national characteristics or identities.[229]

In Sibyl's portrayal of Bubul's feelings and behaviour, the author examines the tensions between new and old modes of behaviour. Bubul's belief that the she and Tigran should be compatible is a radical departure from patriarchal structures of marriage. As discussed in chapter two, in the then common marriage pattern in Armenian society, the family arranged most marriages. What was new among the urban, educated class of Armenians at the turn of the twentieth century, was the notion that women and men should be compatible in marriage. Sibyl was a proponent of this belief, a fact which is clear in *A Girl's Heart* and her subsequent works, notably the play, *The Daughter-in-Law*. In *A Girl's Heart*, Sibyl advocates compatibility, but even more radically, she suggests that women should not have to conform to a man's taste and preferences, because a woman also has preferences as to what sort of husband she wants, based on her personality. In the novel Bubul rebels against loveless marriage, but she is punished for this rebellion, even while the author hints that Bubul's transgressions were justified. Bubul's transgression is her rejection of Tigran Geghamof as her husband. In the final scene between Bubul and Tigran, Bubul tells him that she does not want to marry him, because she does not like him. By saying this Bubul has transgressed what is considered proper feminine behaviour in patriarchal society in which women are not allowed to criticize men or articulate dislike of a man. Bubul's declaration echoes Dussap's statement in *Siranush*, when the heroine tells her husband that since he never inquired about her feelings when he asked for her hand in marriage, he should not expect love. Bubul's statement is perhaps more blunt as she tells Tigran that she actually dislikes him. Bubul's radical behaviour, her audacity in expressing her true feelings, cannot remain unpunished. Although Sibyl supported the moral authority of love and feeling first articulated by Srpuhi Dussap, her treatment of Bubul after this declaration reveals her sense that women who try to live faithful to themselves, are inevitably silenced.

Bubul's punishment begins immediately following her statement to Tigran, when he tells his father of Bubul's treachery. This is the circumstance Bubul has been dreading, and in true Romantic style, Mr. Geghamof has a heart attack upon hearing the news and dies. Bubul is overwhelmed by guilt, causing her to fall ill. Her second punishment is when Tigran forces her out of the house after his father's funeral without a penny; her third punishment is that she loses her social position in Constantinople society; her fourth punishment is that she is consequently too poor to marry her true love; her fifth punishment is when she is forced to return to her natural father's house in Pilechik'; her sixth punishment is that she loses the man she loves, when during their separation, he finds another girl to marry, and finally, she dies at the end of the novel. The way of the transgressor is hard indeed.

Despite the consequences of Bubul's transgression, the portrait Sibyl paints of Bubul is sympathetic. Sibyl allows Bubul one consolation and that is Sofie's continued support and love of Bubul. Although she is portrayed as secondary to the heroine, Sofie acts as a mother figure to Bubul and offers the only image in the novel of a successful professional woman.

In keeping with the importance ascribed to the mother in the educational theories of the time, of which Sibyl was a creator, as the founder of AHË and a teacher, Sibyl attributes many of Bubul's difficulties to her motherlessness. Bubul's mother died at her birth, consequently, Bubul was placed in the care of her aunt, the wife of Mr. Geghamof. Bubul's aunt loved both her adopted children, Tigran and Bubul, but died when they were small children.[230] In the novel, Sibyl regards Bubul's lack of a mother as the origin of her downfall. When Bubul is faced with the problem of confessing to Mr. Geghamof that she does not want to marry his son, Sibyl suggests that if only Bubul had a mother's advice and love, she would not be in this precarious situation:

> Only a mother could free her from this difficult position, but she had never been acquainted with inexhaustible mother love. If her mother had been alive, her experience would have composed the basis of the newly blossoming girl's education and upbringing.[231]

Bubul has a mother figure in her governess, Sofie Gumarian but this is not sufficient to counteract the loss of her mother. Although Sofie is also an ethical young woman, she cannot replace Bubul's mother. She is close in age to Bubul, and although Sibyl downplays the power imbalance between them by saying Sofie was accepted by the Geghamofs as one of the family, Sofie is still a paid employee of Bubul's adopted father. In her description of Sofie's feelings towards Bubul, Sibyl illustrates this power imbalance by representing Sofie's feelings of gratitude:

> [Because] grief, which had so early shattered the bonds of love for that unfortunate soul, in her tender years, first her parents, and then her brother, she was always attracted by love and a smile. She doubled her care of her little pupil, knowing that without her she would remain in Constantinople unaided and without the means to help her adored brother.[232]

Because of her status as a paid employee and her feelings of gratitude Sofie acts to support Bubul but cannot restrain her. This becomes more complicated when Bubul and Sofie's brother, Garrnik, fall in love with each other. Sofie loves both of them and desires that they be happy. She never councils, however, that Bubul break her engagement with Tigran. It is Sofie who remains faithful to Bubul, even when Bubul loses her position in the Geghamof household. It is Sofie who works to support Bubul and Garrnik. It is Sofie who maintains contact with Bubul after the latter is forced to join her father in Pilechik', it is Sofie who argues with Garrnik when he begins to forget his promises to Bubul and finally it is Sofie, after Garrnik's engagement to another girl, who suggests that Bubul and she leave Constantinople to go to the provinces to work as teachers.

In the relationship between Sofie and Bubul, Sibyl portrays strong female friendship and this relationship offers Bubul the only relief, albeit temporary, from her punishments. In her study on female friendship in nineteenth-century English literature Tess Cosslett notes that the model for female friendship:

> . . . is nearly always the maternal one-the friends act as mother-substitutes to each other, providing physical and emotional sustenance, moral influence and example, and social initiation into the world of adult womanhood and marriage. The friendships often spring from an intense "mother-want" on both sides-not just because actual mothers are absent, but because they are inefficient, or because other women have acted as betrayers and oppressors.[233]

Sofie, as friend and governess, provides Bubul with emotional sustenance. Sofie tries to offer Bubul alternatives to marriage, but Bubul is unable to accept it; although she goes with Sofie to Mush to teach at one of AHÉ's schools, she dies there of a "malady of the heart."[234]

It is Sofie, rather than Bubul, who embodies the new professional Armenian woman in this novel. Sofie is from a good family, she is educated and talented, but must work for her living. Sofie is said to have received a good education in her father's house. Her father had an important government position and his family lived well but after his death his family inherited only debts. Therefore after his death, his daughter, Sofie, son, Garrnik, and his widow supported themselves through their own labour. After the mother's death, Sofie searched for a position as governess in order to enable her brother, Garrnik, to go to Italy to pursue a career as a sculptor.[235] Sofie is thus of a good family, fallen upon hard times, however, she is refined and a suitable companion for Bubul. When she takes up the position of governess she quickly recognizes Bubul's artistic talents and encourages them. Sofie is herself artistic and Mr. Geghamof has one of her paintings hung on his wall, which she does not sign, as she is too modest.[236] It is Sofie who requests of Mr. Geghamof that he find excellent art teachers for Bubul.[237] The bond between Sofie and Bubul quickly becomes one of mutual love. Sofie is described as an ethical young woman of the highest order.[238] She encourages Bubul's artistic and intellectual growth. After Tigran leaves for Germany, the young women discuss him with his father, but "when they were alone they talked seriously of literature, art and social issues."[239]

Sofie's employment as Bubul's governess enables her brother Garrnik, to study art in Rome. She appears not to mind working and has four jobs in the course of the novel, each of which she performs well and she is liked by her employers. Sofie is portrayed by Sibyl as hard working and devoted to those she loves. After Bubul is sent away from the Geghamof house, Sofie leaves too. Bubul lives with Sofie and Garrnik, but money is limited and Sofie searches for work. This is a reversal of the usual practice of brothers supporting sisters. In Armenian society at this time, a man's honour was shown by his ability to earn money and support his household. In Dirouhi Highgas' memoir, *Refugee Girl*, of Ottoman Armenian life at the turn of the century, a sister's sewing for money is viewed by her brother as shaming him because it implies that he cannot support her himself.[240]

Garrnik tries to sell his artwork but is largely unsuccessful. Sofie finds a position teaching at a newly opened school in Pera, by searching the Armenian newspapers. She gets a position as a piano teacher.[241] Sofie's position as a music teacher and Bubul's subsequent application for a position as a teacher of drawing indicate, however, that both enter the teaching profession in low positions. Teachers who applied for a teaching certification in handiwork, drawing, music and exercise specialities were granted only a primary school certificate, which Young argues, indicates these disciplines were viewed as holding little weight in terms of intellectual value.[242] The three young people live on Sofie's salary, which is not high and accumulate debts.[243]

Sofie, unlike Bubul, is accustomed to the world of work and can survive. Bubul on the other hand, although educated, has not been prepared to enter the working world. Bubul's education is reflective of an upper-class young woman's education, which was not designed to prepare her for employment. Dussap lamented this in her novels *Mayta* and *Araksia or the Governess*, but Sibyl's position on this issue was more ambivalent because she viewed employment as a sign of a reduction in women's class position. In the article, *Feminism Once More*, written in 1904 Sibyl argued against female employment because women are barred from "respectable" professions with only the unacceptable one of domestic service open to them.[244] Since the creation of the first girls' school, a trade school, in Constantinople in 1830 by Bezdjian amira, working-class Armenian girls were trained to earn wages.[245] Education as training for employment, however, was still not a part of the curriculum for middle and upper class girls. As we have seen from her 1904 article and speech in 1909 Sibyl did advocate employment for working-class girls and women who were left without male support by the Cilicia massacres but not for middle and upper class young women in Constantinople who had male relatives to support them. Zabel Yesayian publicly criticized Sibyl's opinion on women's employment. In an answering article, Yesayian argued that all human beings should be able to provide for their own subsistence and not be dependent on the support of husbands, fathers or brothers. She also attacked the idea that only poor women who have no other options need to work. She argued that work allows all human beings, regardless of gender and social standing, to use their intelligence and exercise their talents.[246] Sibyl's ambivalence about employment, however, reflects a fairly typical position. As we will see in chapter four, employment for Armenian women was the source of controversy in the Armenian press.

The problems facing the professional woman and the sense that work reduced women's class position are demonstrated by Bubul's attempts to secure teaching position. One evening Sofie tells that her school is looking for a drawing teacher. Bubul is excited, she wants the job, but doesn't want to speak about it in front of Garrnik in case it is against his wishes. When Garrnik goes to bed, Bubul speaks with Sofie. At first Sofie is reluctant but then agrees. The next day Sofie brings Bubul with her to the school in Pera. Bubul has some trouble at the school, because she is unaccustomed to the working world. Two men interview her and their "impudent" gazes make her blush. They ask: "How old are you?" "Are you married?" "What have you done until now?" Bubul is angered by their questions. Sibyl interjects into the text at this point to explain that Bubul "has been accustomed to mixing in the capital's highest society—what is there in her situation that should make her feel humbled and ashamed in these men's presence?" The men ask for a reference and it is Sofie who answers, informing them that the municipal chief justice of the quarter, Miabedian Effendi, is well acquainted with Bubul. They tell her that they will get back to her in two days.

After this encounter Bubul walks about Pera and sadly reflects:

> For the first time she realized what the position of a woman is when she has to earn her own living, how she must abase herself. She understood that in that reception there was none of the respect

which a decent woman has the right to expect and that they be-
haved towards her as if she was the lowest sort of person, with
whom it was possible to ignore the rules of decency.[247]

As a consequence of Bubul's visit to the school, not only is
Bubul not hired at the school, but Sofie is fired. The school decided it wasn't proper to have a girl, who had run away with her
lover, to teach children. Sofie is then suspected of being immodest
too since she associates with Bubul.[248] After being fired from the
school, the only employment available to Sofie and Bubul is
sewing.[249] In fact the professions available to Armenian women
were very circumscribed in this period. By the end of the nineteenth century, teaching young girls was one of the few careers to
provide educated Armenian women with a respectable job and
wages and this acceptance is due largely to the efforts of Armenian educational charitable organizations, particularly Sibyl's
AHË. Teaching, which took the figure of the mother-educator
into the public realm, was acceptable to Armenian society and
not viewed by the end of the nineteenth century as threatening to
the social order because it reproduced aspects of women's domestic roles. In addition, teaching which was imbued with a sense
of service to the nation enabled Armenian women to participate
in the national movement for progress and development. As Sofie
tells Bubul at the end of the novel, when she proposes that they
go to the provinces to teach:

> Now Bubul, only our unlucky homeland needs us, and we can do
> good there. You know what poverty and what ignorance there is
> in the provinces. Let's go there to teach our sisters at one of the
> society's schools and let's devote our experience for their benefit.
> At least, we may enjoy the superior consolation of doing good
> works.[250]

The two young women journey to Mush to teach at AHË's
school there. Although Bubul dies while there, the novel is silent
on Sofie's fate.

The character of Sofie is Sibyl's first attempt at representing
Armenian women's professional experience in fiction. The ques-

tion of Armenian patriotism and national development is not fore grounded in this text at all, except in reference to Sofie and her work. Sofie is hired as Bubul's governess because Mr. Geghamof wanted Bubul to be taught Armenian. As is evident from the aforementioned quotation, Sofie views teaching in the provinces as a way to serve the Armenian people. For most of the action the Armenian provinces are not discussed, except when Bubul goes to Pilechik', where the Armenians there are described as Turkish speakers, poor and ignorant, and in need of education, but Bubul rejects any idea of assisting them herself, saying that she is too poor to make any impression on them.[251]

The connection in the novel between women's entry into a profession and the only character associated with patriotism is not accidental. Working for the good of the nation functions in Sibyl's writing as a legitimate alternative to marriage for women, but these two lifestyles are seen as mutual exclusive. In Sibyl's texts a woman cannot be an active patriot and a wife and mother. Therefore the character of Sofie is outside of the romance text, although she is a young woman of talent and education, she is never represented as having a potential husband; instead she is orientated towards work and espouses patriotic values. Patriotism functions as a vocation in Sibyl's writing. At this stage in the formation of public opinion, Sibyl was conscious of obstacles against women's entry into the public sphere. Although women's education was accepted, the idea of employment and public activity was not as widespread. In addition, certain types of theory, including overt discussions of women's rights, were criticized in the Armenian press.[252] Publicly, Sibyl maintained that family ties would be compromised by women's pursuit of active patriotic work, in the form of teaching and living among Armenians in the provinces, so the two callings are always separated in her texts. In her personal life, however, Sibyl was a wife and a mother, as well as a writer, founder of the influential educational association, Azganvér Hayuhyats' Ënkerut'iun, and a teacher of Armenian at various schools in Constantinople. As a young woman, Zaruhi Galémk'earian, who visited Sibyl at home, admired her for being able to successfully combine the roles of wife and mother with that of professional woman and evidently regarded Sibyl as a model for other Armenian women.[253]

Sibyl's construction of patriotism as a kind of vocation is most evident in a play co-authored by Sibyl and Alp'aslan (1859–1919) (the pen name of poet and translator, Aleksandr Panosian) in 1909. The play, *Magnet*, was written to be performed in Constantinople as a fundraiser for the *Patriotic Armenian Women's Association.* Copies of it were sold for five ghrush to fund AHË's charitable activities. The play depicts four types of contemporary young women: the Francophile, the Anglophile, the Armenophile and the Armenian homebody. The Francophile and the Anglophile male and female were stock characters in late nineteenth century Armenian literature. Such characters value French or English culture more than their own and intersperse their speech with French or English phrases. In the play the two most interesting characters are the Armenophile, Vehanush, who is a member of AHË, and the Armenian homebody, Arsine. In fact, Vehanush and Arsine, appear to be the same character split into two. For Arsine also espouses Armenian patriotism and admires and supports Vehanush's work. The difference between Vehanush and Arsine is that Vehanush is devoted to the Armenian people and charitable works and Arsine is devoted to her mother and her fiancé. The splitting of the character of the good Armenian girl is indicative of Sibyl's construction of marriage and active patriotic work as incompatible, one would compromise the calling of the other.

Vehanush's work, however, is described in familial terms. The Armenians of Cilicia are described as mothers and sisters, and the patriotic Armenian girl sees it as women's highest duty to care for them. When the four young women discuss what they would do if they won a large sum of money, Vehanush states:

> "If I had money, I would go directly to Armenia to open schools, in order to spread education and enlightenment in Cilicia's starving villages; in every corner of Mush, Papert, Van, Sassoun, Khus and Pasen, I would bring a kind word, a useful aim, medicine for the ill, clothes for the naked, seeds for the hopeless farmer, and finally an endearment, encouragement and aid for all our kin-the

fathers, mothers, sisters and brothers, who would accept me as a comforting angel, who would love me and bless me . . . How wonderful that would be! Isn't this the Armenian girl's and the Armenian woman's principal calling and first and greatest responsibility in the world?"

Shushan answers: "Oh! Quelle idée! Ma chère Vehanush . . . One day you will be the mother of the Kalfayian Orphanage. . ."[254]

The character Shushan's statement underscores one of the principal concepts of the age, in which the physical role of motherhood, giving birth, is downplayed in relation to the role of nurturing and educating. The mother was to be mother of the nation and therefore if a woman did not marry she could become surrogate mother of the nation through her work with Armenian orphans but not, in Sibyl's writing, if she had a husband and children of her own. Nevertheless the unmarried woman devoted to the nation did create space for women to work and to have a role in the public sphere.

### Mariam Khatisian: On a New Road

Although the plot of Mariam Khatisian's novel *On a New Road* (1894), published three years after Sibyl's *A Girl's Heart* superficially resembles the latter novel, its treatment of the new professional Armenian woman suggests greater ease with women's entry into careers and the public sphere. Like *A Girl's Heart* much of the plot of *On a New Road* revolves around a young woman's love affair with a man, who betrays her. As in *A Girl's Heart* the young woman is an intimate friend of the man's sister and the sister acts as a support to the heroine. The differences between these two novels lies in the fate of their respective heroines, while Sibyl's heroine cannot live and must die after the marriage role is denied her, Khatisian's heroine, after a period of grief over the end of her love affair, begins a career as a teacher and by the end of the novel emerges as a fully-fledged professional woman.

Mariam Khatisian, who has largely been forgotten today and appears in no history of Armenian literature, penned four novels: *Heghine* (1890), *Husband Hunters* (1894), *On a New Road* (1894) and *The Unfortunate Wife* (1899). Khatisian's novels examine urban Caucasian Armenian women's experience of courtship and marriage among the Tiflis bourgeoisie. The novel *Husband Hunters (1*894) describes the main character's search for a wealthy husband, described with great irony by the author, while her final novel, *The Unfortunate Wife* (1899), examines a young, wealthy, but middle-class Armenian woman's marriage into a Russian princely family, and her subsequent alienation and loss of control over her person, her child and her finances. The novel, *On a New Road* is the most interesting of Khatisian's novels as it focuses on the liberation of Armenia movement, female education and the entry of Russian Armenian women into the public sphere.

As Tess Cosslett has stated about nineteenth-century English fiction, "Fiction . . . actually consists in narrative devices and conventions, and these reflect, embody or even create not 'reality' or 'experience,' but ideology."[255] In Khatisian's *On a New Road*, with its suggestive title of change and new paths, the ideology of patriotism and women's role in this movement loams large. The novel set in Tiflis among the educated Armenian middle and upper classes, examines the issues of assimilation to Russian culture of the Armenians living in the Russian Empire, the plight of Western Armenians under Ottoman rule, and response to this issue by Russian-Armenians, and finally the advent of the Russian-Armenian woman into the public, political sphere.

The problem of assimilation to Russian culture and its opposite, how to be a patriotic Armenian, are explored in the novel through the characters of Susan Varts'ian, her daughter, Sofia Meroyeva, and Sofia's daughter, Liza. Each of these women is influenced by a specific historical period and social context, and represents a specific stance towards Armenian culture, relevant to Khatisian's construction of gender and modernity. The eldest, Susan Varts'ian, represents the old, Armenian nobility, closely connected to the Georgian princely court. Khatisian describes the old Armenian princely class of Tiflis as follows:

Since the Armenians have lived in Georgia for centuries, they, especially the noble class, were assimilated to Georgian culture; gradually losing their nationality, customs and language, only through religion did they remain connected to ordinary Armenians. For this reason Princess Susan was educated in Georgian and did not know Armenian.[256]

Khatisian inserts a footnote in the text stating that this was before the Russian takeover of Georgia in 1801. The author states that it was only in the Armenian villages away from Tiflis that Armenians retained their customs and language, but that the Tiflis elite considered them rather coarse. Susan Varts'ian, due to her parents' lack of financial solvency, was married into an Armenian mercantile family, which was from the countryside and therefore practiced Armenian customs and spoke Armenian in the home. In fact, the decline of the nobility in Georgia and the rise of the urban mercantile class is a feature of the incorporation of Georgia into the Russian Empire.[257] Khatisian describes mercantile families and women's position in them as follows:

Armenian girls, who were forced to migrate from the provinces, and were therefore untouched by Georgian ways, were taught blind obedience to adults' desires, household economy, housework, obedience to indigenous customs, and a wrathful and unquestioned religion and humility which prevented arguing with men. They nipped in the bud any sort of independent ideas or interest in the world in their girls by keeping them busy with housework.

Believing in fate, women patiently bore their lot. The protection of family honour and strict responsibility was the sign of a well-regarded family. Thanks to these harsh, definite views, women were shaped as a more or less indistinct type.

It was into such a family that Princess Susan married. Because she had been her family's only daughter, and living under somewhat different conditions, she had grown up rather free, but thanks to her natural capabilities and intellect, she had remained uncorrupted.

Her new family's conversation and style appeared crude, and the closed life didn't come easily, but responsibility, which at that time all classes were well-trained in, forced her to gladly accept her situation.

In time Susan gradually became accustomed to her husband's hardworking family, and day-by-day she was convinced that under their rough exterior, they had warm and loving hearts.[258]

Because she learns to admire her mother-in-law and sister-in-law Susan assimilates into the culture and customs of her husband's family, even learning Armenian. Through her care of her family and her household, Susan represents the traditional Armenian mother but not the mother-educator of the nation because of her lack of connection to Armenians outside of her family.

In contrast to Susan, her daughter, Sofia, rejects Armenian culture. When Susan's husband died suddenly, their two daughters were young and his financial affairs were not in order, therefore Susan was forced to rent out their house in Tiflis and move to the village estate belonging to her husband. The village had no school and as a consequence, Susan sent her daughters to a boarding school in Tiflis. At school the two girls became assimilated to Russian culture. Susan returned to Tiflis every two or three months to visit with her daughters at school, she discovered, however, that with each visit her daughters were increasingly distant with her. The conflict between Susan and her daughters is that the school assimilates them into Russian culture and upper class consumer values. Her daughters are embarrassed because Susan speaks only Georgian and Armenian and because their father was a merchant. Khatisian describes how the daughters have learned to be ashamed of their background at school:

"Mummy, is it true that our father was always a merchant?" Her youngest daughter asked in Russian one day after a long lull in conversation. This daughter had already not spoken with her mother in Armenian or Georgian for a long time, truthfully she was ashamed to speak these languages, but her mother spoke Russian poorly and always answered the child in Armenian or Georgian.

"I don't understand what you are asking, darling, he was always engaged in trade.

"He was never an official?" The eldest daughter asked with surprise.

"It's because of that that all our friends call us "armeashka-dargashka," the two girls exclaimed with tears in their eyes.

The girls continue, asking if their father spoke Russian, because their fellow classmates, say he did not speak Russian. Losing her patience Susan replies:

"Enough of this foolishness. You aren't children anymore, you are fifteen and you, fourteen years old, it's not right that you place such importance on every empty speech. Whether your father spoke Russian or not isn't important, by God, if only all fathers were as good men as your father was!"

"But our grandparents were of noble birth weren't they?" The girls asked with little shame.

"We have heard that they had Russian servants and they decorated their house in Russian style, not those horrid Oriental inlaid things." The younger daughter said with disdain.[259]

Khatisian explains the two girls' fascination with Russian culture and disdain of Armenian as part of a larger trend:

The country fell under Russian influence and began to follow Russian lifestyle trends. The girls, while still in school, had vaguely felt that at present life was on a new road and they yielded to these trends. Under the influence of these trends they didn't find their parents' perspectives and ideals to be sufficient, and were searching for something better. But where should they find these new ideas? These ideas were presented to them in chaotic disarray and they didn't know which to turn to. At the school the girls had absorbed false ideas, about love and self-sacrifice, which they learned in novels, and they confessed to each other that they adored a beloved person above all and worshipped him.[260]

Lacking the ability to judge what are productive values, Sofia and her sister yearn for the world they read about in books. At a party one evening they discuss, with several youths, a Russian novel called, *What is to be done?* The novel, *What is to be done?*, was an actual, controversial work by the Russian radical N.G. Chernyshevsky, written in prison, and published a year before its author's execution. The novel had generated enormous controversy in Russia upon its publication in 1863. It portrays the heroine's struggle to emerge as a full human being, including having intellectual and sexual freedom. In the course of the novel, the heroine discovers that work is the central force in life, and therefore she opens a sewing cooperative, hires women workers, makes partners of them, shares the profits and trains them to become self-reliant. The novel's detractors accused the author of advocating sexual immorality, while admirers and supporters of the novel viewed the novel as having shown women the right path to emancipation. Supporters of the novel in Russia, sometimes even went so far as to open cooperatives modelled after the novel's sewing cooperative in order to put into practice Chernyshevsky's theories on labour and women's emancipation.[261] In Khatisian's *On a New Road*, Susan Varts'ian's two daughters have read this novel at their Russian gymnasium. The two girls proclaim their approval of the novel. They say it is wonderful but are attracted to its discussion of freedom, not its interest in sewing cooperatives, the working class, or "the people," since both girls are contemptuous of the Armenian peasantry they encounter in their mother's village. In the following dialogue Khatisian shows how two girls in Tiflis understood the novel:

> "But what are your life's ideals?" Asked one of the youths with bitter irony.
> "Oh, if it was up to me, first of all men and women's society wouldn't be divided. Second, Russian would be spoken everywhere, and thirdly, it would be permitted for girls to walk everywhere in the city, even along the streets. What else should I say? In short, I wish that our lives be free of all old prejudices.
> "Or to say it differently we should do, whatever is accepted in European civilization," added the plump sister.
> "Very well, then what are your wishes for your people?" The youth asked with interest. Seeing that the girls were at a loss, he

added, "I want to know what is your opinion about the national people's schools?"

"About them we can't say," said the slender sister, helping her sister out of a difficult situation, "the government will take care of the people's education."

"Of course, that is what they told us at school." The other responded happily.[262]

The two Russian educated girls mimic ideas about women's emancipation but cannot think for themselves about the conditions of the Armenians and instead rely on the Russian government to solve any such problems. As will be explored further, Khatisian believed that women should have a role in national development. Although she rejects the confinement in the home model of Susan Varts'ian's family as not beneficial to the Armenians as a whole, she empathetically rejected the idea that women's roles should be merely imitating what they had learned about European social structures from novels. Western and Eastern Armenian intellectuals were concerned with the issue of imitation of European societies, which they viewed as dangerous to Armenian identity. The question of Armenian women's imitation of foreign cultures became especially important when women's role as mothers of the nation was emphasized. For this reason, much of Armenian literature of this period, especially literature by women explored women's roles and their relationship to Armenian identity. Through the creation of various female characters, authors rejected certain behaviours and advocated others, usually portraying in a dramatic form the perils of straying from Armenian values and customs. Khatisian shows the respective consequences of Susan and Sofia's behaviour through the theme of housekeeping.

One of the jobs Armenian women were expected to be responsible for was good household management. Raffi's survey of rural and urban Armenian women in the Caucasus had emphasized that this was one of Armenian women's primary responsibilities.[263] Khatisian, who had read Raffi and was strongly influenced by his essays about women, also constructs household management as a principal attribute of a good Armenian woman:

> Our Armenian women have long been famous for their household
> economy. They are able to spend their husband's money wisely,
> while at the same time saving money for the children.[264]

The consequence of Sofia's imitation of Russian culture, and
specifically of upper-class consumer culture and fashion is that
when she marries she is a poor housekeeper and squanders her
husband's money and even her own dowry, which was meant to
be saved for her daughters' dowries. Susan tries, unsuccessfully,
to intervene and advises Sofia's husband to curb her spending.
Sofia retorts that all upper class people live and spend as she
does. In contrast to Sofia's behaviour as a young bride, Susan in
the same position, considered it a matter of pride that upon her
mother's-in-law death she was able to take over household
management.[265] In Susan Varts'ian's youth the taking over of
household management was seen as a sign of maturity and dignity for an adult woman. Because Sofia refuses this responsibility
she remains childish and irresponsible. As an elderly lady, Susan's
management of the village estate, which she had administered
without male assistance, since her husband's death, is praised by
everyone. One evening Susan explains to the son of the owner of
the neighbouring estate how she manages the estate:

> She enumerated the income she received from the sowed fields,
> gardens, and the sale of vegetables, wood and cattle. She showed
> such interest and practical knowledge that the youths were amazed,
> and were even more amazed when they learned how much she
> was able to get from a relatively small estate.[266]

In contrast to her mother, Susan, Sofia spends money without
restraint and lets the household accounts lapse. Due to her
extravagance there is no money for her daughters' dowries, in
order to get them married, her husband borrows money and goes
into debt. The family is financially ruined and the family loses
their home.[267]

In the novel, the character of Susan functions as a positive example of the traditional Armenian woman. She is a good housekeeper, was obedient to her husband and his family, tried to be a good mother and grandmother and learned Armenian when required. Khatisian treats the character of Susan Varts'ian with respect but Susan is a character of the past and not the ideal modern woman. In contrast, Susan's daughter, Sofia is not treated respectfully and is a cautionary example of what not to become. Liza, the heroine of the novel represents Khatisian's ideal modern woman. She is close to her grandmother, Susan, throughout her childhood Liza spent long summers with Susan on the village estate. She follows Susan's directives on household economy and familial respect and obedience. In attributing these qualities to Liza, Khatisian attempts to synthesize what she considers valuable from the past, with a new vision of the future. But Khatisian adds to Liza several qualities that Susan lacks. Firstly, Liza, unlike Susan, is educated and believes in the importance of education and secondly, she is patriotic. When living on the estate Liza teaches the village children Armenian. Although Susan supports some education, she does not value the education of the villagers to the extent Liza does. In addition, Susan Varts'ian has a much more hierarchical relationship to the villagers than does Liza. Until 1870 peasants in Transcaucasia were serfs and their land was owned by Muslim and Christian landlords. The land reform of 1870 permitted peasants to own land, but they had to purchase it from the landlord, and most were too poor to purchase the land.[268] Susan's relations with the peasants on her estate reflects the former feudal state, she expects complete obedience to her orders from them. Although never embracing socialist ideas, which had already entered Transcaucasia, Liza disagrees with her grandmother's attitude towards the peasants, the only time disagreement between them is mentioned in the novel.[269]

The final criticism levelled against Susan Varts'ian's generation in *On a New Road* is that Armenians of that era did not have a sense of solidarity with Armenians beyond family members. In the novel, the son of the neighbouring estate owner, Levon Bagruni, brings his elderly aunt to visit with Susan Varts'ian. The two elderly women speak of the manners and mores of their youth, and reserve particular praise for the sacredness of family life and love towards relatives:

> "Yes, today they aren't acquainted with love of family." Susan sighed.
> "What family? What relatives?" Angrily cut in Aunt Katerina.
> "The other day I was in society, and a young woman was shown one of her close female relatives and she said 'Who's that?' Bah, did you ever hear such a thing! What days have we entered into?" The old lady asked with a deep sigh."

Levon's response to the elderly ladies' speech, emphasizes the new ideology of patriotism, espoused by Khatisian:

> "In reality, it is impossible to not favourably regard the patriarchal life in some ways, however, in other ways, we should be happy that those times have passed." Bagruni said turning to Mrs. Varts'ian.
> "In the past they lived in a limited family environment, and outside of their kin and close relatives, other people could die of starvation, and no one would concern themselves with their circumstances. And now, if people don't respect their relatives, as they did in the past, at least now societal good is close to their hearts."[270]

Levon's statement is the key to understanding Khatisian's conceptualization of the ideal role of the Armenian women in the public sphere. The Armenian woman is expected to bring the values of maternal care to the public sphere so that the members of the Armenian nation are cared for like fellow family members. This notion of Khatisian's was also expressed by other female intellectuals, notably Zabel Yesayian, who advocated an active, public role for Armenian women, justifying women's entry into public work by arguing that the Armenian woman should have both rights and duties in the public sphere, as her help was necessary in eradicating social problems. Yesayian wrote:

What we desire of our women, whatever social class they belong to, and whatever the level of their progress, is that every one of them must do her share in educational and charitable work. Women's place alongside men is necessary and valuable. This is of particular importance when we look around us and see that there are children who go to school hungry and half-naked, that there are unemployed women who need to work for a living, unfortunate girls alone in their misfortune, sick people who have no medicine and children who are dying because of their parents' ignorance and poverty.

Yesayian concluded this article by advocating that women's traditional domestic responsibilities extend to the public sphere:

Assuredly the future will show that for humanity, they [women] have an important and valuable contribution, which until now has been confined to the benefit of their families.[271]

The notion of doing societal good is what distinguishes, in Khatisian's novel, Liza and Levon's generation from the generation of the elderly Susan and Aunt Katerina and certainly from the self-centred and Russified, Sofia. Patriotism by doing societal good plays an important role in this novel. Love of the Armenian nation is shown through concern with the oppression of the Western Armenians and closer to home, the education of Armenians in Russian Armenia.

The oppression of the Western Armenians living under Turkish rule was a central issue in Russian Armenian intellectual circles. The political parties, the Hnchak and the Dashnak, were founded by Russian Armenian intellectuals. Young Russian Armenians formed circles, as does the character of Ruben in this novel, to study and discuss political and philosophical issues and to read the novels of Raffi and the poetry of Rafael Patkanian (1830–1892).[272] The political and social conditions in Western Armenia are of supreme importance in Khatisian's *On a New Road*. In fact, the influence of Raffi on this novel is quite evident, particularly his novel, *Kaytser* [Sparks], first published in Tiflis in 1883. *Kaytser* is mentioned by name in Khatisian's *On a New Road* and her novel reads in part as an accompaniment to Raffi's *Kaytser*. The novel, *Kaytser* focused on a group of Armenian students who visit Western Armenia, where they analyze and observe Armenian life under Ottoman rule. They explore options and possible ways of alleviating the plight of the Ottoman Armenians. Khatisian's novel portrays a similar process, all the young men in her novel visit Western Armenia, and discuss the treatment of the Ottoman Armenians and debate how they can work to improve conditions. One of the characters, Ruben Geokch'ian, sums up the prevalent attitude among the young Russian Armenians of the novel, thus:

> "We, Russian Armenians, who live under better conditions," Ruben continued hotly, "are duty bound to help our oppressed brothers with all of our strength and capabilities. And they justly put all their hopes on us."[273]

Believing it is their duty to aid the Western Armenians, the youths in Tiflis discuss strategies to do so. The strategies they discuss range from setting up schools and hospitals in Western Armenia to supporting armed struggle. Some of the youths argue for a "cultural road" which includes educating the populace and argue against armed struggle because they fear it would result in massacre of the Western Armenians. They debate the possibility of European, particularly English, support of the Armenians:

> "Indeed England has an advantage in this issue, but it is very dangerous to place hopes on their help," objected Geokch'ian. "It is evidently sympathetic and will encourage rebellion, but in difficult moments it will not help Armenians, because as always it doesn't want to incur harm to itself. It is frightening to envision the terrible images of what will happen to the Armenians left with only their own defences. The troops, principally composed of Turks, will totally wipe them out, and at that time you can say goodbye, for a long time, or forever, to the hope of liberation. Everywhere the Armenian element is oppressed."
> "It's true," several voices were raised in agreement with Geokch'ian.

"Finally Ruben, you agree with us," called out Manukian, "All far-sighted and right thinking men have always of the opinion that at present sedition in Turkey would result in massacre; with half of the Armenians being killed and the other half subjected to such severity that it would be impossible to imagine cultural development in Western Armenia. Therefore it is necessary to resist the present movement with all our might. Yes, gentlemen, there is only one path in the goal of ensuring the country's progress and that is the cultural path," Manukian confidently asserted. "It is necessary to go there with the intention of studying the country, to find the means of awakening the people to the awareness of their situation and not to incite rebellion at present."[274]

Khatisian states that such discussions of the situation were common to all progressive and patriotic minded Russian Armenian youths. Discussion of the Western Armenian situation always occurs in the novel among young men. (Older men are invariably against this movement and concentrate on making money and curbing youthful enthusiasm). Armenian women are not portrayed as being interested in such issues. The exception to this rule is Liza. In Liza, Khatisian explores how a female patriot is formed and the obstacles to her participation in active patriotic work. Liza's devotion to Armenian identity is demonstrated by her desire to learn Armenian well and her teaching career. However, Liza is also interested and sympathetic to the living conditions of the Armenians in Western Armenia and like her male counterparts, she desires to assist them, what makes this impossible is her gender. When males visit Western Armenia in this novel, as part of a "depi erkire" [towards the homeland] movement,[275] Liza is conscious of how she is prevented from doing the same. When a group of her male compatriots plan a trip to Western Armenia she thinks:

Is there really nothing we women can do to better the conditions of the Turkish Armenians? Won't there be the wounded and the ill there who will need our help?[276]

Throughout the novel Liza's interest in Western Armenia is perceived by society to be unusual in an Armenian girl. During a visit to the Geokch'ian house, the female guests go to one room, the male guests to another. The women gossip, while the men discuss politics. Liza bored by the women's gossip, desires to join the men, but feels uncomfortable about going into their room alone. The young men are portrayed as admiring of Liza's patriotic interests and sympathetic to her, but when she joins their conversations her awkwardness reveals the difficulties she faces in crossing the gender divide into the public sphere. Sensing Liza's desire to join the men Ruben invites her to join the men's conversation. Liza enters saying that she hopes she is not disturbing them. Ruben answers:

> "On the contrary, your sympathy gives heart to all those in service to this sacred task." He said loudly, the other youths hearing this looked respectfully at the young woman.
> "We are very pleased to witness this," added Geokch'ian's close friend, Levon Bagruni, "especially since we are not accustomed to the fair sex's sympathy in social and national questions."
> Blushing Liza shyly sat in the room's farthest corner.
> After distributing the tea, Hrrip'simé entered the room too.
> The conversation's principal theme was the Turkish government's treatment of the hapless Armenians and possible ways to improve the situation of the unfortunates. From there they turned to a discussion of the lack of medical care in Turkish Armenia. Earlier Geokch'ian had discussed the necessity of opening a hospital in Van and about the possibility of collecting money for such a project.[277]

In the novel, Liza and Ruben fall in love with each other. Unlike Sibyl's heroine, Bubul, however, this love is not for Liza an end in itself. In fact, Khatisian's portrayal of Liza's and Ruben's relationship hints that Liza's primary attraction to him is her belief that if married they would be able to go to Western Armenia together to aid the Armenian people. Ruben has been to Western Armenia and he speaks eloquently with Liza about what he witnessed there. He is well educated in Armenian and helps her with her language studies. When a student at the university in Moscow, we are told, Ruben gave speeches and wrote articles on the topic of the Armenian Question, thereby gathering a group of admirers and supporters around him.[278] Liza and others view him as a committed patriot. Upon examining how both discuss their future marriage it is clear that the lure of going to Western Armenia together infuses this relationship. When courting, Ruben brings Raffi's novel, *Kaytzer*, which he reads to Liza. Interrupting the reading, Ruben asks Liza, if she is listening, she answers:

> "You understood. I was thinking about your essay and I want to know how things are progressing? You have said that its success is related to your going to Turkish Armenia, where you will fulfil the role of the hero of this novel we are reading."
> "The essay is going ahead, darling. From the day that I learned that you returned my love, my mind has received extra courage and is more capable."
> Liza squeezes his hand and happily asks: "You will take me there with you, won't you?"
> "Of course, darling. You will be my guiding star, you will ease my chosen work.
> "We will work together."[279]

Both Ruben and Liza describe their coming union as a chance to achieve societal good together. Ruben's vision of marriage is revealed by his advice to his friend, Levon:

> I advise you to marry Olia, [Liza's sister] she is a wonderful girl. We would be neighbours and together with our wives we could work. We will enter into a new level of familial governance and we will open a school and hospital. Oh what a wonderful life it will be![280]

Liza likewise invites another person to join them in their work. She tells, Hrip'simé, her friend and Ruben's sister:

> You will come with us won't you Hrrip'simé? I am quite breathless from happiness when I think of how we can participate in this

great work, which earlier we only dreamed of. If only we could go there soon, where we are so needed," Liza said enthusiastically.[281]

Liza's need to marry in order to fulfil her desire to go to Western Armenia is highlighted at the end of the novel, when having been betrayed by Ruben, who has abandoned her to marry a wealthy girl, and in addition, has subsequently lost interest in the Western Armenians in favour of his medical career, Liza more cold bloodedly, because she knows she is not in love, contemplates marriage to Levon in order to go to Western Armenia. In the end Liza, decides that it is not fair to marry Levon when she knows her feelings toward him are based solely on friendship not love.[282] Thus ends Liza's opportunity to go to Western Armenia.

Despite the fact that working in Western Armenia does not turn out to be a viable option, Khatisian allows Liza an outlet for her desire to do patriotic work, when she becomes a committed schoolteacher in Eastern Armenia. Khatisian's Liza as schoolteacher is the first fully-fledged portrayal in Armenian literature of a career-orientated Armenian girl. Unlike Sibyl's Bubul, Liza does not do this work because her love affair ends. Prior to her betrayal by Ruben, Liza already had exhibited passionate commitment to patriotic work; education is the path by which Liza can achieve her goal of engaging in socially productive labour.

*On a New Road* is a bildungsroman, in the sense that it outlines the development of a young woman from the intelligent but pampered daughter of a wealthy family interested in intellectual and social issues, to a woman committed to education and serious enough about her profession to be able to leave her family and risk their disapproval to go to abroad to study pedagogy in Switzerland. From the beginning of the novel, Khatisian depicts Liza as a young woman committed to Armenian identity. Unlike her sister Olia, who studies French, Liza studies Armenian. From the start Liza desires to utilize her ability in Armenian for the benefit of others. In the first chapter of *On a New Road* it is stated that over the winter Liza translated a children's book into Armenian.[283] It is revealed that she has also been teaching the village children on her grandmother's estate to read and write during her summer visits. She is disheartened to learn, however, that the children have largely forgotten what she has taught them from one summer to the next. She wishes that there were a school in the vicinity, which the children could attend all year round.[284] At this point in the novel, although Liza, teaches the children the Armenian language and arithmetic every summer, and is certainly sincere in her commitment to them, her attitude to teaching is amateurish. At the beginning of the novel, Liza's attention is captivated by her love for Ruben and the promise of their great work in Western Armenia. The turning point in Liza's development as a professional woman is when the relationship with Ruben is ended. Initially, Liza falls into a state of extreme depression, rather like Sibyl's Bubul, but what saves Liza is her family and friends' support and her already existing commitment to education. Liza's father and grandmother provide the emotional support, which enables Liza to overcome her grief, something orphaned and uncommitted Bubul could not do.

At the same time, Khatisian clearly shows that Liza needs to overcome societal injunctions against women's entry into the public sphere in order to emerge as a professional woman. As discussed earlier, Liza's interest in Western Armenia was considered unusual in an Armenian girl. Society, and Liza's family expect her to marry. The notion that young women can work is rejected by all. When Liza's family loses all their money and are forced to move into humbler quarters, Liza's mother becomes extremely depressed, undaunted, Liza offers to work to improve the family's situation:

> "Of course, dear mother, poverty is not as terrible as it seems to you. If only the debts were paid, they more than anything disturb father. I am young, I can work. Several of my girlfriends support their entire families, I will do likewise, and you will see how well we will live."
>
> But Sofia refuses this emphatically saying: "If you want to improve our situation, get married."
>
> "Then I will die happy," said Meroyeva in a weak voice interrupting his wife, while entering the room, barely able to stand.

"Free me from that. It is better to die than to be offered to someone as a payment of debt. That is beyond my endurance, dear parents," cries Liza collapsing into the armchair.[285]

Liza's refusal to enter into marriage for financial reasons is part of a larger movement in Armenian letters in which marriage as a financial transaction was fiercely rejected by women authors. Srpuhi Dussap had argued against it in the novel, *Siranush* (1884), and Marie Beylerian argued against it in the pages of *Artemis*, in favour of marriage based on compatibility and love between the partners.

Liza's family are not cruel, however, they simply cannot envision a life for a woman that does not include marriage. As Susan Varts'ian's worrying over Liza's future reveals:

How is it possible for her to live alone? What other goal can a woman have in her life, other than the care of home and children? What can her future possibly be if she doesn't marry?[286]

This question is not illogical, given the fact that in the late nineteenth century few career options were available to upper-class women in the Caucasus. Despite limited opportunities and society's condemnation Liza determines to forge a new path for herself. She decides to become a schoolteacher and asks Levon Bagruni to help her find a position as a headmistress at a parochial school. He does so and a position is found for her in the Akhaltskha province. Bagruni inquires if her grandmother will consent to Liza living away from home. Susan Varts'ian will not consent to Liza living away from her because Liza is "young, beautiful and naïve." Seeing Liza's determination, however, her grandmother talks with Bagruni and persuades him to finance the opening of a school in Liza's grandmother's village, which will benefit the children on both estates and allow Liza to remain within the protection of her family.[287]

At this juncture the novel begins to describe the new school and Liza's activities there. The description of the school offers insight into the conditions of village schools in the late nineteenth century. The school consists of: "two large rooms with rows of desks and benches, blackboards and cupboards containing school supplies and books, and even a clock on the wall."[288] The children are dressed in new, clean clothes, purchased by Bagruni. "The girls are wearing clean dresses. Their dresses are of a dark coloured printed cotton with grey aprons; all of this gives Liza an encouraging impression."[289] The social and political function of the school-it teaches adherence to concepts of time and punctuality through the clock, trains the children to conform by wearing uniforms, and teaches obedience to authority are evident in the description, but not criticized by the author.

Liza's teaching consists of reading the children advisory tales, teaching them about the surrounding environment and "raising their level of progress." As Young's research on Armenian education in the nineteenth century has revealed, language textbooks often contained a combination of history, business, moral stories, with animals being used to explain morality lessons, object lessons, proverbs, and grammar.[290] Khatisian portrayal of Liza's practices confirms this model. Liza teaches the children in the mornings and devotes her evening hours to "her little pupils."[291]

An assistant, Miss Sat'enik, who is described as a graduate of a parochial school, aids Liza in her teaching. She was hired by Bagruni as a teacher of women's handicrafts. Handicrafts were viewed by charitable organizations as particularly important as they prepared working class pupils for a trade. In 1888 the Tiflis Women's Benevolent Association, of which Khatisian was a member, got the chance to make into a reality its longstanding wish to open a trade school. On September 21, 1888 the school of dressmaking and handicrafts opened. The pupils were taught-sewing, embroidery and ironing, drawing, accounting, and household economy. Eventually, the curriculum was extended to include cookery, laundering, hat and stocking making.[292]

Khatisian portrays teaching as having a healing effect on Liza. Her love for the profession increases and the pupils' hard work and interest inspires her. When she thinks of the past and particularly her depression over the end of her affair with Ruben, she thinks:

> How wrong my view of life was, I thought that life had lost all
> its significance, but what a source of happiness my little pupils
> are to me.[293]

As Liza teaches on a daily basis she begins to lament the lack
of good textbooks in Armenian for the children's use.[294] With a
male friend, Arshak Manukian, who teaches boys, Liza discuss
the problem of acquiring good textbooks. They confer with Levon
Bagruni about the idea of forming an organization for the translation of books into Armenian for girls.[295] Witnessing Liza's devotion to education, Khatisian has Arshak, who has always criticized Armenian girls as artificial and self-absorbed in the novel,
reflect upon the good a woman who is interested in intellectual
activities can have on society:

> He prepared to say to Liza that she was responsible for a change
> within him, he wanted to explain that when a woman's heart was
> imbued with intellectual benefits, she with unavoidable strength
> affected the world around her, but he restrained himself not
> regarding it as his right to behave so freely.[296]

He informs Bagruni, however, of his change of heart stating:

> If among us ten or twenty women, could become so interested in
> social issues [as Liza], our country would be a happy
> place…Unfortunately our girls think only of their own advance-
> ment, which serves as an advertisement for their various (per-
> sonal) goals.[297]

Arshak's statement, which echoes Raffi's discussion of the
importance of women's education and participation in the public
sphere for the benefit of the nation, is based on a new
conceptualization of the family as the foundation of the country
and the woman as mother was seen as the foundation of the family. As Najmabadi has argued about Iranian society in the same
period:

The envisaging of the family as the foundation of the nation, as
standing for a building block of the nation, also meant reenvisaging
relationships within it. Ignorant women were not only unsuitable
as mothers but also unfit as spouses . . . a sentiment comparable to
friendship between men was proposed to constitute the right bond
between husband and wife.[298]

When women began to be viewed as a foundation of the nation
and a companion to men greater importance was ascribed to their
intellectual and moral qualities. For this reason Liza's interest in
Western Armenia and education, which is viewed as ridiculous
by her mother, is admired by nationalist men as a model for other
women and an example of the ideal woman.

At this stage in Liza's development, however, teaching functions partly as a way of forgetting her disappointments over the
affair with Ruben and the end of her dream of going to Western
Armenia. This is demonstrated in the novel by the frantic quality
of Liza's work. She works virtually all day and in the evening
with her pupils. The village women and Liza's grandmother
become alarmed as they believe she is compromising her health.
Susan attempts to persuade her to slow her pace of work, arguing
that even if she doesn't care about her own health she should at
least think of her pupils who are in class all day and are looking
pale. Liza responds by splitting her pupils into two groups-seeing
the younger ones in the morning and the older ones in the after-
noon. Her grandmother is not satisfied as Liza herself is still working all day.[299] Due to this hectic pace, Liza falls ill and the doctor
orders her return to Tiflis for medical attention and rest. Liza is
very upset by this because she does not want to discontinue teaching at the school and informs her grandmother that the school is
not a toy to her. In order to ease her mind about the school Bagruni
offers to hire a replacement teacher for the year. After much
deliberation Liza determines that he should hire Hrrip'simé, who
teaches private pupils, because she will be able to understand the
course of study Liza has established at the school.[300]

In Tiflis Liza recovers, and it is at this stage that the last
impediment to Liza's development as a teacher occurs. She sees

Ruben one evening at the opera with his wife and realizes that she now views their relationship as being unimportant. This is in contrast to Sibyl's Bubul who cannot see her lover as unimportant and who has no alternative to death, despite her governess and friend, Sofie's attempts to channel her interest into teaching Armenian girls in the provinces. In contrast, Liza becomes healthier and her attitude to teaching becomes healthier too. She is greatly interested in it but not to the detriment of her physical and mental health. She begins to reflect upon the lack of Armenian women in the professions. She tells Bagruni that she thinks that it is a great pity that there are no women doctors, because they could be of great benefit to the villagers. Liza statement about medicine and women echoes Chernyshevsky's novel, *What is to be done?*, when the heroine Vera Pavlovna, argues that women should be doctors as it would make women patients feel more comfortable, and therefore would eliminate much suffering and pain.[301] It seems certain that Mariam Khatisian had read *What is to be done?* What is interesting is the ways in which she diverges from Chernyshevsky's novel. She rejected sexual licence, but creates a version of acceptable work. Khatisian also added dimensions not perceived by Chernyshevsky and other male writers, namely, she was at pains to find fulfilling work for women, while at the same time representing the enormous obstacles women confronted when forging new roles. After lamenting the lack of female doctors, Liza says:

> "I am convinced that in the village many children die not so much due to poverty but due to ignorance."

Levon responds that Armenian girls aren't interested in such issues. Liza argues that lack of interest is not the girls' fault:

> "Of what are they guilty when from childhood they are surrounded by circumstances that strangle any such thoughts."

Bagruni answers:

"You want to say, Miss, that our environment is hostile to any new ideas, that a young heart cannot easily struggle against this inequality, but you must observe although, at present, it is an up-hill battle, without it nothing will happen. You will see that the development of this issue shall be the principal question in my article."

Liza interrupted, "But do you know what it is like in our country for a woman who has risen above the crowd?" She stopped not wanting to continue, she remembered how estranged she had been from her mother and her social circle, she remembered the arguments that had amounted to dislike, and her anger came, but she didn't want to reveal her personal life to Bagruni . . . [302]

Liza's thoughts about the enormous social and familial pressures against women's entry into the public sphere reveals the knowledge that female intellectuals carried with them, that to go beyond society's injunctions is a lonely path, a psychological state that even sympathetic male intellectuals can never fully understand. Liza's realization of the societal restrictions against women's professionalism comes at a time when she has also begun to reflect upon the inadequate teaching preparation most women teachers enter into teaching with.[303] This marks Liza's emergence as a fully-fledged professional woman. No longer is teaching merely a second prize after the failure of marriage nor is it viewed as a sort of religious vocation, although Khatisian never represented work and marriage as incompatible as Sibyl had done. It is a career that women must prepare for. The novel ends with Liza's leaving Tiflis for Switzerland to learn contemporary pedagogical practices at a university in order to return home to implement this knowledge.

Liza's decision to go abroad to university and attain further training in her profession represents the culmination of her development. She has developed from the patriotic but immature girl, who could not leave her grandmother's estate to teach in the provinces to a confident young woman. The final scene makes it clear that Liza's grandmother and mother still disapprove of the whole enterprise. When Liza's grandmother wishes her good-bye, she says that they won't meet again and hugs Liza tightly. Liza begs her not to say that. Liza's mother responds, "We have begged you to not go and stay with us." But Liza has overcome such societal restrictions and she leaves the shelter of her family for higher education.

Tempering her grandmother's sadness and her mother's sharpness is the encouragement of Levon Bagruni and Arshak Manukian. All the youths wish Liza success on the new road to higher education. Their usage of the term, "on the new road" echoes the title of the novel. Khatisian used this phrase earlier in the novel, to denote, the false road travelled by Liza's mother, Sofia, but its use at the end of the novel, indicates that Liza's path is the true "new road" that is expected to bring beneficial results to the Armenian people. Everyone praises Liza and believes that she will set a good example for others. Khatisian comments, "That hope, which was not far away at that time, was that the Armenian woman would bring enlightenment and desired to benefit her society."[304]

Most importantly is the final image of the novel in which, Liza's sister, Olia, with her two-year old daughter in her arms, says:

> Return soon with all your knowledge. You promised to teach my little daughter." "Certainly, she is my future pupil." Liza replied.[305]

This final image of Khatisian's reflects the ultimate goal of the teaching and social work of Armenian women: to return home and to educate the future generations. For Khatisian education is the key to the progress of the nation. She viewed the amelioration of the status of the Armenian woman as entwined with the status of the Armenian nation. She and other women writers recognized that Armenian women could not achieve emancipation without a corresponding advancement in the overall conditions of the Armenian people, while at the same time they asserted that the Armenian community could not progress without a change in the status of women. It is due to this understanding of the mutuality of female and national efforts for advancement that Armenian women writers advocated greater female participation in all aspects of Armenian community life. The concepts of women's education and national loyalty were emphasized in Armenian women's writing in order to demonstrate the connection between Armenian national autonomy and Armenian women's liberation.

In the novels, *A Girl's Heart* and *On a New Road*, Sibyl and Mariam Khatisian, created four middle and upper class female characters, to represent Armenian women's first forays into the profession of education. The authors, recognized that in order for the Armenian woman to participate in the public sphere and alter existing patterns in marital relations a new concept of Armenian femininity had to be articulated: one in which Armenian women's participation in national affairs and the economic and political spheres was not viewed as unnatural but as legitimate. The first step in this process was the creation of heroines with a developed sense of self. Sibyl began this process when she portrayed Bubul as free from hypocrisy and true to her own values and beliefs, in this novel, however, Bubul cannot emerge from the romance text to forge an identity separate from that of wife. Sibyl portrays the character of Sofie as more comfortable with her role as a professional woman, but her story is overshadowed in *A Girl's Heart* by Bubul's story. The failure to represent an alternative to the romance plot by Sibyl suggests some of the difficulties women writers felt in trying to conceive of new roles for women.

It is in Khatisian's novel, *On a New Road*, that true alternatives to the romance plot are fashioned and this enabled the author to portray the development of a fully-fledged professional woman. One of the key elements in enabling Liza's development as a professional teacher is through her friendship with Hrrip'simé. She is Liza's best friend and Ruben's sister, and is not explicitly associated with patriotic action. In fact, when Liza tells her friend that she wishes Hrrip'simé to accompany Ruben and herself to Western Armenia, Hrrip'simé although sympathetic to patriotic ideas, thinks that it is premature for women to participate in this work.[306] Instead of being inspired by notions of patriotism, Hrrip'simé has always worked since graduation from school, this is partly due to her family's poverty and her desire to assist her brother's study at university, but what is also clear in the text is that Hrrip'simé derives personal satisfaction from work. When her brother betrays Liza and his ideals and marries for money, his standard of living improves and he invites Hrrip'simé and their mother join his new household. Hrrip'simé does not want to give up her independent life and tells her brother that she has worked for so long that she cannot live without some sort of employment. Under pressure from her mother and brother, Hrrip'simé consents to move in with Ruben and his wife. She quickly becomes uncomfortable with the arrangement, in part because his wife makes it clear that they are living on her money, but also due to her own enforced idleness. When Levon approaches her about teaching at Liza's school for a year, Hrrip'simé gladly agrees. By consenting to teach at the village school she receives her own salary of 500 rubles a year, half of that salary will be paid for by the Charitable Organization.[307] Employment enables Hrrip'simé to provide a home for herself and her mother. Her brother, Ruben, is against the idea of Hrrip'simé's working when he can support her, but her reply indicates the pleasure it is possible for women to derive from employment:

> At present I am perfectly healthy and there is no reason for me to remain unoccupied. I must confess to you Ruben, that without teaching, I have quickly become bored and with pleasure agreed to take up the running of a school when the opportunity was presented. This was always my desire. The village air, as you yourself always say, will be good for mother and I. If mother doesn't like it in the village, as you suggest, she can always return to the city.[308]

Hrrip'simé is a successful teacher and assists in Liza's progress in becoming a fully-fledged professional woman. Hrrip'simé writes Liza about the progress of the school and pupils while Liza convalesces in Tiflis and finally, when Liza decides to go to Switzerland for higher education, it is Hrrip'simé who once again takes over the running of the village school in Liza's absence, promising to keep her informed of the school's progress.[309] In the novel Hrrip'simé provides Liza with the support, emotional and practical, she needs in order to overcome her family's objections to her employment. In addition, Hrrip'simé offers an example, for Liza

of a woman satisfied with employment and able to support herself and her family.

In this novel the support Liza derives from her friend,
Hrrip'simé and her sister, Olia, creates a world in which women's
friendships offer strength to the heroine to move beyond the
romance plot, into the public sphere. The ending of the novel also
suggests Liza's future transformation of the public sphere, through
her projected education of Armenian girls, like her niece, who
presumably are not expected to encounter the restrictions Liza
experienced.

# CHAPTER FOUR

# WOMEN'S JOURNALS: MARIE BEYLERIAN
## AND *ARTEMIS*

The salon, the charitable organization and the journal facilitated woman's writing in early twentieth-century Armenian intellectual circles by creating a discursive public space in which
women could attempt to influence social and political ideology.
The salon and the charitable organization have been discussed in
chapters two and three. This chapter will explore the third institution of importance to women writers: the journal. The nineteenth-
century Armenian journal was the main forum in which male and
female intellectuals were able to debate and discuss new ideas
concerning social and educational issues, modernization, literature and science. The journal enabled Armenian women to express their views and discuss issues, including women's rights, in
a public forum, read by both women and men thereby participating in the formation of public opinion. Publishing in journals allowed women writers to become more visible and to make their
reputations as writers. Both Sibyl and Zabel Yesayian made their
literary debuts through writing short stories, novels and poetry
for the Armenian language press. The journal, unlike the salon
and charitable organization, allowed women of different social
classes to participate in intellectual debates. It is therefore not
surprising that Zabel Yesayian, Marie Beylerian and Shushanik
Kurghinian, who were writers from modest households, each
became well known through her writings in journals as writing
for a journal, unlike hosting a salon or founding a charitable organization, did not require great wealth. Journals opened up new

possibilities for publishing and ways of earning some money. The
journal widely disseminated women's concerns to Armenians
throughout the Diaspora and helped create a shared discourse in
Armenian of women's social, political and educational issues.[310]

The first known Western Armenian journal published and edited by a woman, Élpis Kesarats'ian, was a monthly, entitled
*Kit'arr* [Guitar], begun in Constantinople on August 1, 1862.
*Guitar* remained in print for a mere seven months and apparently
generated much controversy. Intellectuals writing in the journals
*Masis*, *Meghu*, and Smyrna's *Tsaghik* warmly received *Kit'arr*,
but it also had its detractors, for example, Stepan Voskan in
*Arevmutk'* (Paris, 1864).[311] The second journal published and edited by a woman, was Srbuhi Yerits'ian's *Tomar Ëntanekani* [Fam-
ily Almanac], in Tiflis in 1874. Due to financial difficulties, however, only one issue of this journal ever appeared.[312] Although
both ventures were short-lived they did provide models for later
women's journals, including Marie Beylerian's *Artemis* (1902–
1903) and Haykanush Marrk's *Tsaghik* (1905–1907) and *Hay Kin*
(1919–1932).[313] After Mark's forced closure of *Hay Gin* in 1932,
the Armenian women's press continued, notably in Beirut, Lebanon with the publication of *Yeritasard Hayuhi*, which ran (intermittently) from 1932 to its final issue in 1968, under the editorship
of Constantinople born, Seza.[314]

Although the first two attempts by Armenian women to publish and edit journals were of short duration, female contributors
and writers were writing and being published by the Armenian
press throughout the late nineteenth century. Some stigma was
attached to women's writing in the nineteenth century, but the
inclusion of women's sections [Kanants' Bazhin] in journals
helped legitimize women's publications. Proof of the opportunities opened up by women's sections in journals is attested to by
Zaruhi Galémk'earian (1874–1971), who wrote in her autobiography that after having published two small volumes of poetry in
Constantinople in the 1890s, she was advised by the editor of
*Puzantion*, Puzant Kech'ian, that she should concentrate on writing about women's place in the family and home. He also warned

her that young women who wrote freely of their emotions and desires would be judged harshly by society. Galémk'earian, while lamenting this attitude, states that what slowly changed the status of the woman writer, from being thought of as immodest, was the advent of the women's sections of journals, which signalled acceptance of women's writing and provided a forum for female authors.[315] Editors sympathetic to women's entry into the public sphere invited women to submit essays and articles about women and social issues. In the early 1880s the editor of *Arevelian Mamul*, Matteos Mamurian (1830–1901) invited Srpuhi Dussap to write several essays on topics such as women's employment, female education and Armenian charitable associations for publication in the journal. The acceptance of women's issues as a relevant topic is attested to by the fact that by 1900 several Armenian journals, for example *Tsaghik*, published in Constantinople, edited by Arshak Chobanian and *Arakatz*, published in New York, included women's sections in which female contributors wrote of issues affecting women and Armenian society. Titles of articles by women include: *The Armenian Woman's Role in Society, A Heart to Heart Talk with my Sisters, My Life as a Student in England* and many others. Journals such as *Masis* and *Arakatz* printed laudatory articles about Armenian women writers and their advent into the public sphere. Such articles include *Mer Kin Groghnerë* [Our Women Writers], in *Masis* (1905) and *Hay Kin Groghnerë* [Armenian Women Writers] in *Arakatz* (1911). The latter series indicates, however, that men did try to control literary content through the praising of women writers deemed acceptable, for example, Sibyl and Arshakuhi Teodik, which contrasts markedly with the harsh criticism the author directed at what he deemed the unacceptable feminist content of Haykanush Marrk's journal *Tsaghik* (1905–1907).

Despite opposition, the women's sections of journals were influential forums for women to debate and discuss the political and socio-economic issues confronting women and society. The press also provided models of women engaged in public activity as writers and by publicizing the works of charitable organizations, including membership lists, and the mandates of the associations, as well as information about schools and educators, the principal profession of turn of the century Armenian women. The hopes and expectations of the women's sections of the journals are demonstrated by an early editorial by Zabel Yesayian in which the author wrote:

> The "women's section" of *Tsaghik* must endeavour to publish useful and masterful articles in a popular and clear way. It should keep our women informed of the work in the areas of education and charity that women in other countries are doing. For this series of publications, which has all the difficulties of being the first of its kind, we have great hopes of our women's contributions. These pages are open to all who have something to express or a cause to defend and we are sure that from our women writers' efforts, all classes of women will be able to contribute to this "Women's Section," which has definite educational and charitable goals.[316]

From Yesayian's editorial it is clear that its organizers envisioned the "women's sections" to provide a forum for all classes of Armenian women, but at the same time, they had a definite goal of promoting education and charitable work as suitable activities for Armenian women. Yesayian's statement highlights the fact that as women entered the public sphere they also gained a sense of responsibility for what occurred in the public domain, particularly issues affecting children and the welfare of the Armenian community.

From a reading of several women's journals and women's section of other journals, it is clear that the principal concerns of the women's press were: women's rights, motherhood, education and employment. The press and women's novels and short stories reveal that these four concepts were subject to extensive reevaluation and re-creation in the context of modernity and national development and that women sought to shape this process through the written text.

The third Armenian journal published and edited by a woman was Marie Beylerian's *Artemis*. This journal was published in Alexandria, Egypt from January 1902 to December 1903. Its editor, Marie Beylerian (1880–1915), was a native of Constantinople, where she received her education at the Esayian School. Due to Marie Beylerian's participation in the Bab Ali demonstrations in 1895, she was forced to flee to Alexandria, Egypt in 1896 in order to avoid imprisonment by the Ottoman authorities. In Alexandria she held a position in that city's Armenian school. After the declaration of the Ottoman Constitution in 1908 Beylerian taught at Smyrna's Central School and later Tokat's Armenian School. She died during the Armenian Genocide in 1915.[317]

*Artemis* is an important part of the history of Armenian women's writing because women's journals acted as forums for the dissemination of women's perspectives. In her first editorial Beylerian made this explicit when she wrote that she had dreamt since her schooldays of creating a journal for Armenian women to present women's free voice.[318] *Artemis* assisted in the legitimization of women's entry into the public sphere by presenting women's opinions and discussing them among readers. As numerous scholars have shown, Habermas was mistaken in his assumption that women did not participate in the creation of the public sphere. Women did participate in the public sphere through women's magazines and journals. Beylerian's *Artemis* enabled women to enter the Armenian public sphere. In fact, the literary public sphere was ideally suited to Armenian women who for various reasons lacked access to non-discursive spheres. *Artemis* attracted the attention and praise of Armenian women readers throughout the Diaspora, many of whom became correspondents and contributors to the journal. The articles by women readers are typically reports on the contemporary state of Armenian women's lives and activities in the town or city the writer is currently living in. Letters and articles from Armenian women in Kars, Nor Jugha, Tiflis, Moscow, Paris and New York appeared in the pages of *Artemis*. The practice of publishing such a wide range of women's articles, by women who were not famous authors, in contrast to the practice in other journals, was a unique feature of Marie Beylerian's journal. *Artemis* thus made an attempt to represent Armenian women's voices from all over the globe. The final aspect making *Artemis* of interest to the history of Armenian women's writing was Marie Beylerian's strong editorial leadership and her interest in Armenian women's place in national identity and development. Beylerian's editorials discuss the four themes of women's rights, motherhood, education and employment within the context of the challenge of western discourse on women roles in society and as central to Armenian national development. Beylerian, perhaps because of her own status as a political exile, also introduced the problem of exile and dispersion into her discussions of Armenian women's roles in society.

Beylerian's choice of the title *Artemis* highlights many of her principal concerns in the contemporary discussions of Armenian women's roles, as well as what she considered important for Armenian women to safeguard. The Greek goddess, Artemis, was the daughter of Zeus and Leto, twin of Apollo. She was a virgin goddess whose domain was wild places, mountains and springs and because of this she was viewed as free and independent. In Greek mythology she was the helper of hunters as well as protector of young animals. She was also the protector of young children and newborns and of their mothers, especially in childbirth.[319] In ancient times, at the time of marriage, young women honoured her, and she was considered to be the "promoter of healthy development" in girls.[320] Her care for the young, for mothers and girls' healthy development must have made her appealing to Beylerian, whose journals advocated all of these. The excavation of the temple of Artemis in Ephesus, located south of Smyrna, had begun in 1869 funded by the British Museum and work on the site had continued in the early years of the twentieth century. It is possible Beylerian had heard of the excavations and this too stimulated her interest in the figure of Artemis.

In art Artemis was commonly represented as a hunter. In several issues of Beylerian's *Artemis* the end pieces depict the goddess as a huntress with a bow and arrow, stepping on the head of a lion. Doves are nearby and next to her there appears an inkpot, a scroll, a large, open book, a painter's palette, a harp, a globe, and a hand press, under these appear the journal's name *Artemis*: Family and Literary Monthly Magazine, The Twentieth-Century

Armenian Women's Organ [Amsahandés Ëntanekan ev Grakan, Organ K'sanerord Daru Hay Kanants'] and a quote attributed to Solomon: The intelligent woman is a crown to her husband. The depiction of Artemis beside symbols of the humanities and technology (the hand press) reveal Beylerian's firm alliance of the "Twentieth-Century Armenian woman" with art, science and modernity. The remainder of the chapter will explore Beylerian's writings in *Artemis* on women's rights, motherhood, education and employment and the problems and solutions she identified and advocated for these issues in the public domain.

## Women's Rights

As Kumari Jayawardena has stated the concept of feminism has suffered many misapprehensions. It has been alleged by traditionalists, political conservatives and leftists alike that feminism is either a product of 'decadent' western capitalism or that it is based on a foreign culture of no relevance to women in the third world or that it is the ideology of women of the local bourgeoisie or that it alienates or diverts women from their culture, religion and family responsibilities or from revolutionary struggles for national liberation or socialism.[321] In Armenian intellectual history the question of women's rights is likewise viewed as a sign of westernization. Scholars frequently discuss the influence of missionary women on discourse on women and claim any discussion of women's rights is "not Armenian." Several misconceptions are at work in such discussions of women's rights. Firstly, the question of what is feminism, is frequently unstated and yet is vaguely understood as conforming to contemporary definitions, despite the fact that feminism has a well documented history, and its theories of women's social, intellectual and political place have never conformed to a single model. Nineteenth-century European feminisms were principally divided into two primary theories of women's nature, which influenced discussions of women's social and political circumstances, these are the sameness or difference arguments. The sameness argument posits that women and men

are absolutely equal in terms of intellectual and spiritual qualities, and the only difference between the two is biological difference. Supporters of the difference argument stated that women
and men have different characteristics and qualities, specifically
that women were more moral, nurturing and peaceful while men
were competitive, aggressive and self-interested. Feminists who
supported the difference argument, and this argument was particularly popular in the nineteenth century, argued that because
women had those different characteristics they should have equal
access to education, work and citizenship in order to represent
themselves and use their unique and positive characteristic for
the benefit of society.[322]

Armenian women writers, including Marie Beylerian, generally subscribed to a unique version of the difference argument.
They argued that Armenian women were by nature moral and
nurturing and that as a mother the Armenian woman should extend her maternal care for her family to the nation. As has been
stated earlier in chapters two and three this coincided with the
reconceptualization of the nation as a family with national brothers and sisters, and enabled Armenian women's participation in
the public sphere as mothers and sisters. It is clear that Armenian
women saw their roles as care takers of the nation.

In answer to the charge of Western influence through missionary activity it is important to remember that for the most part
missionaries were not feminists in their own countries and there
is nothing to suggest that they exposed Armenian women to feminist ideas. What they did do, by example at least, if not design, is
to provide an alternative model of womanhood. This model was
by no means feminist, although it was a powerful one given the
economic and political status of Europe and North America in
the world. I would like to suggest, however, that while western-
inspired discourse about women's proper roles and place in the
social order, was a challenge no nation in contact with the European powers could ignore, this does not mean that women blindly
imitated these models. Beth Baron's suggestion that in Egypt
"female intellectuals wrote in the tradition of nineteenth-twenti-
eth century intellectuals responding to the challenge of the West"

is useful in discussing Armenian discourse on women's rights.[323] In examining, Marie Beylerian's editorials, and indeed all the women writers discussed in this book, it is evident that women writers discuss Armenian women's social and familial status conscious of an alternative, western model, but this does not mean that they advocated that alternative model. In fact, the western model was usually rejected as unviable or often as a downright undesirable model for Armenian women and society. Instead of the western model, Armenian female intellectuals sought to redefine womanhood in a way that was distinct from the immediate past, which was considered inadequate to prepare Armenian women for their place in the modern world. The new model of women was designed to ensure Armenian women a central and influential role in contemporary Armenian political and social life, but would at the same time harmonize with Armenian culture and socio-political conditions.

How Armenian women sought to shape new definitions of women's roles is clear in Marie Beylerian's editorials, when she enters into a dialogue with European feminisms and their supporters among Armenians. Beylerian directly responded to the question of the compatibility of European feminism and Armenian women's rights by comparing the two ideologies and the respective political and social conditions of each group of women. In the editorial of *Artemis* entitled: *The Armenian Woman Question or the Demands of "Feminism"* after having carefully outlined her stance on Armenian women's rights in previous editorials, Beylerian responded to the question of whether or not Armenian women should join the "international women's movement". Beylerian rejected Armenian women's participation in a European feminist movement from a theoretical stance, which concurs with historian Nancy Cott's statement that feminism or women's movements "take part in" and "comprise part of–the general cultural order, while it has its own tradition, logic and trajectory"[324]

Beylerian states, what she terms the *Armenian Woman Question* [Hay Knoj Harts'], has already entered into Armenian intellectual and political discourse and has divided intellectuals into two camps. The first camp she describes is the one she herself supports. Beylerian describes this group's ideological position as follows:

> There is a group of people who view the "Woman Question" as directly connected to and reconciled with the nationalist perspective. This group desires that the Armenian woman direct her emancipation within the framework of her position in national circumstances and realities, and that she become mistress of her own fate through steady advancement without reducing our national strength. And at least at present, to leave to the future, and to circumstances and necessities, the plan of greater emancipation and sufficiency.[325]

In this statement two important elements of Beylerian's theory of Armenian women's rights are evident. One is the emphasis on the Armenian woman becoming mistress of her own fate and the second that any changes within Armenian family and social structure should be directed at strengthening the Armenian nation. Both these elements shall be discussed subsequently in this chapter, however, at this stage it is important to note that both these issues, control of women's fate and the need to benefit the Armenian nation, firmly situate Beylerian's discourse within her contemporary social and political context.

Beylerian's basis for rejecting western feminism resembles the current academic trend of linking European and American feminisms to political and social movements.[326] Beylerian argued that the solution to a Woman Question lies in that nation's political position, social structure and the implementation of governmental laws and statutes.[327] Therefore, Beylerian states, due to the very different political and social structures, which make up European women circumstances and determine their demands, European women's feminism is not compatible with Armenian women's needs or demands.

Implicit in her argument is Beylerian's distinction between two types of rights, what she calls: "societal and political rights" and "natural rights."[328] She states that European women, who already have natural rights, presently are demanding their societal and political rights. Given the publicity concerning the women's suffrage movement in this period, it seems likely that by political equality Beylerian means suffrage. Because Armenian women did not live under political systems in the Ottoman or Russian Empires based on electoral systems, suffrage, the principal political demand of turn-of-the-century western feminisms, had little meaning for Armenian female intellectuals. Beylerian viewed European women as able to struggle for social and political rights because they already possessed natural rights. It is in the realm of "natural rights" that Beylerian locates the Armenian women's struggle.

All of Beylerian's editorials in *Artemis* advocate "natural rights" for Armenian women. The French Revolution was perhaps the event most directly influential of discussion of rights. The 1789 Declaration of the Rights of Man and of the Citizen posited that men had the natural right to possess property and be admitted to all public functions. It is a political theory that maintains that an individual enters into society with certain basic rights and that no government can deny these rights. From its inception, a group of French women had demanded a share in these rights. They were supported by such persons as the Marquis de Condorcet, who in his *Essai sur l'admission des femmes au droit de cité* [Essay on the Admission of Women to the Rights of Citizenship] (1790) had argued for the Rights to include the rights of women to civil and political equality; as had Olympe de Gouges in her *Déclaration des droits de la femme et de la citoyenne* [Declaration of the Rights of Woman and the Female Citizen] (1791).[329]

Natural rights in Beylerian's discourse means a woman's right to control her fate, her right to have a public voice, to have her opinions respected and listened to both in the public and private spheres and finally the right to choose her own husband. Beylerian saw women's natural rights as subjugated by "old prejudices." She identified old prejudices as customs injurious to women. In an editorial entitled, *A Glance at the Armenian Woman's Past*, Beylerian identified specific past customs and practices as contributing to women's subjugation. Unlike Sibyl and Zabel Yesayian who saw the ancient Armenian past as providing contemporary women with activist foremothers, Beylerian rejected, as examples of by-gone respect for Armenian women, the women described by Yeghishe, Khorenatsi and Mkhitar Gosh. She stated that the positive portrayal of Armenian women in these texts is related to their class status as ladies of the ruling elite, rather than indicative of respect for their sex. Respect, Beylerian says, was not shown to ordinary women.[330]

In this same editorial she presents a picture of Armenian women's social and economic conditions, which have denied women their "natural" rights. Beylerian identifies the custom of calling women, by no other name than "mer tan spasuhin" [our household servant] or "dzer aghakhine" [your maidservant] as indicative of her voicelessness in the family, where Beylerian says, she should actually occupy the highest place.[331]

Beylerian viewed the custom of arranged marriage as being a dehumanizing sale of women. She says of arranged marriage:

> The voice of the heart wasn't listened to, ideas, character, feelings, age, all of this counted for nothing.
> The governing principle was money and it remains money until today.[332]

Beylerian is critical of the prescribed social relations governing husband and wife's interaction in such marriages. She says:

> For Armenian women of the past, family life was hell. She was forced to be a shadow, nothing more. It was considered shameful for a young man to speak openly, friendly and lovingly to his wife. In that case, those around him would call him effeminate. He would be reproached and insulted by them. If he had something important to say to his wife, he did so without looking at her face.[333]

Sociological data of Armenian family structure indicates that upon marriage the new bride entered into a period of silence, called *moonch*, or "the bride swallowed her tongue." She was not allowed to speak to older family members and was not allowed to speak to her husband except when they were alone and opportunities to be alone were few in the extended family household.[334]

It is because of this historical legacy of silence and supporting customs that Beylerian saw Armenian women as being without "natural" rights and why she placed such emphasis on a woman having the right to be mistress of her fate, to speak and voice her opinions and to be listened to. In an editorial entitled *The Child*, Beylerian created a manifesto outlining her stance on women's rights:

> We, Armenian women, see more hardships and tyranny than others. Civilization has barely weakened our chains of slavery. And the provincial Armenian woman still sobs under the same load of hardship . . .
>
> We are moderate in our demands, recognizing, however, that we have equal rights, but agreeing to moderate them. We struggle fiercely against those prejudices, which have plagued us for centuries and today threaten our well-being.
>
> We demand to have the right to love completely and freely; we have the right to chose, without coercion and with a free will, our life's partner, whose heart is tied to our own heart.
>
> We have the right to speak freely and to reveal our bold opinions about all issues, which touch communal life, and we demand our opinions to be taken seriously and our ideas respected.
>
> We are free in our family life, free and independent in our activities and thoughts, free to pursue whatever idea or goal that is beautiful to us, in short, we are free in everything that is pure and free from prejudice and to allow what is ethical and does not damage the work of raising the next generation.
>
> Beyond this limit we won't pass. We voluntarily and with love remain in our sacred role and remember that the greatest satisfaction and the greatest joy consist of perfect fulfillment of responsibility.[335]

As is evident from the above quoted passage, Beylerian viewed women as having rights, but advocated not demanding some of those rights if they compromised national unity. One of the features of European feminism that frightened Beylerian was the vision of internal national disunity, for this reason, in editorials, Beylerian always emphasized the unity of the group, specifically the unity of Armenians, as sacred. In her discussion of women's rights, therefore, she sought to elevate Armenian women's status, and she could be quite critical of certain institutions, such as the family, but her analysis consistently tries to avoid conflict leading to disunity.

The "natural" rights identified by Beylerian, were extremely important to all Armenian women writers of this period. Srpuhi Dussap had forcefully argued against marriage for financial profit in her novel *Siranush* (1884), as had Mariam Khatisian in *On a New Road* (1894); while Sibyl had advocated women's self-knowledge in *A Girl's Heart* (1891). Marie Beylerian's editorials participate in the intellectual dialogue about women's rights that had begun in the nineteenth century. Beylerian's editorials often summarize many of the standard arguments common to this debate, while adding new insights from her own perspective as a political exile and educator.

In Beylerian's discourse the key to achieving women's natural rights is through a reinterpretation of motherhood, the availability of female education and employment. These three subjects were redefined in such a way as to give women new status in both public and family life.

## Motherhood

We have already discussed the mother-educator and her role in nation-building, by the turn of the century when Beylerian began publishing *Artemis,* this figure was firmly established. The mother-educator is envisioned in Armenian intellectual discourse as the figure who will educate her children in the Armenian language and teach them to love their nation. Elise Hagopian Taft's description of her own mother, before her deportation in 1915, epitomizes the good qualities associated with the mother-educator figure:

> Typical of most Armenian women of the time, she was hard-working and resourceful and kept an immaculately clean home... Blessed with a gentle disposition, she weighed every word and

never raised her voice to us children. In times of trouble and distress people looked to mother for comfort and advice. Whenever friends, relatives or neighbours became sick, she spent sleepless nights at their homes nursing them.[336]

The concept of the mother-educator entailed a radical re-envisioning of the relationship between motherhood, familial relationships and the national entity. As Afsaneh Najmabadi has argued in the case of Iran, the notion that the family was the foundation of the country and that within the family, woman as mother was its foundation, meant that woman's "intellectual development or underdevelopment becomes the primary factor in determining the development or underdevelopment of the country."[337] The new mother-educator could no longer be illiterate, especially not in the Armenian language, and care of her children could no longer be given up to her mother-in-law. It is due to this latter fact that advocates of the mother-educator also emphasised nuclear family structures rather than the extended family (gerdastan) as the ideal structure. Women's writing from the turn-of-century routinely portrays the family as a nuclear one with husband and wife and their children. The heroine struggles to marry the man of her choosing and to compose another nuclear family. If the extended family is depicted in women's writing, the focus is on the relationship between the mother-in-law and daughter-in-law, and to a lesser extent the relationship between the son and his mother, although this second relationship is of lesser interest to women writers than the first. In this literature the character of the mother-in-law rarely fares well. She is commonly portrayed as the source of reactionary traditional customs, which are seen as injurious to the development of the modern Armenian family and by extension the nation.

Marie Beylerian's short story *The Mother-in-Law: A Tale from Provincial Life*, crystallizes many of the common complaints against the mother-in-law and the extended family structure in a dramatic form. The greatest sin of the mother-in-law in this story is that she is cruel to the daughter-in-law, and when her daughter-in-law gives birth to a baby girl, the mother-in-law is angry, but still insists on her prerogative of deciding how her grandchild will be cared for. In many regions, it was the grandmother's prerogative to care for her grandchildren and especially to perform specific tasks, such as bathing the child.[338] In this story, because the child is female, however, she neglects her, but won't allow her daughter-in-law, the baby's mother, to care adequately for the child. In consequence of the mother's-in-law behaviour, the baby dies.[339]

The second sin of the mother-in-law in this story is that she interferes with the relationship between husband and wife. The daughter-in-law and son of the household, although married, actually have little contact and rarely speak to each other. On the sole occasion when the son protests the harsh treatment of his wife, his mother yells at him and accuses him of betraying her.[340]

One of the other important features of the mother-educator was that she was expected to be a companion to her husband. For this reason, the extended family structure with its emphasis on the son's relationship to his parents and not with his wife was rejected by women writers in favour of a model of the husband and wife as companions. In the traditional system of child brides and arranged matches, Beylerian sees the creation of companionate marriage as impossible. In the short story, Beylerian characterizes the young bride's feeling as follows:

> And towards her husband who should be Almast's "life companion" she feels only hatred. She regards him as her greatest enemy, because it was he who separated her from her parents and brought her to this miserable house, ending her childhood and the freedom of her innocent and happy years.[341]

The protagonist's feelings hinder the creation of a bond in marriage and thus the development of a strong nation. The emphasis on companionate marriage at this time was in part based on Christian doctrine and its conceptualization of a woman as helpmeet to her husband. Its connection to nation building and systems of governance, however, was of a more recent origin. In historian Nancy Cott's discussion of marriage and republican government she argues that based on their reading of Baron de Montesquieu's

*L'Esprit des lois* [Spirit of the Laws] (1784) the early American republicans viewed marriage and the form of government as mirroring each other. Christian monogamy as a voluntary union based on consent was viewed as parallel to the new republican government, which was theoretically based on voluntary consent to be governed by delegated representatives.[342] Marriage and the social position of women as connected to political systems, was a connection also made by early visitors to Europe. For example in his work discussing Persian travellers to Europe, Mohamad Tavakoli-Targhi notes, that the travellers linked European women's seeming freedom and the restrictions of power of the sovereign to new definitions of freedom. To strengthen their nation some nineteenth-century Persian travellers called for the establishment of constitutional government and the participation of women in the public sphere.[343] As Christians, the Armenians already practiced monogamous marriage, however, in the nineteenth century, companionate marriage based on mutual love between husband and wife was promoted as the ideal for strengthening the nation. When companionate marriage became the ideal among Armenian intellectual, this had an enormous impact on how the Armenian girl was perceived in literature and in society.

The nuclear family as the ideal family was disseminated in Armenian literature of the period. In the nineteenth century, whether the extended family, which ideally included a husband and wife, their sons and the sons' families, was the norm or not is difficult to say. Susie Hoogasian Villa's research, which is based on interviews with Armenians who lived in Western Armenia before 1914, suggests that by the turn of the century most Armenian households were probably nuclear due to natural causes, such as times when there were no grandparents living and no grandchildren had been born. She argues that the shorter the life expectancy of the people of a particular community was, the smaller in size was the family household. In addition, Hoogasian Villa argues for regional variations, by suggesting that the extended household was prevalent in areas where Armenians had the greatest need for self-defense. The principal function of the gerdastan in this situation was mutual self-defense.[344] In addition, to Hoogasian Villa's discussion of natural causes, I would add that perhaps premature deaths by massacre and violence resulted in some regions in the decline of the gerdastan. Her suggestion of regional variation and defensive measures is also useful. Susie Hoogasian Villa's research indicates that there was a connection between domestic architecture, family structure and security. She states that in the villages of Western Armenia houses, stables and neighbouring dwellings were often interconnected, creating a "semi underground warren in which people could hide themselves and their valuables."[345] The English traveller, Lucy Garnett, who visited the Ottoman Empire in the late nineteenth century, commented on the fortress-like appearance of older Armenian houses designed to protect the occupants. Garnett, notes that by the 1890s, in the cities of Constantinople and Smyrna, Armenian middle class houses were more open reflecting a sense of greater physical safety.[346] The gerdastan along with defensive household architecture was less prevalent in the urban centres, where the vast majority of women writers lived. This was especially true for the emerging professional class, trained in the new professions of lawyer, engineer and doctor. Sometimes these men moved to different towns in the Ottoman Empire taking their wives with them, thereby creating nuclear family structures. This is evident in the case of Sibyl's first marriage, in which she and her husband, the lawyer, Garapet Tonelian, left their families in Constantinople and lived in various provincial towns throughout their marriage. Sibyl only returned to her family in Constantinople after her husband's early death. On the other hand, many memoirs describing rural life before 1915, portray extended families living under one roof.

Whatever may have been the sociological reality, it is clear that in terms of political theory, the companionate marriage, with its emphasis on the relationship between the husband and wife, and not on the relationships between the husband and his parents or brothers, was promoted. The ideal of companionate marriage, and the duties of the mother-educator are closely linked in political theory and literature of the period, and deserve special attention. As Najmabadi suggests: "The envisaging of the family as the foundation of the nation, as standing for a building block of the nation, also meant reenvisgaing relationships within it. Ignorant women were not only unsuitable as mothers but also unfit as spouses . . . sentiment comparable to friendship between men was proposed to constitute the right bond between husband and wife."[347] In order to be a good wife and companion to her husband the wife had to know more about the world than had been thought necessary in the past. She was expected to be able to talk intelligently with her husband and for this reason rudimentary education was viewed as necessary. The words of American missionary, Mary Van Lennep, describe the impetus for female education as follows:

> The Armenian gentlemen feel that a thorough reformation cannot take place in their nation, until those who will be wives and mothers shall come under Christian influence. And they take a deep interest in this enterprise [the establishment of an American missionary secondary school for girls].[348]

Within this new family paradigm, however, women were not constructed as passively as may first appear. As female intellectuals participated in the redefinition of familial relationships they sought to position women in a powerful place within the family. Sibyl's play *The Daughter-in-Law* (1918) demonstrated how the concept of the love match undermined the traditional power structures of relationships within the family. *The Daughter-in-Law is* concerned with the position of women in the extended family structure. The daughter-in-law, Arusiak, lives with her husband, Arshak, his widowed mother, Mrs. Tiruhi, and his unmarried sister, Hanëmik. Traditionally the daughter-in-law had the least power in the extended family, while the mother-in-law had great authority over her children, and especially her daughters-in-law, giving the younger woman orders on how to perform chores and how to rear her children.[349] The tension of this play revolves around the fact that while Arusiak is always polite and good-natured in contrast to the hostility and ill-temper shown by her mother-in-law and sister-in-law, the traditional subordination of the daughter-in-law has been subverted because Arusiak and Arshak's marriage is a love match and hence the daughter-in-law does not have to fear her mother-in-law. As a consequence, traditional rules governing the status of the daughter-in-law have ceased to have power or meaning, a fact shown to be well understood by Arusiak's mother-in-law when she states:

> Akh, what can I say to my Arshak now, since he didn't even ask for my permission but simply went out and hastily got married? If I had been there I wouldn't have given permission![350]

Mrs. Tiruhi's lament demonstrates the threat that love was seen as having upon traditional structures of power and the potential threat to the authority of the extended family. The threat to the extended family posed by a love match is made clear by Arusiak's wish that she and her husband live separate from his family:

> I would have preferred a small apartment of my own, decorated according to my tastes, with lots of plants and flowers, and everything prepared by my own hands. They threaten me with having to work in the kitchen but to me it would be a pleasure if I could be alone with my beloved husband, without being endlessly attacked by those two critics.[351]

This wish is one, which Arusiak only expresses to herself; she does not utter it or make any plans to divide her husband and herself from his family. Although love is a potentially destructive force to the extended family, Sibyl does not allow this potential to come to the forefront in this play and the same time, however, Sibyl was at pains to illustrate that the existent relationship between the mother-in-law and daughter-in-law was not beneficial to society. Raffi also criticized the extended family structure as the root of women's oppression.[352] The contemporary academic emphasis, especially in anthropological studies of the Armenian family, on the power of the mother-in-law as an example of female power, was not promoted by turn-of-the-century women writers, because, they for the most part, were writing of young women who were trying to escape this sort of female power. Rather, they

attempted to place a higher value on women in the family by attributing higher value to the work performed by women in the
(nuclear) family and by paying more attention to childhood.

In Marie Beylerian's writing the role of motherhood both el-
evates women and gives them greater status than men. In the editorial entitled *The Child* Beylerian argues against the sameness
argument, endorsed by some feminists of the nineteenth and twentieth centuries, in favour of women's unique role and authority as
mothers.

Beylerian constructs a version of the difference argument in
her discussions of Armenian motherhood. She states that for
women to desire to have the same freedoms as men will be detrimental to the raising of children and thus of national development. Although this argument limits women's roles within the
boundaries of motherhood, the position of motherhood is elevated
in her discourse. Because of their freedom of movement and action,
men are considered prisoners of "passion and bestial instincts,"
while the woman is considered the "protector and guardian of
reason and sense."[353] The role of motherhood is constructed as
infinitely superior to that of fatherhood. Beylerian wrote:

> A national poet explained the difference between paternal and
> maternal love: "When a child dies, the father cries with deep grief
> but in time, this grief won't predominate more than other sor-
> rows, but look at the mother's heart years later, the same wound is
> still bleeding."
>
> It is the same among animals. Who is it that cares for her young?
> Who is it that protects them against enemies? Who is it, with love
> and affection, nurses them with her milk? It's the female . . .
>
> Among humanity knowledge is much more developed. The
> father, although careless and indifferent when compared to the
> mother, at least has a definite love and care for his child, unlike
> the animal father who forgets his children and leaves them to the
> female who looks after their every need.[354]

Endowed with superior feeling, Beylerian states, the mother
can take heart in the notion that her influence is everlasting and
will always remain in the child's soul and heart, and will inspire

goodness, beauty and benefit in them.[355] The inspiration and influence the mother has on her children is then linked to national development. By having such a significant impact on children and future generations, the woman will be able to participate in national development.

Beylerian states that because woman is reasonable and sensible she will decline equal freedom with men because by nature she has been called to a higher state and that calling is to be the mother-educator. She wrote:

> [W]oman's most suitable and agreeable place is under the familial roof, and while it may appear that she is confined to a limited space, she actually has an unlimitedly high place when fulfilling her heavenly role, for which she was called to by nature, that is to create and educate man, and through man, humanity and through humanity, nations and peoples.
>
> Devoted to their familial obligations through conviction and zeal, they are modest and serious mothers completely conscious of their responsibilities, by which they give to the world modest, serious and responsible nations.[356]

In Beylerian's construction women can influence social and political development through raising good, patriotic children. In the same editorial, Beylerian continues saying:

> A great thinker once said: Give me your mothers and I will give you a nation. *Artemis'* goal must be to prepare girls, spouses, and mothers for the day when it can be said with pride: Here are your mothers, give us the nation. [357]

As Najmabadi has noted the discourse on women's role as mothers of the nation and their entry into the public sphere contains elements both disciplinary and emancipatory.[358] The discourse of the mother-educator in Beylerian's writing is both confining and liberating. It ensures women a respected position in the construction of the Armenian nation, because she is mother of that nation, which legitimizes her education and right to speak in matters affecting the nation, but at the same time, not challenging men's dominance in the governing and economic spheres.

To a contemporary reader of these texts, the disciplinary elements of the role of mother-educator are striking. It is important, however, to recognize the liberatory elements of this position. It is based precisely on women's role as mother that Marie Beylerian was able to make her bold declaration of women's rights:

> We have the right to speak freely and to reveal our bold opinions about all issues, which touch communal life, and we demand our opinions to be taken seriously and our ideas respected.
>
> We are free in our family life, free and independent in our activities and thoughts, free to pursue whatever idea or goal that is beautiful to us, in short, we are free in everything that is pure and free from prejudice and to allow what is ethical and to not damage the work of raising the next generation.[359]

The power of being the mother-educator was attractive to women and ensured a legitimate platform on which to speak publicly and to be listened to and respected, on issues previously regarded as the exclusive domain of men.

To be a mother-educator, however, women had to be properly educated. This education included not only literacy but also preparation for women's role as mother. In the short story, *The Mother-in-Law: A Tale from Provincial Life,* which should be read as Beylerian's criticism of the "old prejudices" mentioned earlier, she describes the young married daughter-in-law as follows

> She is a woman, and she waits for instruction, she waits for them to acquaint her with her responsibilities. She is a mother who waits for them to teach her how to care for her child. She has a family and she waits to be shown how to govern her household."

Beylerian remarks:

> It is those ill-timed marriages, which occur in our provinces that are the cause of great misfortune. They are the cause of strife in the composition of serious and knowledgeable families, these

customs  physically and mentally harm our wretched provincial girls...[360]

It was to prepare girls for marriage and motherhood, and to delay marriage until girls were old enough to understand their responsibilities, and to not weaken the nation with "ill-timed" marriages, that female education was advocated for girls in the pages of *Artemis*.

## Education

The earliest discussions of female education in the Armenian press began with articles designed to persuade journal readers of the necessity and desirability of educating girls. For example, an article in 1881, about a charitable association established to finance Hrrip'simé Secondary School in Smyrna, includes a long explanation of the benefits of female education to the Armenian nation. The author argues that the goal of female education is "to return and spread usefulness, general knowledge and morality in the Armenian family and national life."[361] Supporters of female education knew that they had to overcome anxieties around the figure of the educated woman before achieving the goal of educating girls. Female literacy traditionally was viewed as detrimental to the social and sexual order of Armenian society. A literate girl was seen as threatening to the family's control over her sexual behaviour, demonstrated by the common maxim that girls who could write would write love letters.[362] The danger of this, of course, was that she would form attachments independent of her family's will. Beylerian argued that the educated woman was derided in the past because she was regarded as upsetting gender conventions by appropriating male prerogatives:

> Heart, mind, education, not a thought was spared to these. It was considered shameful for a woman to say an educated and progressive word. A woman who could read and write was considered a new type, outside of her place and sex, an unnatural

mannish creature, who other women looked upon with bitterness and as scandalous.[363]

The advent of the figure of the mother-educator, helped to dispel the stigma attached to educating girls, by connecting knowledge to national development and by disproving the notion that the educated woman was "immodest." It is for this reason that educational associations, like Sibyl's AHË, focused primarily on establishing girls' schools in order to teach girls the Armenian language in preparation for their future roles as mothers. As a mother the Armenian woman now had to be educated in order to teach her children their ancestral language and to instil in them an understanding of their duties and responsibilities to the Armenian nation. In the early twentieth-century, such theories had justified primary education for girls. The second stage of writing on education focused on the curriculum and the objectives of education. The teaching of the Armenian language was still the primary objective but complexities were added to the goal of basic literacy by the beginning of the twentieth century, especially in larger towns, where the many primary schools had already provided basic Armenian language education.

Marie Beylerian, a schoolteacher in various Armenian schools in the Ottoman Empire and Egypt, was particularly interested in the question of education for girls. Her editorials in *Artemis* treat the issues of curriculum, quality of teachers within the context of female and national development. In the editorial entitled *The School* Beylerian criticized the current curriculum taught to girls. She argued that it was based on "theoretical and abstract plans and principles," which did not prepare Armenian girls for hardship.[364] One of the elements that make Marie Beylerian's writings on education distinct from other Armenian intellectuals is her awareness of the precariousness of the Armenians' position in the Ottoman Empire. Beylerian had been forced into exile in 1896, as a consequence, when she discusses education and employment, she often emphasizes that Armenian women should be prepared to enter what she calls "life's struggle." To a certain extent, Beylerian accepts an ideal in which men of the family financially support women, but because of her experience of exile, she knows that this is not always feasible. She states:

> It is time for education to strengthen our girls' minds and hearts. They need practical classes to prepare them, using real examples, to go along life's path. In order that the wind doesn't carry her here and there, and so that evil events and massacres don't take advantage of their weakness and throw them to the ground.[365]

Beylerian's statement, written only thirteen years before the Armenian Genocide, eerily prefigures the situation in which many women and young girls and boys would be left without family care and were forced to support themselves. In 1915 knowledge of practical skills, such as sewing and tailoring could sometimes make the difference between survival and death.[366]

Because of her knowledge of exile, how to prepare Armenian girls to enter into Armenian national life as a mother-educator and to withstand evil events was the subject of Beylerian's discussion on school curriculum. She divides this discussion into two main parts: psychological development and practical training.

In terms of psychological development, Beylerian viewed education as the means of improving Armenian women's status and intellectual development. As stated earlier, when the theory of national development became linked to women's knowledge or lack thereof, much focus was paid to women's minds. Beylerian was interested in the development of women's minds as well, for the good of the nation, and also for the benefit of women. She desired women to become educated to take their place as rational beings:

> Self-respect and self- knowledge are the marks of a rational human being and of the most sublime feelings.
>
> The person who is not acquainted with the self, and has no understanding of responsibility to the self or others, isn't a worthy person and can't be called a rational being.
>
> What will give birth to and develop those attributes in the heart and mind of a human being?

The School . . .

We, the Armenian women, who, just yesterday, were more or less valuable possessions, pretty playthings, today the school has opened up to us enlightenment, instead of ignorance. From today we begin to feel that we are becoming human beings, with our minds, free hearts and independent wills, with which we can, without external pressure or influence, think, feel and work.

The school is the weapon to shatter the unjust fate of the female sex.

The school is the force, which awoke the Armenian woman's slumbering self- respect and self-knowledge.[367]

To understand Beylerian's advocacy of self-knowledge, a concept also significant in Dussap's, Sibyl and Zabel Yesayian's writings, it is useful to think of the function of self-knowledge in the English feminist, Mary Wollstonecraft's discourse. Western Armenian women, probably through French translation, knew Wollstonecraft, Yesayian mentions her works in an article on contemporary Armenian women's roles.[368] In a discussion of Mary Wollstonecraft's *A Vindication of the Rights of Woman* (1792), Jan Wellington argues that "Wollstonecraft suggests, the socially determined lack of opportunity to develop their intellects or their moral sentiments makes women and the rich, paradoxically, both selfish and selfless, for in flying from themselves they fail to realize their human potential by acquiring "virtues which they may call their own."[369] A similar conceptualization of self-knowledge is found in Beylerian's writings. For it is self-knowledge that enables women to behave responsibly, or in Wollstonecraft's words to become less "selfish." Beylerian believed that self-knowledge and respect would enable women to raise their own status, acquaint them with their responsibilities and shield them from moral corruption if forced by circumstances to enter the workforce:

We need to encourage and pay serious attention to the need for our young girls to study and prepare to enter life's struggle, with a strong mind and heart through exercise and by raising self-respect and knowledge.[370]

The goal of instilling self-knowledge was to enable women to successfully enter the public sphere:

> We must educate our girls in a hard-working, respectful spirit and inspire them with faith in their abilities, so that they may courageously and successfully perform the work they have undertaken.[371]

The second function of education in Beylerian's discourse was to provide women with practical training. Because the ideal economic arrangement in Armenian society of the period was a model of men rather than women as wage earners, the notion of education as preparation for employment was not central to most discussions of women's education. The failure to prepare women for employment was criticized by Srpuhi Dussap in 1883, who in a sophisticated analysis in *Mayta*, argued that men benefit from women's unpaid work and lack of competition as follows:

> It is difficult for me to pardon men for perpetuating this injustice against women, by pushing women out of jobs, they kept these jobs for themselves. I don't understand why society gives us the responsibility of the family which requires so much knowledge. Why are they giving women a job [motherhood] which is so elevated they cannot successfully achieve it? What is going to be the result of this conduct?[372]

In this passage Dussap clearly identified women's unpaid work in the family as beneficial to men by providing free domestic labour and keeping women away from economic competition with men in the workforce. Most theorists of education were slower to take this issue up, although they did agree that a woman should be educated to know her responsibility as a mother. Gradually, however, the press began to acknowledge that girls, especially working-class girls would have to assist the household economy through waged labour. In fact, benevolent associations had been aware of this for some time, and had been tacitly educating girls in handicrafts as both necessary for household use and for professional use. In 1888 the Tiflis Women's Association got the chance to make into a reality its longstanding wish to open a trade school. On September 21, 1888 it opened the school of dressmaking and handicrafts. The school accepted graduates of the three-year primary school, and taught the pupils sewing, embroidery, ironing, drawing, accounting and household economy. In the future the curriculum would be extended to include cookery, laundering, hat and stocking making. In its first year the school accepted eleven pupils, but the number increased to 100–120 pupils, demonstrating that girls and their parents regarded such a curriculum as worthwhile.[373] In the Ottoman Empire, Sibyl voiced in 1909, what had been a policy of AHË for some time, namely that the Armenian girl was being trained in order to "earn her own bread." [374] Foreign orphanages with Armenian pupils also concentrated on the teaching of trade skills. Prior to 1915 the German run orphanage in Marash trained girls in sewing, cooking, needlework, childcare and some nursing skills. These were viewed necessary primarily for household management but could be transferred, if necessary, to wage earning labour. At the same time, boys at the orphanage were prepared for weaving, shoemaking and carpentry.[375]

In *Artemis* Marie Beylerian criticized curriculum which taught girls only theories and delivered dry sermons on how to be a responsible human being. She provides the example of Constantinople's Pera Girls' Trade School, which taught girls reading and writing as well as trade skills: tailoring, dressmaking, and needlework. According to Beylerian, the guiding principal of this school was to enable women to support themselves "honourably" in case of need.[376]

Beylerian states that although the school closed after six or seven years and had been forgotten by almost everyone, its pupils did not forget it:

> However, the Trade School's former pupils still remember it with deep gratitude for as long as they live, that blessed place where they were taught to love, to live and to fight . . .
> Some of these girls became exemplary mothers, others became teachers, workers and dressmakers, and the majority are self-

supporting and through responsible labour earn their own living today. [377]

This passage emphasis both Beylerian's belief that women need to learn how to "live and fight" in order to survive and that education should prepare women to have a responsible place in national life, as "exemplary mothers" or "self-supporting" workers.

For Beylerian a middle-class girl and a working-class girl can both be prepared for their destiny as mother-educators through education. She argued that the goal of education should not be preparing girls to be adornments in the salon but rather real mothers and women upon whom the basis of the home is founded. And that in place of teaching piano and singing, "let's teach our girls' their responsibilities to their parents, nation and homeland."[378] Najmabadi has argued that it is in the school that Iranian women began to construct themselves as citizens.[379] In theories of education among Armenian theorists, such as Beylerian's, we see a similar phenomenon: it is the school that teaches Armenian girls to become members of the Armenian nation through instruction in the national language, religion, and history. In addition, as Pamela Young's research has demonstrated, textbooks for girls emphasized socialization paying special attention friendships, communication and honesty.[380] These qualities are also designed to ensure national development. Beylerian's statement that girls should be taught "their responsibilities to their parents, nation and homeland" is part of the reconceptualization of Armenian women as active participants in the nation and not simply as bearers of children. Women had reconceptualized their role as mothers, and motherhood was not confined to the physical act of giving birth, motherhood now entailed training the children to understand their responsibilities as members of the Armenian nation. The school, as did the charitable association, facilitated this process by teaching Armenian women what constituted a national member (a citizen in Najmabadi's words) and enabling its expression through the charitable association. As Najmabadi describes it: "At these schools and associations women were constituting at once a new individual self through literacy and a new social self through patriotic political activities."[381]

The final issue that occupied Marie Beylerian's discussion of education was the quality of teaching. Because the school was considered so central to national development, the teacher was of great significance. Adequate teacher training, however, was a persistent problem. Initially, there were few teachers available and numerous charitable associations were founded with the specific aim of training teachers. The association headed by Srpuhi Dussap, *Dbrots'aser Hayuhyats' Ënkerut'iun*, which was devoted to the preparation of teachers to work in Armenian schools in the provinces, was one such example.[382] They were many more, including the *Krt'asér Ënkerut'iun* [Education Society] founded in Smyrna in 1881.[383] In *Artemis* Beylerian outlined the qualities expected of an ideal teacher of girls:

> [M]ust be skilled and proficient in her task. She must know how to inspire young girls' minds, hearts and natures. She must see into the depths of their souls and hearts.
>
> Above all else she must know how to attract their hearts in order to love and be loved by the children, for it is through love that an experienced teacher can direct them and by her desired model form their characters.[384]

Beylerian laments, however, that the Armenians do not have very well trained and educated teachers. She says that generally teachers have no idea what it means to "build a mind, heart and soul." They become teachers merely in order to earn some money. Sometimes, schools like Ketronakan and Sanasarian, would send teachers for extra training at special summer schools or to Europe,[385] but teachers at these schools constituted an elite, not the untrained female teacher, usually recruited to teach Armenian girls in small, village or town schools. Although Beylerian appears to admire the teachers who were able to go to Europe to study, she acknowledges, however, that most women who become teachers are too poor to go to Europe to study pedagogy. In lieu of higher education she advocates that such women teachers study at home.[386] In a subsequent editorial, Beylerian advocated reading as a means of self-improvement for the student and for any woman who has not had sufficient formal education.[387] Education is the key in Beylerian's construction of the desired, modern Armenian woman, because at its best, education was designed to promote self-knowledge and to teach women how to become responsible members of the Armenian nation. The issue of employment for women was more contentious than female education because its usefulness to the woman, the nation and family was less obvious to intellectuals of the period.

## Employment

As discussed in the previous section, Beylerian viewed education as the means of preparing a woman for her role as mother-educator and if necessary, due to family poverty or massacre and exile, for training to earn money. In the editorial entitled: *Work is Necessary for Women* Beylerian added to her discussion of women and work. She divided her discussion of work into two categories. The first is how work will raise the status of women in society and the family and secondly, she called for a re-evaluation of what constitutes work.

In discussing women's employment Beylerian argues that women's low status in the family and by extension society is due to the fact that women do not typically engage in paid employment. Beylerian examines the contemporary Armenian family, stating that upon the birth of a baby girl no one is happy because of the sex of the child. She states that although a well off, urban father will hide his disappointment knowing it to be "uncivilized," the rural or poor father will not bother to hide his contempt.[388] Beylerian suggests that the reason for dislike of girls is based on economics. The girl, in contrast to the boy, is costly. The parents must provide for her food and clothing in childhood and then give her a dowry when she marries. Thereby losing the benefit of her household labour and cost of upbringing. This is in complete contrast to the male child who at his birth is welcomed with joy and by the time he is ten or twelve years old is already working alongside his father. Beylerian comments that the upbringing of the boy is never considered wasteful because he is not expected to leave home and his labour will always be channelled to benefit his family.[389]

Beylerian suggests that the way this situation can be rectified is for women to engage in paid employment. She argues that if women were employed and "participated equally in the worries of the household economy" they would be valued as boys are valued. She also suggests that women's employment could eliminate the need for dowries. She states that men demand dowries because they claim once women are married they sit idly at home, and therefore the man needs this money to compensate for having to care for his wife. Beylerian argues that if women were not accused of idleness, dowries would not be demanded.[390]

As historians of the Egypt and Iran have shown, housework in the nineteenth century was elevated to a science called "household management." Female intellectuals constructed this as the women's special work on par with men's work outside of the home. In Armenian discourse on women's roles, the management of the household was ascribed an important place. As we have already seen in Mariam Khatisian's novel, *On a New Road*, the successful completion of the care of the household was the mark of a responsible, *adult* woman. In Marie Beylerian's editorials she argues for a redefinition of work, which places value on non-waged work and counters accusations of women's idleness:

> Women prepare meals, do the cleaning, laundry, and ironing and are responsible for the housekeeping expenditure. In addition, she carries the weight of motherhood, she gives birth, suckles the infant, and raises the child and cares for the child day and night, often with little or no sleep. Can all this really not be considered work? Unfortunately it is not valued as work by our male companions because it does not bring money into the house. All that labour has merited us is the title "household servant . . ."[391]

In fact, a perusal of all that the Armenian village woman was responsible for in the household and the ways she contributed to the economy, supports Beylerian's contention that women already worked very hard. In the rural regions women were responsible for the drying and storing of fruits and vegetables; the grinding and sorting, and storage of grains, baking bread, and feeding the household three meals a day. They were also responsible for laundry and childcare. In addition, while men were primarily engaged in field work, when extra help was needed during harvest season, women also worked in the fields.[392] Nor was difficult work confined to the village woman; women of families engaged in artisanal trades also worked at home. For example, Zabel Yesayian portrays her maternal aunts as working at their home in Constantinople in the dyeing of cloth for wages.[393]

The editorial *Work is Necessary for Women* connected women's low status with her lack of waged employment, the next editorial Beylerian wrote on women's employment entitled: *A few words to those who misunderstand us* explored what sort of work would be most beneficial to women and the nation. In the latter editorial, Beylerian writes that she is responding to attacks on her stance on women's role in society. Unfortunately, these opposing arguments were not published in *Artemis*, but Beylerian does give some hints of what was criticized. She says that the editorial board of *Artemis* was accused of wanting "the woman confined within the family, and to be occupied solely with children, the kitchen and household worries . . ."[394] Beylerian answered that she and the staff at *Artemis* do not want women to be confined solely to the house but nor do they want women to work at just any sort of profession. This statement highlights one of the primary concerns of Armenian intellectuals on the topic of women's employment. Women writers generally supported the principal of women's work, however, they were not agreed on what sort of work was acceptable for women. For example, Srpuhi Dussap lamented the fact that employment was restricted on the basis of gender. In her novel, *Araksia or the Governess*, the main character, who is good at mathematics states:

I have a talent for book-keeping, if social conditions permitted I would have pursued accounting because I have a particular inclination for that area. But to my sex every dream of entering such a career is hindered.

She resolves therefore to: "chose the only work available to me, that is to be employed as a governess in a respectable family."[395]

Later Sibyl expressed concern over the lack of good employment available to middle-class women and deplored the degrading factory work performed by working-class women in Pilechik'. Sibyl had witnessed female factory workers in Pilechik', where she had lived as a young wife with her first husband and wrote about in *A Girl's Heart*. Her portrayal of the homes of women forced to work in Pilechik' reveals both the necessity of women's work in the home and the ill-effects of factory work:

Many households have no one to prepare their food. Those that didn't have a mother or mother-in-law to prepare food were forced many times to be content with a piece of dry bread. Upon returning home from school little children need to be given food. Others were to be found in front of the factories, brought by a nine year old sister, who could no longer stand the cries of starvation of the little nursing baby. The mothers would try to nurse these babies from their dry breasts, and passers-by would stare at the half-naked women, unconscious of her sex's most sacred and most devoted feeling-modesty.[396]

Beylerian entered the fray by arguing against any employment in which Armenian women would be exposed to humiliation and degradation. Although not explicitly stated what concerned women when writing about employment was the idea that women could be subject to sexual exploitation. In several short stories the author, Krikor Zohrab had described the sexual exploitation of domestic servants in wealthy homes in Constantinople. For example in the short story, *Postal* [Whore] he suggested that attractive domestic servants were procured by the family for sons in order to ensure familial control over male sexuality while holding the young women responsible in the advent of pregnancy or scandal.[397]

Beylerian expresses similar worries when she states that Armenian women, when required to work outside of the home, are naive and unprepared for the outside world, and therefore will be susceptible to exploitation, again in Beylerian's writing work is associated with exile:

> The inexperienced and naïve Armenian woman, by an unforeseen and cruel fate, is thrust out of her country and her beloved home and is forced to inhospitable shores, where everything looks harsh to her-the air, the earth, the water, manners, customs and language. By mind and spirit she is completely unprepared and unable to digest outside ideas, unable to correctly ponder, to see clearly, to judge rightly and is susceptible to be deceived by a pretty speech, or a tender glance. It is understandable that she cannot without moral injury take on, indiscriminately, every sort of work. We believe that above all else she should work in a career with definite regulations and rules. For example, we don't consider it desirable that our straightforward and innocent Armenian girls serve in restaurants, taverns, coffeehouses and bars, as waitresses, singers or dancers. We have seen this, although fortunately in small numbers, (although we can not be certain that the numbers won't increase in the future) and the blood froze in our veins . . .[398]

As is evident in past editorials, the type of work Beylerian saw as acceptable for working-class girls and women was in trades such as dressmaking, while middle and upper-class women were advised to "establish a woman's association, run a school, create a body for the care of the poor, found an orphanage. . ."[399] Interestingly, although a teacher herself, Beylerian does not give much concrete information on the teaching profession. Nevertheless, teaching and eventually nursing, became the most respectable employment outside of the household management. Although, initially, in the first half of the nineteenth century, teaching school had been viewed as an unsuitable job for an Armenian woman. In 1864 the Protestant missionary Josephine Coffing described the difficulties a young Armenian woman graduate of the mission school experienced when she attempted to administer a school for girls in the provincial town of Marash. The young woman was very discouraged and nearly all her pupils had left the school:

> The men called her a brazen-faced thing for trying to teach, a thing no woman could do. The women called her crazy, because she did not improve her opportunities for matrimony. Some called her proud; some accused her of wishing to turn a 'Frank;' and all turned from her with scorn and cutting indifference.[400]

By 1878, however, there were ten schools in Marash taught by Armenian women and Mrs. Coffing comments that by this time:

> So rapid had been the change in public sentiment that the people thought they [the women] excelled men in teaching.[401]

In fact, the numbers of Armenian women teachers associated with Armenian national schools increased in Constantinople throughout the nineteenth century. In 1865 there were nineteen female teachers in the capital, by 1897 there were fifty-nine and by 1908 one hundred and twenty six.[402] Teaching was also the most popular career among Armenian girls educated in Protestant Mission schools. Mary Patrick, the principal of the American College for Girls in Constantinople, noted that of the college's large number of Armenian students between the years 1871 and 1924 eighty percent were reported to have become teachers.[403] Presumably because it reproduced women's domestic roles, teaching was an acceptable profession for women.

However, like her counterparts in the Egyptian women's press, Marie Beylerian concentrated not on waged employment, but rather on improving the domestic environment in discussions of women's employment. Baron comments, "enhancing this sphere was seen as the best strategy for raising women's status, and the outpouring of domestic literature instructing the wife, mother, and "mistress of the house" showed pursuit of this goal."[404] Beylerian's final conclusion in her discussion of women's employment is that if women must work outside of home:

> At present the Armenian woman must become accustomed to a certain sort of work and can survive on a modest salary if she moderates unnecessary demands.[405]

The occupation of mother-educator, however, remained women's primary calling in Beylerian's theoretical constructions of women's role in society.

Marie Beylerian's journal *Artemis* participated in the creation of a discursive public sphere by discussing issues of rights, motherhood, and education and to a lesser extent employment as they affected women. This is not to suggest that Armenian women all had the same opinions and views, they did not, but as writers and readers women could participate in the creation of public space through writing for and reading journals such as *Artemis*. Marie Beylerian's bold discussion of women's right to be free of oppression in the family and in the state, as well as her re-evaluation of motherhood and marriage, ascribed women a central place in ideological constructions of the nation. Armenian women's writings in novels, short stories and essays of the turn-of-the-century consciously represent the interests of women, children and the family and display a sense of responsibility to the future development of the Armenian nation and society by focusing on social and institutional reforms.

# CHAPTER FIVE

# SOCIALISM AND REVOLUTION:
# THE POETRY OF SHUSHANIK KURGHINIAN

The construction of the railroad connection from Tiflis to the Black Sea port of Poti, the opening of a textile mill, which by 1872 employed 800 workers, the majority of them Armenian, the oil industry in Baku and the refineries in Batumi, were the nascent stages of industrialization and caused the growth of an urban working class in the Caucasus. As historian Ronald Suny suggests, although the economy remained agricultural, the expansion of industry and railroad links caused a disintegration of the economy of the rural areas of Transcaucasia.[406] The economic disparities, social upheaval, and the development of revolutionary movements in Russia, all caused Armenian intellectuals in the Caucasus to rethink the nature of society, including economic and class disparities, the role of the peasantry and the conditions of the Armenians in the Ottoman Empire. In the 1880s and 1890s, influenced by Russian populism, young Armenian intellectuals went out among the people to learn from them and to inspire them with revolutionary zeal. The Armenians restated the Russian populist slogan "going to the people" to suit their reality, as a people divided between three empires, by calling for a movement "depi erkire" [going to the homeland].[407] Socialist and nationalist trends are present in Armenian political thought of this period. In chapter three, Mariam Khatisian's portrayal of the arguments typical in Armenian circles in Tiflis about going to the homeland, was explored. This chapter will focus on the poetry of Shushanik Kurghinian (1876–1927), whose political stance represents the

169

socialist trend of the Transcaucasian intelligentsia, yet engages, like other Armenian women writers, with the question of Armenian women's place in this configuration.

The literature of Eastern Armenia in the nineteenth century critically examined the customs and beliefs of the Caucasian Armenians. The most notable of these writers is Hovhannes Toumanian (1869–1923) whose works, such as *Anush* and *Gikor*, portray rural customs, poverty and the exploitation of the peasantry and working class. As Kevork Bardakjian states in *A Reference Guide to Modern Armenian Literature*, Toumanian's works illustrate "the devastating consequences of superstition, ignorance and long-standing customs."[408] The reader of Toumanian cannot doubt that the author is not simply representing custom in the narrative poem, *Anush*, nor is he merely narrating a simple story of a rural boy's migration to Tiflis in *Gikor*, rather the author told these stories to make his audience conscious of what was wrong with contemporary social and economic structures.

Shushanik Kurghinian is considered one of the creators of proletarian literature in Armenian. She was sympathetic to the socialists and later the Bolsheviks and consequently was accorded great significance in literary historiography after the creation of Soviet Armenia in 1921. A biography about her life and work appeared as early as 1955 by Hovhannes Ghazarian, she is an important figure in Zvart Ghukasyan's short volume, *Hay Kin Groghner* (1978); a lengthy chapter is devoted to her work in *Hay Nor Grakanut'ian Patmut'iun*, Volume 5, (1979), and she is credited as being the Armenian poet of the 1917 Revolution in a work entitled *Mets Payk'ari Herosuhinerë* (1985) written in celebration of the Armenian women who contributed to the Bolshevik victory. Although Kurghinian's poems and short stories have been studied primarily from the perspective of her commitment to the Russian Revolution and socialism, her poetry also contains common nineteenth-century literary themes such as: plight of the poor (a concern not limited to socialists), representation of the natural beauty of Armenia and a secular world view.

By the end of the nineteenth century, many Armenian intellectuals, both in Russia and the Ottoman Empire, expressed an anticlerical, secular nationalism. Stepan Vosgan (1825–1901) had extorted his friends  to: "Rally around the concept of Armenia and not that of religion."[409] Some poets offered the pre-Christian Armenian religion as an alternative to Christianity; since the latter was viewed as encouraging passivity in the face of oppression. For example, the poet Siamanto (1878–1915), in the poem, *Prayer to Anahit on the Feast of Navasard* (1914) wrote:

> Take your revenge now, after twenty centuries,
> Oh my goddess Anahit, now as I throw
> Into the fires of your altar, the two poisonous arms
> Of my cross . . .

In contrast to Christianity, which the poet sees as having weakened Armenians, he calls for strength to come from the ancient Armenian past, through the pagan goddess Anahit:

> I beg of you, oh powerful, unequalled beauty,
> Give your body to the sun and be fertilized,
> Give birth to a formidable god for the Armenians.
> For us, from your diamond hard uterus bear an invincible god.[410]

Kurghinian's poem *Begone with your Cross* is part of the secular trend in Armenian poetry. In this poem, first published on January 20, 1907, a revolutionary on his way to execution declines the "consolation" of the cross, because he views religion as the historic tool of oppression, saying:

> Begone with your cross-instrument of countless,
> Endless falsehoods, shameless hypocrisy . . .
> The exploiters' weapon-four armed
> Long worshipped,
> Whenever a person groaned in pain
> With their minds blinded and wingless . . .
> Begone with it, blood is pouring from it.[411]

In this stanza Kurghinian, like other secular intellectuals, represents Christianity, as having weakened the people and caused them to look to religion in their anguish instead of action. Unlike Siamanto, however, Kurghinian locates salvation, not in history, but in socialist revolutionary struggle. Besides these themes, Kurghinian, like other women writers discussed in this book, explores the role of motherhood and the position of women in society. The latter themes shall be the principal focus of this chapter.

Shushanik Kurghinian (nee Popolchian) was born in Aleksandropol (present-day, Gyumri) on August 18, 1876, her father Harutiun Popolchian was an artisan. The young Shushanik benefited from the expansion of Armenian education to the working-classes and attended an all-girl's primary school at a local monastery where nuns taught her, before attending the Alexandropol Arghut'iun Girls' School. In 1895 she studied at a Russian gymnasium. As Mariam Khatisian was at pains to show in her novel, *On a New Road*, the objective of the educational system of this period was to Russify students in the Caucasus. The Russian tsar Alexander III (r.1881–1894) had instituted a policy of Russification in the Caucasus. Hundreds of Armenian schools, with approximately 20,000 students were closed down.[412] The primary school Kurghinian attended was forcibly closed down by the Russian government in 1879, 1884 and 1896. Kurghinian later stated of the period of her schooling: "The Russian bureaucracy was busy forcing development and Russification on the small nations of the Caucasus."[413] At school Kurghinian's literary inclinations appears to have been known and encouraged by her teachers. In a letter written in 1895 a teacher encouraged Kurghinian to examine the Armenian people's literary traditions and learn from them. This advice may account for why, of the majority of women writers of the period, Kurghinian was primarily a poet, the traditional literary form of the Armenians. Although other women writers in this period wrote poetry, they experimented primarily with the new forms of the short story and the novel. Kurghinian's first poem, *Verjaluysi varr shoghk'erov* was published in 1899 in *Taraz* and in 1900 her short story, *Poch'at Katvi Patmutiunë*, written in 1898, appeared in the journal *Aghbyur*. Despite her early experimentation with prose and poetry, Kurghinian is primarily identified as a poet.[414] Kurghinian's writing of poetry, the traditional and immensely popular literary form in Armenian letters, is perhaps her way of learning from and appealing to the Armenian masses. If her objective was to inspire the people, this was facilitated by composing short, rhyming verses, which are easy to memorize and recite. Kurghinian's poems were usually called songs [yerg] and employ a simple, rhyming, couplet form and like the verses of songs are easily remembered.

Kurghinian participated in political activities from an early age. In 1893 she organized, with other young women, the first Hnchakian young women's group. The Hnchak party had been organized in Geneva in 1886, when Caucasian Armenians, Avetis Nazarbekian and his fiancée Maro Vardanian, and Gevork Ghara-jian wrote a draft programme for a new party. The immediate goal of the party was independence for Western Armenia; the eventual goal was a socialist republic. In August 1887 in Geneva, six Armenians formally established the revolutionary party and their principal means of recruiting support was through their news-paper *Hnchak* [The Bell]. The party was socialist although not specifically Marxist. Suny states the Hnchak programme contained elements of Marxism and populism and divided people into two parts-shahagortsogh [the exploiters] and the shahagortsvogh [the exploited].[415] Kurhginian employed the language of exploiter and exploited in her poetry. In 1889–1890, Hnchak organizer, Ruben Khanazatian, traveled to the Caucasus to organize Hnchak groups and arrange for monthly deliveries of the newspaper, Hnchak.[416] Perhaps it was at this time, that Kurghinian first came into contact with Hnchak's ideology. Kurghinian's youth, she was seventeen when the Hnchakian young women's group was organized, is fairly typical, as many of the members of the various parties, were very young.[417] Kurghinian remained committed to socialism for the rest of her life.

It is generally noted that Eastern and Western Armenian litera-ture was influenced by two different geographic and literary in-fluences, the former directed towards Russian and German edu-cation and literature, and the latter towards French culture, edu-cation and literature. As a result of her education at a Russian gymnasium, Kurghinian looking toward Russia, had desired to go to Moscow in 1896 in order to further her education, however, due to financial constraints, she was not able to go. It was not until 1903 that Shushanik, her husband and their children, set out for Moscow. On the journey, however, the children became seriously ill and the family was forced to stop in Rostov. In her (unpublished) autobiography, Kurghinian dates her stay in Rostov as the beginning of her political awakening. It is not perhaps surprising that Kurghinian's interest in the urban working class began in Rostov, as this city was one of the early industrial cities in Russia, and therefore witnessed the dissatisfaction of an industrial, urban working class and the development of a labour movement.[418]

The Russian Revolution of 1905, stirred Kurghinian, she called it her "rebirth" and wrote many poems dedicated to the working class and the revolution. The 1905 Revolution began on January 9, 1905 when troops fired on Petersburg workers demonstrating in front of the Winter Palace. During the first nine months of 1905 throughout the empire, solidarity against the tsarist government, blossomed. There were workers strikes, student demonstrations, peasant uprisings and mutinies in the armed forces. Workers formed worker councils in Petersburg and Moscow, these were violently put down and there were many casualties. As a consequence of the 1905 Revolution the autocracy had to legalize political parties and consult with the parliament. At the same time, however, the tsar asserted that Russia was still an autocracy and parliament was dissolved by him when it was considered insubordinate.[419]

Kurghinian's first volume of poetry, *The Ringing of the Dawn*, (Nor Nakhichevan, 1907), was a collection of new poems and those formerly published in Armenian journals. It responded to the workers uprisings and to the reaction of autocracy. The overall tone of *The Ringing of the Dawn* is exemplified by the popular poem, *Extinguish the Lamps,* (December 14, 1906), addressed to the "bourgeoisie" who Kurghinian describes as sitting in front of full tables, while the children of dead workers starve:

And let the bloody, exhausted, black ghosts
From the damp, dry coffins
Visit you and scare you with their deadly looks.
Let them celebrate with you and have fun with you
Let them sing the song of their lives,
The song of that dry bread—with that deadly whisper
And let them break all the cruel chains of injustice.
Extinguish the Lamps![420]

The volume "Ringing of the Dawn" was published with the assistance of Aleksandr Myasnikian, first president of Soviet Armenia, and his brother Sahak in 1907, both of whom encouraged Kurghinian's works.[421] Following the reaction to the 1905 Revolution, Kurghinian's obvious support of socialist revolution meant that her poems were not published in newspapers and journals. A new collection of poetry remained unpublished as Kurghinian did not want to be forced to alter its contents due to censorship.[422]

In 1910 Kurghinian's health began to deteriorate and she was in a sanatorium from 1910–1916. Her Soviet biographer, Ghazarian, says that "during world war one she wrote 'nationalistic' pieces."[423] The "nationalistic" texts are those that deal with the Armenian Genocide and the influx of Western Armenian refugees into the Caucasus. For a variety of reasons the official Soviet policy in 1955, when Ghazarian wrote his biography on Shushanik Kurghinian, was to downplay the Armenian Genocide and its consequences. Kurghinian's concern with the plight of the Armenian refugees and the ways in which her writing altered after 1915 are worthy of more critical attention than they have received. This chapter will begin to address this question, but it is worthy of more space than can be afforded here.

In 1921, Kurghinian moved to Yerevan and from 1923 to 1925 she lived in the city of her birth, Aleksandropol. After receiving medical care in Moscow, she returned to Armenia in 1926 and lived in the Nor Malatia district of Yerevan until her death on November 24, 1927.

## Womanhood and Social Practice

Critical attention focusing on Kurghinian's politics has neglected aspects of her work, which did not conform to dominant
Soviet ideology; these neglected aspects include Kurghinian's
treatment of women and society and the refugees of the Armenian Genocide. The former has been ignored, even in such texts
explicitly focused on women writers, such as Zvart Ghukasyan's
*Hay Kin Groghner*, published in Yerevan in 1978. Following
Ghazarian's lead, Zvart Ghukasyan says that concurrent with
Kurghinian's calling for Armenian (male) workers to join the revolutionary struggle, she extends her invitation to Armenian working-class women. In fact, Kurghinian's treatment of the role of
Armenian women is more complex than simply a call to revolutionary struggle with men. Like her contemporaries, Kurghinian's
poetry acknowledges that women experience gender specific social inequalities. In common with Marie Beylerian and Zabel
Yesayian's texts, Kurghinian identifies lack of freedom and opportunity for young women, women's position in marriage, and
social customs governing sexuality, as sites of oppression. Where
Kurghinian differed from her contemporary women writers was
in her solutions to women's problems, for Kurghinian working
women's problems were expected to be solved by socialist revolution. Nevertheless, Kurghinian's identification of problems
experienced by Armenian women fits into prevailing trends in
Armenian women's writing and offers new insights into the
Armenian women's situation from the perspective of the non-elite.
Kurghinian was one of the first Armenian women writers who
was not a member of the Constantinople or Tiflis upper-middle
class, and her writings add the perspective of the urban working-
class woman.

Although Kurghinian's poetry following the Russian Revolution of 1905 does include odes to the revolution and the working
class in such poems as *Hangts'rek' Jaherë* [Extinguish the Lamps],
*Banvornerë* [The Workers] and *Hay Banvornerin* [To the Armenian Workers], from 1906 to 1910 Kurghinian's poetry also explored women's lack of freedom within contemporary society.

One of her earliest poems tells of a young Armenian girl and forbidden love in a manner reminiscent of Hovhannes Toumanian's famous narrative poem *Anush* (1890–1902). Kurghinian's poem entitled *The Village Girl's Lament*, was published in 1906. In its first stanza the poem portrays a girl in love, in which the world of nature around her encourages her sensuality with tragic results. The following rendition in English is done to illustrate meaning and is more literal than poetic. In the original Armenian Kurghinian's poems rhyme, no attempt has been made to reproduce this feature here.

> The sky said to me—love!
> The flower gave me a kiss
> The wind also said—don't grieve!
> The nightingale sang of love.

> The (water) spring said—in the early morning
> Come to my source to see your beloved
> The mist said—beautiful girl
> I will veil you like a bride.

> The deep valley gave me space,
> I hid with my beloved,
> The cold stream's murmur
> Shielded our voices from being overheard . . .

> But the evil doers denounced us
> The village talked of us . . .
> The fortune-teller said our stars
> Never came near each other . . .

> They gave word to my father
> Akh . . . he grabbed me by the braid
> They gave me to a despised boy,
> Red, my day darkened . . .

> Hadn't the sky said to me—love!
> Didn't the flower give me a kiss?
> Hadn't the wind said—don't grieve!
> Didn't the nightingale sing of love?[424]

Bardakjian's description of Toumanian's narrative poem, *Anush*, as a "total negation of outdated and disastrous notions of honour and tradition" can be applied to Kurghinian's *The Village Girl's Lament*.[425] Like Toumanian's *Anush* this poem occurs in a mountain village, two young people are in love, but due to outdated customs, in this poem, the use of astrology to determine marital compatibility, the lovers are betrayed by the customs and gossips of the village, and are punished. The young woman is forced into marriage with a despised other man. Many Armenian writers of this period rejected the notion of forced marriage viewing it as a violation of human dignity and a national injury. Shushanik Kurghinian, like Toumanian and Marie Beylerian, wrote against forced marriages, especially of very young girls. For instance, Toumanian, rejected child marriages in his poem *Maro* (1887), by telling the story of a young girl, who is forced into marriage as a child and when not allowed to return home, kills herself.[426] Kurghinian's *The Village Girl's Lament* is part of the literary movement against forced marriages.

In the poem, *The Village Girl's Lament*, Kurghinian established a dichotomy between nature and custom. Nature encourages the girl and boy, by shielding their talk by the river's murmur, and the mist, which veils the girl. In this poem nature is a positive force, while people's attitudes are based on ignorance and superstition. This suggests a sort of natural right found in the works of Srpuhi Dussap and Sibyl, in which certain behaviour is accepted because it is natural and therefore correct, rather than adherence to custom or "old prejudices" to use Beylerian's terminology. As stated in the introduction, the theory of nature in Armenian women's writing, beginning with Dussap, posited that in the natural world gender equality existed. In Dussap's discourse, if the rules of the "natural world" dominated, social harmony between different genders and classes would exist:

> In nature everything is in harmony. Where power is equal there is no oppression, there is no exploitation, there is no abuse, there is no perversion of nature's laws and when power is balanced everything works calmly and efficiently.[427]

In Kurghinian's poetic universe, nature is conceptualized as freedom for women. Kurghinian's exploration of women's lack of freedom is continued in one of her most popular poems, *The Eagle's Love*. This poem, like many of Kurghinian's other poems, employs the imagery of the natural world as being freer, in this case the world of the eagle, than the human world, represented by the girl. It is one of the few poems by Kurghinian commonly understood to be written about women's lack of freedom:

> The eagle sat on the rocky shelf,
> He sat and sang;
> He saw the girl in the valley below—
> He observed her beauty.
>
> "Girl, gazelle girl,
> It's a pity you don't know how to fly;
> In that cool, moist and silent valley,
> You will wither up and like a flower, die.
>
> If only you could fly—to my rocky heights
> I would chose you as my queen
> When sleep came to your eyes, upon my wing
> I would lull you to sleep with sweet songs . . .
>
> To me your eyes are like black night,
> Your smile, the brilliant sun;
> The immense sky would not rule over you
> But would be beneath you.
>
> Is it true that you don't know how to fly?
> Who gave you life without wings?
> Have you never in your life desired
> To fly in the air, free and light?"
>
> Thus on the rocky height
> Sang the proud eagle
> He flew over mountains and valleys,
> Mourning the girl's fate.[428]

This poem was published on September 26, 1907 and was translated into English as early as 1917, in Alice Blackwell Stone's collection of Armenian poetry. It indicates Kurghinian's early interest in women's lack of freedom. The portrayal in the poem of the sky, flying and freedom available to the eagle contrasts with the girl's immobility, because she has no wings with which to fly. Flying is a motif of freedom, and Kurghinian's emphasis in this poem, on the girl's lack of wings, highlights her lack of freedom. Even the girl's beauty, which attracts the attention of the eagle, is likened to a flower that will wither up and die, if she remains down below in the valley. The girl viewed by the eagle is not portrayed as part of any particular class and is intended to represent all women, who are born without wings. That she is an Armenian girl, is suggested by her eyes "black like night," a common illusion in Armenian poetry, and the fact that the physical landscape of this poem, with its mountains and valleys, even its wildflowers, suggests Armenia. Another poem, *Like a Sweet May Rose*, published in 1908 repeats some of these same images, including the dark eyes of an Armenian woman, and again likens her to a flower that will fade:

Like a sweet May rose
The Armenian girl blossoms—
I wish him, to whom by obedience
You will be enslaved, beautiful.

The days pass . . . on your pretty face
Wrinkles dominate,
Silent grief in your black eyes
The gleam completely erased.

And your life's conditions
To eat, to sleep and to give birth,
A sort of female slavery
That is what it is to be born a girl.

And by an obscure death your life's
End will occur uninterrupted

And who were you, what was your soul?
That the grave will know . . .

In *The Eagle's Love* and *Like a Sweet May Rose*, Kurghinian uses flower imagery, so beloved of medieval Armenian poetry, to represent woman's beauty. Srpuhi Hairapetian has stated that in medieval Armenian poetry, it was common for a woman to be described as "luminous figure, a matchless beauty," who is compared to "fruit, flowers, trees, fragrant plants, honey [and] fire."[429] Kurghinian, obviously harkening back to the medieval tradition, uses the image of flowers as a signifier of beauty. In her poetry, however, while signifying beauty, flowers inevitably fade and are associated with death. The imagery of the girl as a fading flower was employed in *The Eagle's Love*; why the Armenian girl fades is explained in this poem as due to her lot within marriage, when she is expected to be obedient and pass her days "eating, sleeping and giving birth." Kurghinian's poem echoes, Marie Beylerian's statement in 1902, that the Armenian woman's fate was marriage and silence:

> she is born and marries, and she is born only to be the household servant, and dies like an animal, like a plant, like grass, she passes through the world unnoticed, without specific activity, without a goal, without ideals . . .[430]

The turn-of-the-century Armenian women writers objected to the silent woman as the ideal Armenian woman. Kurghinian's poem, as does Marie Beylerian's editorial, struggles against the obscurity of women's lives. The final lines of this poem, "And what were you, what was your soul?/That the grave will know…" highlights the loss of self, found in Dussap's and Sibyl's writings, in which the authors argue that a woman must gain knowledge of herself in order to take her rightful place in society. In this poem, ending with the image of the grave, the search for the self seems doomed to inevitable and tragic failure.

In Kurghinian's oeuvre what will save women from isolation and oppression is revolution. Her most famous poem, *Let's Unite* calls for Armenian women to enter into the revolutionary struggle:

> This empty world is full of grief and sorrow
> Enough of carrying each burden on our shoulders;
> Enough of heart-rending tears and continual crying
> Enough of extinguishing the light from our eyes.
>
> Enough of these cruel laws
> Sacrificing our Spring, our youthful days,
> Forgotten behind four walls
> Enough of doors closed against us.
>
> Come, sister, let's awaken the world,
> Let's shake up our friends
> From this black, unbecoming life
> Let's exit and forge a new path.
>
> Come sister, let us unite,
> Let's become participants in that big "holy fight"
> Enough of being slaves and being chained
> With foggy thoughts and drunk from want.
>
> Let our lucky ones, our men,
> Not be too proud,
> Without us, believe me, sister
> They could not have reached anywhere—
> They would be scattered...
>
> Let's go, sister, bravely and together
> Sacrifice everything to our just cause
> For the sake of freedom's sacred light
> We are all equal and worthy fighters...[431]

As a reading of the poem indicates Kurghinian's call for women's participation in the revolution is not gender-blind. Soviet literary criticism ignored the gender specific aspects of Kurhginian's works because they posited that socialist society would eliminate women's problems, and any specific addressing of women's issues was condemned as "bourgeois." For this reason, Kurghinian's *Let's Unite* is usually described as simply calling Armenian women to join the revolution. But upon reading the poem it is clear that Kurghinian's call to women is not confined to participation in the revolutionary struggle. In stanza two Kurghinian's mentioning of cruel laws, which force women to spend their days within four walls and closed doors, is a reaction against women's confinement in the home and the prohibition of women entering the public sphere. For Kurghinian, participation in the revolution should break down old customs and "cruel laws" and usher in a new dawn for women in society. It has been suggested that Marxism in countries outside of Europe was associated with modernization.[432] As has been discussed, discourses on women's rights in Armenian intellectual circles, was connected to the themes of modernization and nation-building. Kurghinian's socialism, with its particular inclusion of women, and its emphasis on the consequences of economic inequality on women and children, participates in contemporary Armenian debates on what constitutes modernity and what should be women's role in that paradigm. In this poem, Kurghinian emphasizes the significant role Armenian women have performed in society in stanza five, in which she admonishes men not to be too proud of their achievements since these accomplishments are the result of women's assistance. The final stanza calls for women's participation in the "just cause" for the sake of freedom, based on the entire poem, however, it is evident that Kurghinian's "holy fight" is multi-layered including both proletariat revolution and women's emancipation.

## Women and Work

In the 1890s the Armenian workers of Transcaucasia consisted of artisans, day labourers, factory workers and peasants seasonally employed in towns. The majority of the approximately 30,000

Armenian workers in Transcaucasia were employed in the oil industry of Baku, the refineries of Batumi, or the factories and workshops of Tiflis. Increasingly, the experience of industrialization and capitalist development was represented in the literature of the period. For example, the novelist and playwright, Aleksandr Shirvanzade (1858–1935), set many of his novels and plays against the background of the industrializing city of Baku and the resultant socio-economic upheaval. His most famous work dealing with this theme was his novel, *Kaos* [Chaos], written in 1896–1897. Like Kurghinian, Shirvanzade had been a member of the Hnchaks in the 1890s.[433]

The Armenian workers were almost completely unprotected by the law and uprisings and strikes by workers occurred in the 1890s. Shushanik Kurghinian composed many poems on the plight of the working class. For example the poem *The Workers* published in 1907, describes the suffering of the underfed and downtrodden:

> We are coming,
> With dirty old jackets, covered in soot,
> With torn hats, and dirty hair
> Mostly pale, hungry and barefoot,
> Sometimes pale, sometimes resigned
> A clear sign of hunger and that silent misery.
> Sometimes with uncontrollable anger, eager for revenge,
> Looking old before our time, from the awful pain,
> With the desire for light and fresh air on our faces
> With the hope of one day living like human beings
> And with deep wounds in our broken hearts
> We are coming . . .

The poem ends with workers confident readiness to destroy the old order:

> Yes, we are coming
> From the forgotten darkness of torture and pain,
> Poverty, persecution and slavery,
> To destroy your tyranny,

To break the chains of slavery,
To forge a new road for the ones like us
Who deserve equality.
This is how we are coming![434]

There appears to be no full scale study of the gendered nature of employment and the conditions of the working class in the turn-of-the-century Caucasus, however, industrialization did affect women and men as workers. This is illustrated by the 1894 strike of Armenian tobacco workers at the Bozarjian factory in Tiflis. The male workers went on strike when they discovered their sick fund had been confiscated by the owners. The workers demonstrated in the streets until the police came and arrested the leaders. The factory was closed and workers laid off. Later when the owners reopened the factory they hired women workers whom they considered to be "obedient and neat."[435] The socialist movement in Russia largely ignored the question of the exploitation of women workers. Because women workers were preferred to male workers by factory managers, male workers were hostile to women workers, and the leaders of the socialist movement had little interest in organizing women, until the advent of Aleksandra Kollontai (1872–1952). Like Kurghinian, Kollontai later stated that the 1905 Revolution was decisive in the transformation of her life and thinking. Kollontai became a full time revolutionary and it was at this period that she began to pay particular attention to the organizing potential of the women workers in Russia. She lectured on the "Woman Question" from the Marxist perspective and wrote *The Social Bases of the Woman Question* (1909). Kollontai was one of the founders of the "proletarian women's movement" of the years 1905–1914, the record of which, according to historian Richard Stites, was mixed. Kollontai faced much hostility from other socialists who believed that the problems faced by women workers would be solved through the establishment of a socialist state.[436] Although it is not known if Shushanik Kurghinian read Alexandra Kollontai's work, there is little doubt that Kurghinian was interested in the conditions of women workers, who were considered more malleable than their male counterparts, and usually paid less. In contrast, to the epic style odes to male workers, Kurghinian's poems about women workers, explore the plight of the working-class mother who must struggle to feed her child or the young girl who must support her elderly relatives. In several poems Kurghinian portrays the female worker, sewing for a pittance, selling flowers and even in desperation selling her body. Perhaps we can understand the women workers at the Bozarjian factory, when we read of Kurghinian's portrayal of women workers' lack of options. In the poem the *Flower Seller* Kurghinian portrays a young girl's despair as she tries to support herself and her aged grandmother:

> She was a girl, blonde, thin . . .
> She had nothing—not intelligence, not even a smile . . .
> She journeyed through the green fields,
> For a fresh flower to bring to market.
>
> And in the field, lovely, dressed in gold—
> The flower's bloom wilts;
> The girl's hands are empty of fresh flowers,
> She looks stunned and quietly cries.

Unable to find flowers to sell at market, the girl fears returning to her grandmother with no money:

> In truth why is she a bad girl?
> She has nothing—she knows nothing . . .
> Why is she not cherished in love by anyone?
> Why is she hungry, beaten without mercy . . . ?
>
> In the tranquil fields, there are no flowers anymore . . .
> And the grandmother will say to the pitiable girl,
> —Either help your elder, spoilt girl,
> Or go to the street homeless and barefoot . . .

Unable to earn money any other way she sells her body in order to bring money home:

Uncertain hands slithered on her breast,
Someone breathes heavily in her face,
The thin, desired body trembles,
In eyes of the woman a stupid evil smile . . .

She came home late, pale a little drunk . . .
"Hey Granny, it's me, open the door."
The grandmother with a stick in hand went to the girl—
"In the tranquil fields there were no flowers . . ."

This poem published in 1908 hints at the taboo topic of prostitution. Sexuality and prostitution are not common themes in Armenian women's writing at the turn of the twentieth century. Male writers, such as Krikor Zohrab, did occasionally portray prostitution and sexual exploitation, however, women writers usually avoided the topic. The reason for this appears to have been the sense that women's writing itself had only recently become socially acceptable, and only just, with most women writers having to overcome injunctions against writing and calls to focus on motherhood.[437] Kurghinian, witnessing the economic conditions for the working class in industrializing Russia and the Caucasus, noted the lack of adequate and good paying opportunities for both male and female workers, and especially women's occasional, lapses into prostitution in desperation. She would return to this theme following the Armenian Genocide, World War One and insecurity during the Russian Revolution, in a poem entitled *The Girl*:

With clothes, old and tattered
The eyes beautiful and blue,
She is the child of great pain.

Upon her face, an ungrudging smile
And a vague, impudent glance,
From early experienced lust

And to the populous market
She goes pale, hungry
Searching for an "acquaintance". . .

She heart-rendering cries—"Take me,
For the price of a piece of bread,
Or a glass of wine."

"Take my body, little poor one,
My soul alone unconsoled
My heart for sale, unashamed."

—Come, I said, wretched sister,
—Come, I will ease your pain,
To free you from shame.

She cursed me unashamed
And laughed "You are purer than me?
Who has been abandoned by blind fate."[438]

This poem, published in 1917, continues the theme of prostitution, begun in the 1908 poem, but is perhaps even more despairing. The girl in this poem seems destined to an unhappy fate. Unlike the flower seller who can sometimes earn money from selling flowers this girl's degradation appears of longer duration, she is a "child of great pain." Her desire for wine suggests her hopelessness and her need for temporary relief from the pains she experiences. The last stanza challenges the scorn and moral judgements of passers-by. It was a firm belief of Kurghinian's, stated in her poetry many times, that it is fate and not special virtue that causes one woman to sell herself in the marketplace, while another is loved and protected. She asks the reader to view the girl's fate with compassion instead of derision because the crushing weight of poverty and homelessness could be the fate of anyone.

## Motherhood

The topic of motherhood and especially the modern mother-educator, was one of intense debate and great importance in

Armenian intellectual and literary history. The Armenian mother was conceptualized as the creator of the Armenian nation and defender of Armenian culture through her raising of children, which in turn was related to nation-building by providing the nation with responsible and patriotic citizens. The ideological connections between the Armenian mother and the nation has a discernible genealogy in Armenian intellectual history. As we have seen in Mariam Khatisian's portrayal of Susan Varts'ian in *On a New Road*, the older concept of Armenian motherhood was based on the mother's care of her children and other family members, which was channelled towards her immediate and extended family, while the nineteenth-century intelligentsia saw the extending of maternal care to the nation as a modern, patriotic act. Kurghinian's poetry often depicts the working-class Armenian mother, in ways, which adhere to the older vision. Kurghinian's mothers cannot raise their children to be patriotic Armenians because they are too worried about keeping the said children alive. This is clearly visible in a poem entitled *The (Female) Worker*, published on October 20, 1907:

Don't cry child, let me sew,
There isn't much light,
Certainly, I will bring you bread
Only a little sewing remains.

Close your eyes, sleep well,
Your nights aren't bartered;
You will grow up and you won't find
A sweet night's sleep or bread.

I was once a little girl like you,
In a poor house,
Whether there would be bread or not, I never knew
But I wanted it unceasingly . . .

I still wasn't fully grown
When they married me to your father
There was no subsistence, there was not even a piece of dry bread-

They sold [me] for bread.

The house where I went as bride—
Was poor and bare like ours—
I became a prisoner and cried much,
I cried secretly, every day . . .

My mother-in-law never gave me a day,
She always complained to your father;
Your father came home drunk
In a rage, he beat me.

Who can I tell of my suffering?
When you grow up, you will understand;
Fate is black for an Armenian girl,
The anguish never diminishes . . .

Don't cry child, let me sew,
There isn't much light,
Certainly, I will bring you bread
Only a little sewing remains.[439]

Kurghinian's vision of motherhood is unromantic but never-theless the reader feels the mother's love and her pain as she desperately sews in order to earn money to feed her child. At the same time, the mother's sadness is clear because she knows that if her child lives to adulthood, she will be condemned to the same sort of sorrow and unrelenting poverty as the mother. Typical of most women's writing of this period, the mother-in-law is viewed as a negative figure. In this poem poverty affects the girl in gender specific ways, in order to get bread she is married, where she is subjected to abuse. The poem alludes to the cyclical aspects of poverty. The girl is born into a poor family and is transferred to another indigent family. Her children inherit this same legacy and so the cycle of birth and death in poverty continues without an end in sight.

Kurghinian wrote another poem with the same title as this one, *The (Female) Worker*, less than a year later and like the earlier poem it is about a working-class mother, with the focus on the mother-child bond, and the hopelessness of poverty. This poem is bleaker than the first, because it implies that soon both the mother and child will be dead from starvation:

> Arise sun, red sun, brilliant sun,
> My sleep disappeared with the pained night
> Give my musty, cold cellar a warm hello
> With you, sun, hope is inextinguishable—there is no pain.
>
> Near you, sun, under your rays, today
> I will leave my hungry and naked child
> Give to him, instead of bread, crimson rays
> Which will cause my soul no pain
>
> Caress him, merciful sun, with warm breath,
> So a lively smile will shine on his face,
> In his deprived life, he has lived with nothing—
> Yearning for air, yearning for warmth and light.
>
> And when he is tired, lie down on the dirty ground,
> Shine a pure arc of light on his curly head
> Put my wretched child asleep with dreams,
> Say, your mother will bring bread for you…
>
> And if death suddenly greets my life,
> And the wheel of fortune embraces my emaciated corpse,
> I'm not coming home,
> When he wants bread, say to my child, brilliant sun
> —The unjust, merciless bread ate your mother! …[440]

In this poem, published on March 18, 1908, the mother pleads for the sun to offer the consolation that she is unable to, because the struggle for bread consumes her. In Kurghinian's works the Armenian mother cannot be mother of the nation if she cannot look after her own child's basic needs. Kurghinian's vision of motherhood is gritty and bleak. Unlike Kurghinian's contemporaries, whose portrayal of the Armenian woman as mother-educator is as a positive and empowering figure,

Kurghinian's mothers are occupied with basic survival and have not time to worry about education or concern with the nation.

## The Refugee Poems

Following the Armenian Genocide in 1915, scores of refugees from Western Armenia entered the Caucasus. Some charitable associations provided aid, medical care and food, to the refugees. But the Caucasus region itself was strapped for money and aid workers, due to World War One, and then in 1917, the Russian Revolution. Illness and warfare raged in the Caucasus as the Armenians fought to prevent Turkish takeover of Eastern Armenia. Zabel Yesayian's description of doctors and nurses who attempted to care for the ill and the wounded reveals the difficulties and risks attendant in such work. As does the following portrait of Sat'enik Ohandjanian, a founder of the Constantinople Women's Red Cross: [441]

> Miss Sat'enik Ohandjanian, whom I had already met in Adana during the Cilician massacres and whose tireless activity, modesty and absolute dedication never ceased to inspire me and all others who knew her, rushed to Etchmiadzin before the refugees. Cholera and typhus epidemics claimed the lives of thousands of unfortunates every day. Doctors and nurses were obliged to live in close contact with the sick. There was no way to lessen the contagion. They were engulfed in a wave of invalids and the wounded whose numbers only dropped due to death. In such circumstances, Miss Ohandjanian, with some others, began her charitable work with her customary modesty. It wasn't long before she became ill with typhoid and died in October 1915.[442]

In 1918, when the independent republic of Armenia came into being, the government was faced with tens of thousands of starving and homeless refugees, disease, and the threat of the Turkish army.[443] The winter of 1918–1919 was a terrible one. People lacked bread, fuel, medicine and shelter and riots ensued. At the end of the winter some 200,000 people died from hunger, cold and typhus.[444] In this period Shushanik Kurghinian was ill and confined to a sanatorium. She wrote short stories, such as *Kuyr Harse*, on the Western Armenian refugees fleeing deportation, starvation and death. As stated earlier, the Soviet biographer, Hovhannes Ghazarian called these works "nationalistic" because they veer away from calls to proletarian revolution to concentrate on the traumatic impact of the Armenian Genocide and the appalling conditions of the refugees in the Caucasus.  In January 1922, Kurghinian, who had moved to Yerevan at this time, wrote poems about the plight of the refugees. Two of these poems depict the refugee's struggles, sorrows and the Eastern Armenian observer's response, particularly her feelings of guilt, and a sense of kinship with the Armenian refugee.  In the poem, published on January 9, 1922, called *The Refugee Woman* Kurghinian writes:

> Under the protection of ruined walls
> The refugee woman has built her nest,
> Clothing her body and the ground,
> Her roof [is] the arc of the sky.
>
> Sun, rain, wild wind
> They are her guests-inseparable companions,
> In the depths of her mind, there is no treasure,
> Where affliction, unafraid, has planted its cross.
>
> Hers is the hungry and barefoot generation
> Growing up freely, in the poor and dirty streets;
> Plentiful dirt falls on her shoulders,
> Cruelly wounding her heart, which has not even lived.
> My sister, let me kneel before your anguish,
> I am the eternal prisoner of the pleasure,
> Let me, taking a bright spark from your hopes,
> Give light in the night to my abandoned thoughts...[445]

Kurghinian's portrayal of the refugee woman is poignant and touching.  The poet expresses her sense of kinship with the woman, by calling her sister, and feeling that the woman's anguish is an emotion the poet must acknowledge and "kneel before." In the poem, *The Refugee Family*, published a week after the poem, *The Refugee Woman*, on January 14, 1922, Kurghinian explores the bride's role in the refugee family. As we have seen the bride or daughter-in-law [hars] was frequently depicted in Armenian women's writing of this period, often as an oppressed figure, but in this poem she cares for her parents-in-law who "cower in memories," while suffering her own private grief:

> . . . The damp firewood of the bonfire hisses
> The dirty kettle bubbles;
> Near it sits an old man and woman
> They cower in memories—what a day they have reached.
>
> The beautiful-eyed bride spins the thread on the spindle,
> And secretly cries, for life's destruction;
> She rocks by foot the unnamed baby,
> For love of whom, grief isn't enough . . .
>
> She spins, submissive, silent, uncomplaining
> The grief is tangled in the spun thread,
> And her maternal compassion, love
> Has not nurtured in her mind a protest or a quarrel . . .
>
> She spins steadily, she spins from the beginning of the day until night,
> So the grief will be consumed with the soft wool,
> So the owl will not hoot in her hearth,
> And go back through its worn-out road . . .
>
> A terror of violent anger or fear,
> Is growing in my heart's depths
> The woman whom I left asleep, as a captive,
> Has not yet seen the day . . . and has entered into a deep sleep . . .[446]

The image of the young mother, rocking her baby and spinning, the traditional occupations of the rural Armenian woman, connects her with the past and women's traditional industry, but the landscape, the young mother's tears and grief, mingled with the thread indicates the violent rupturing of the past.

Shushanik Kurghinian's poetry added new elements to Armenian women's writing, it shifts away from the urban elites found in Dussap, Sibyl and Khatisian's writings towards the peasantry and the urban working class. Kurghinian and Yesayian, in novels such as *In the Waiting Room* (1903) and *When they don't love anymore* (1914), were the first women writers to write of the Armenian working class. This is not surprising as they are also the first of the women writers to not come from wealthy households. The expansion of Armenian language education to include working class and rural girls, made possible by the charitable educational organizations, like the ones founded by Dussap, Sibyl and Khatisian, facilitated the development of women's writing from a greater variety of class perspectives. Armenian women's writing of the nineteenth and twentieth centuries was more a product of the urban elite than men's writing, simply because female education was made available to women later than men, which meant that the development of women's writing was slower than men's. In addition, while boys of poor families were sponsored by amira and the like to pursue higher education abroad, fears about Armenian girls' chastity and ability to cope, hindered their venturing abroad for higher education. Kurghinian desired higher education, but was never able to receive it, yet she did attend Armenian primary school and a Russian high school, and through additional personal study, furthered her own education.

The new ideas coming into the Caucasus in the 1890s informed Kurghinian's mind and political activism, witnessing the social upheaval of the beginning of industrialization, Kurghinian, like her contemporary Shirvanzade, responded to the impact of industrialization. Her poetry depicted the human cost wrought by the Armenian Genocide, the conditions of refugees, and the aftermath of World War One, from the unique perspective of the affects of these socio-economic and political trends and events on working class women and mothers. Like other women writers, Shushanik Kurghinian was concerned with women's entry into the public sphere. Her socialism, like Kollontai's in Russia, paid attention to women workers, and advocated women's liberation from class and gender hierarchies.

# CHAPTER SIX

# EXILE AND GENOCIDE: ZABEL YESAYIAN

The presiding genius of Armenian women's writing was Zabel Yesayian, whose novels, short stories and essays explored orientalism, migration and exile from the perspective of women. In addition, Yesayian's writing, before and after the Armenian Genocide, reveals significant changes in the representation of Armenian female identity, thereby demonstrating some of the ideological shift, which occurred as a result of the Genocide.

This extraordinary woman's life and writing career encompasses the most turbulent periods of modern Armenian history. Born Zabel Hovhannisian on February 4, 1878 in the district of Silihtar in Constantinople, as a child she attended the well-known primary school Holy Cross in Scutari, graduating from there in 1892.[447] In common with Marie Beylerian, the political unrest and massacres of Armenians in Constantinople and the provinces in 1895, resulted in Yesayian leaving the city in that year.[448] Consequently, Yesayian went to Paris to study at the Sorbonne and was one of the first Armenian women of that period to study abroad, although young Armenian men had been studying in Paris in earnest since 1839.[449] In 1900, still a student in Paris, Yesayian married Constantinople-born painter Dikran Yesayian (1874–1921). They had two children, Sophie and Hrant. Yesayian returned to Constantinople in 1902 where she continued her writing career. Yesayian was a prolific writer who wrote non-fiction articles about France, the Armenian community, women, literature and social issues. Her fictional texts of the period from 1903–1922 reveal the author's interest in women, particularly female subjectivity and systems of oppression.[450] Such thematic novels include: *When They Don't Love Anymore* (1914), *The Last Cup* (1917) and *My Exiled Soul* (1922).

In 1909, Yesayian was a member of the Constantinople Patriarchate's Commission, which journeyed to Cilicia to investigate the aftermath of the massacres of the Armenian population there.[451] Her report, which contains her interviews with survivors, as well as her impressions and descriptions of the aftermath of the massacres was published in Constantinople in 1911 under the title of *Among the Ruins*. This work was widely acclaimed upon publication as one of the best depictions of the effects and the suffering brought about by the Cilician massacres. Zabel Yesayian is also prominent today and especially remembered for two books: *Among the Ruins* and *The Gardens of Silihtar* (1935). The popularity of these two books can be attributed to the fact that they address two principal concerns of the Diaspora today: the representation of genocidal violence against the Armenians and the portrayal of the vanished pre-1915 Armenian world.

In 1915, Yesayian was one of the Armenian intellectuals in Constantinople designated to be arrested in April of that year. Yesayian escaped arrest because she was out visiting when the police arrived at her house, and her family managed to secretly send word to her not to return. She hid for several weeks in Constantinople before eventually escaping to Bulgaria. Her mother and young son remained in Constantinople while her husband, daughter and sisters were settled in Paris. Yesayian was reunited with her son when he was brought to Bulgaria. From Bulgaria, Yesayian went east to the Caucasus. In 1917, she was in Baku assisting in the care of Armenian refugees and orphans. Travelling through Iran, Iraq and Egypt, Yesayian and her son were not reunited with their family in France until 1919. In 1920, Yesayian went to Cilicia with her two children in order to help with the Armenian orphanages there. When the French army withdrew from the region, Yesayian endeavoured to have the orphans moved to a safer place. She returned to Paris shortly before her husband's death in 1921.[452]

Following 1915, Yesayian's life was a life of exile. During this period she wrote numerous appeals seeking to draw world attention to the plight of the survivors of the Armenian Genocide, including *The Agony of A People* (1917) and *Le rôle de la femme arménienne pendant la guerre* (1922). She also continued to write fiction: *The Last Cup* (1917), *My Soul in Exile* (1922) and *Retreating Forces* (1923).

In 1922 Yesayian rented a house in Paris with her two children and her mother. Money was scarce and she supplemented her income by writing and giving lectures. In 1926–1927, Yesayian visited Soviet Armenia and published her impressions in a lengthy work entitled *Prometheus Unchained* (1928). In 1933, at the invitation of the Soviet Armenian government, Yesayian settled in Yerevan. She lectured on French literature at Yerevan State University and wrote important new works including *Shirt of Flame* (1934), *Gardens of Silihtar* (1935), as well as the posthumously published *Uncle Khachik* (1966). In 1936–1937, during the Stalinist arrests of the Armenian intellectuals Eghishe Charents (1897–1937), Aksel Bakounts (1899–1936) and Vahan Totovents (1894–1937), Yesayian was arrested and sent into exile in Siberia. She died in prison in 1942 or 1943, the exact circumstances of which are not known.

### The Paris Years 1895–1902: Emigration and Alienation

In 1895, Zabel Yesayian went to Paris where she studied literature and philosophy at the Sorbonne. A notebook belonging to Yesayian's student days, in the archives of the Museum of Art and Literature in Yerevan, reveals that her studies in 1896 at the Sorbonne concentrated on medieval and modern French literature and history, Greek philosophy, Latin literature and the history and literature of the Middle East.[453] When Zabel Yesayian arrived in Paris, she had already rejected the only career then open to a middle-class Armenian woman, that of a teacher. She later stated that she had no desire to teach, although she had been offered a position as teacher of the Armenian language at a school in Constantinople. Yesayian had already decided upon being a writer.[454] Zabel's commitment to writing is shown by her professional attitude to this career. In 1934, Yesayian wrote an essay on her writing, which emphasizes the changes that occurred in her writing when she first went to France:

> In France, during my student days, I understood what poor specimens my already published works were, and contrary to the empty praise, I began, with seriousness and severe self-criticism, to free myself from the influence of the "Bolis" literary environment. For nearly seven years, I never wrote a line, without cruelly erasing what I had written, and I devoted all of my time to my education.[455]

Yesayian's definition of education was highly unconventional to her circle of friends:

> At that time I comprehended that to be a true writer, it was necessary to have a wide range of knowledge, I don't mean that I have reached my goal, but at least, I have endeavoured to obtain knowledge. With immense interest I pursued every subject, except literature, and concentrated on socializing, and social and political issues. Many of my friends, who had also come from Bolis as students, jeered and criticized me. They were not stimulated in the same direction as me and thought that my broad interests would detract from my literary path and hinder my creative development.[456]

Yesayian's undaunted dedication to her writing continued throughout her life, as is demonstrated by a glimpse into her life provided by her son, Hrant. Following Dikran Yesayian's death in 1921, Zabel Yesayian and Hrant stayed for a time with Zabel's sister, who had married a Frenchman, Paul Cox. Hrant comments, "Although Mr. Cox didn't have a bad nature, he was in principle against women writers, and particularly foreign women writers."

Hrant described Cox as a precise man who demanded that meals and bedtimes occur at a set time every day. Hrant wrote:

> Sometimes he would wake up at midnight and seeing a light on in our room, where my mother was working, he would come into the room in his nightshirt and in carping tones grumble . . . It was in those days that *Retreating Forces* was born."[457]

It is a testament to Yesayian's commitment to writing and her professionalism that she continued to write despite such inhospitable circumstances. Her professional writing career began in 1895 with the publication of a narrative poem, *Yerg ar Gisher* [Ode to the Night] in the pages of the Armenian journal, *Tsaghik*. It was in the Paris years that Yesayian would make a name for herself in Armenian language journals and some French journals. From 1903–1904, she contributed a series of articles for the women's pages of the *Tsaghik*. These articles include *The Woman Question*, *The New Woman* and *The Parisian Woman* and are reports of the European women's movement. Later articles in the journal *Arakatz* in 1911, such as *The Role of the Armenian Woman in Communal Life* and *The Armenian Woman After the Constitution*, examined Armenian women's activities in Armenian national and charitable work. Her first novel, *In the Waiting Room*, was published in 1903.

By the time Yesayian returned to stay in Constantinople in 1902, she was a well-known and admired figure in the Armenian literary community, particularly among those committed to realism. As Yesayian's biographer, Sevak Arzumanyan, notes between 1898–1906 Yesayian was a literary legend in Armenian circles with article after article published about her and her work.[458] Hagop Oshagan called her the most talented author of the psychological novel in Armenian literature.[459] Yesayian's good literary reputation is deserved and is in part due to her treatment of her writing career as a serious profession.

From 1895 to 1902, Zabel Yesayian lived and wrote in Paris. She later stated that she was sent abroad in that year, 1895, by her father, as he feared for her safety, following the Bab Ali demonstrations, as Yesayian was known to frequent salons where politics and the platforms of the Hnchak and Dashnak parties were discussed.[460] Yesayian's journey to Paris was the beginning of her exile from the city of her birth, Constantinople, for although she would return in 1902, her lifestyle was what is now called "transnational," with her journeying between Constantinople and Paris, where her husband and daughter continued to reside. Due to her journey to Paris in 1895, Zabel Yesayian explored emigration in literary texts, as Marie Beylerian was doing in Alexandria in the pages of *Artemis*. Zabel Yesayian's writing between 1895–1905 touched upon the difficulties of emigration for women, concerns, which after 1915 would beset the Western Armenian people and would not be confined to a small group of intellectuals. The focus in this chapter is on two important themes of Yesayian's writings that of exile and the Armenian Genocide in 1915. These themes will be examined from the perspective of Yesayian's treatment of contemporaneous debates on women's place in the public sphere and motherhood. It is through comparing such themes that the changes in Armenian women's writing from 1880 to 1922 and shifts in the ideological constructions of women become visible.

## Identity and Migration: *The Man*

Yesayian later described her early Paris years as "liberated" and the beginning of her social and political interests.[461] Several autobiographical pieces from this period, however, also attest to Yesayian's sense of homesickness and exile. In *Artemis*, Marie Beylerian discussed exile in abstract terms, namely how it affected the abstract "Armenian Woman," in Zabel Yesayian's writing, she discussed how exile affected her personally and psychologically. As a young Armenian woman in Paris, pursuing higher education, Yesayian was in a unique, exciting, but often lonely, position. Although Armenian male students had been pursuing higher education in Paris and other European cities since at least the early nineteenth century, the same is not true of Armenian women.

Although the idea of Armenian women going abroad to study was gaining legitimacy, the numbers of such students were still small.[462] The author's feelings of alienation and the resulting identity disintegration are found in a short autobiographical sketch published in 1905. The action of *The Man* occurs in 1896, during Yesayian's second year of study in Paris. The story explores the psychological affects of higher education and migration aboard on two students, the Armenian Zabel Yesayian and the Russian, Miss Zavatska. The Paris of this story, like other stories depicting Yesayian's life in France, is a dark and gloomy city, as demonstrated by Yesayian's description of the building and area where she lived:

> It was the beginning of my second year in Paris. At that time I was living in the Boulevard Arago in a small room on the sixth floor which overlooked a courtyard, that is to say a small square space, resembling, from the sixth floor, a deep hole, the bottom of which I never saw. Twice a day the smell of badly prepared food seemed to endlessly float up from small windows, nauseating us. Above me I saw only a square patch of sky, which was often covered with the black, polluting smoke and hopeless, damp fog from the nearby factories. On the days when I saw a clear blue sky, a childlike joy filled my soul and it seemed to me that for human being's complete and pure happiness a blue and sunny sky was all that was necessary.[463]

The physical environment where she lived shaped the author's psychological state:

> Sometimes from the depths of the courtyard, with the smell of grease and oily particles covering the four walls, the voice of a itinerant singer would spiral upward, I would stop my work, and standing next to the window I dreamed . . . I dreamed . . . if an organ barrel went by playing its stifled and mournful music, I don't know why, but it filled my soul with unequalled sadness and sentimental yearnings as I cried in my sunless and melancholy room.[464]

Yesayian's melancholy was exacerbated by her feelings of loneliness. She says she had friends in Paris but they were frequently
busy with exams and she spent her leisure time reading Edgar
Allen Poe (1809–1849) and Charles Baudelaire (1821–1867).[465]
Her loneliness was intensified by the fact that she did not meet
very often with other Armenians and consequently rarely spoke
her native tongue:

> If I said that I felt hopeless and bitter at that time, the reason will
> be understood when I say that not one of my fellow countrymen
> came to call and it happened that for days, sometimes weeks, I
> didn't utter a word in my own language. It was by these means
> that I lost my habit of thinking in Armenian.[466]

This passage clearly demonstrates that for Yesayian the loss of
speaking her native tongue was one of the problems of living
abroad. Although this was a problem presumably experienced by
both female and male foreign students, Yesayian's alienation was
exacerbated by the fact that she lived without other Armenian
students. Unlike her male counterparts, or the Russian girls she
lived with, Yesayian did not have a female Armenian student to
live with and speak her native language. Therefore the experience of living in France is portrayed as separating Yesayian from
elements of herself. Her statement, "I didn't utter a word in my
*own* language" reveals a disintegration in Yesayian's sense of identity, and raises the question: "if she is not speaking her own language, who is she?" This is a particularly pertinent question in
the Armenian context in which the speaking of the Armenian language is held to be one of the principal features of Armenian
identity.

The action of *The Man* revolves around one of the Russian
girls, Miss Zavatska, who like Yesayian, studied literature. The
story is concerned with national and female identity. In Paris,
Yesayian came into contact with women of many nationalities. In
the 1890s, when Yesayian attended the Sorbonne, foreign women
outnumbered French women as university students in
France.[467] The Russian women students captured Yesayian's imagi-

nation. She wrote an article about the young Russian women she
met and lived amongst, who were for the most part students of
medicine and the social sciences.[468] This is accurate as many Russian women studied abroad at this time and concentrated on medicine, which was seen as the most useful way of contacting and
serving the Russian people.[469] To a certain extent, after this experience, Zabel Yesayian looked to Russian women as a model for
Armenian women. Yesayian admired the women's dedication to
their people and country, which harmonized with the current concept of service to Armenia and the Armenian people. The Russian women's way of achieving this, through education and service to the people, was similar to current Armenian theory and
practice.

In the story, Miss Zavatska suffers from a respiratory disease
and her years are said to be numbered, although Yesayian does
not understand why, in this case, she chose to spend her youth in
the poor student quarters of Paris, the two young women are
friendly.[470] One evening Zavatska entered Yesayian's room in a
frightened state and told her of a strange occurrence she had experienced for the past several nights. Each night as she prepared
to sleep she heard someone at her door. Initially, the man said
nothing, but after she called out, he began begging for money and
trying to enter her room. Frightened the girl asked the concierge
if someone had been in the building in the night. The concierge
merely laughed at her and told her it was her imagination.[471]
Yesayian offered to spend the night in Zavatska's room in order
to ascertain what or who was there. That evening the two girls
gathered in Zavatska's room, talking and drinking rum.[472] In the
night, while Zavatska slept, Yesayian thought she heard someone
at the door and was very frightened. The next morning she advised Zavatska not to stay in the house any longer. Very soon
after this, Zavatska, because of her worsening health, was taken
to hospital where she was described as subject to delusions.
Yesayian concludes the story by stating that she herself was never
sure if there was, in reality, a man at the door, or if, when she
heard someone at the door she had somehow entered into
Zavatska's melancholy state of mind.[473]

The style of *The Man* resembles the supernatural stories of Edgar Allen Poe, whose works Yesayian tells the reader at the beginning of the tale, she had been reading during this period.[474] The influence of Poe's supernatural and psychologically charged stories is found in the suggestion of a mysterious presence and the state of heightened mental awareness of the two girls. What is uniquely Yesayian's work, in this piece, is how she takes elements found in Poe and transfers them to depict the psychological state of two young foreign women living and studying in nineteenth-century Paris. Yesayian implies that the two girls entered into the same delusion because they share similar psychological feelings. That this story is about psychological states rather than socio-logical conditions is clear from Yesayian's treatment of the man at the door. The overwhelmingly implication in the story is that there is no one there, from the concierge's denial of the possibil-ity of anyone's entering the building at night, to Miss Zavatska's removal to the hospital where she suffers delusions soon after the incident occurs. Yet why does Yesayian imply that the man is not corporeal? The novels of the Norwegian author, Cora Sandel (1880–1974), who went to Paris in 1906, and wrote about a young woman's struggle to become an artist there, living in the same cheap hotels described by Yesayian, offer an illuminating com-parison. Sandel offers a very different portrait of the occurrence of the "man at the door." In Sandel's novel, *Alberta and Freedom* (1931), the action of which takes place in 1912, the young, for-eign women in Paris, who live in the attics of such buildings, must be careful to lock their doors and push out any male visitors who try to enter their rooms.[475] Yesayian and Sandel's characters occupy the same space in Paris. Sandel's protagonist, Alberta, lives in a working-class district, not far from Yesayian's Boule-vard Arago, which Sandel describes as grey and depressing, as does Yesayian.[476] Both women's protagonists walk in the Luxem-bourg Gardens because it provides inexpensive and pleasant sur-roundings for the poor. The similarities in location suggest that Yesayian and Sandel had occupied similar spaces in Paris. There-fore, Yesayian's decision, when writing the story, to make "the man at the door" a figment of imagination, rather than questioning if the "man at the door" is real, for example he could be a man from one of the other floors in the building, suggests that *The Man*, although it contains elements of realism, is about psychological states and anxiety around female identity. In Yesayian's story, the narrator and Miss Zavatska, are both lonely and feel vulnerable due to the condition of being foreign in an alien city but also based on their gender and their reason for being in Paris.

In an article on feminist thought in nineteenth-century England Mary Maynard noted that one of the main issues feminists discussed at this time was the threat which uncontrolled male sexuality, such as rape and sexual harassment, posed to women's safety.[477] In *The Man*, Yesayian confronts this reality in women's lives, through her depiction of women's vulnerability and fears about attack. For this reason, the voice heard outside the young woman's door, occurs at night when she is alone. This is why Zavatska can sleep the night Zabel stays with her, but is frightened when she is alone. The two young women's terror is a result of their feelings of vulnerability, regarding living alone in a foreign country, without any family. This sense of being entirely alone and helpless is demonstrated when Zavatska hears the voice for the first time:

> . . . around me everything was silent and it seemed to me that the city was empty. My heart was pounding so hard that for a minute I thought that its beats were the knocks [at the door] I had heard earlier.[478]

In addition to feeling alone and vulnerable in a foreign city this story hints at anxiety about women's entry into new roles in the public sphere. In part, *The Man* may be read as a story of women's advent into higher education and its impact on female identity. As has been discussed in chapter three, education for girls was a new experience and the majority did not go beyond primary school education at this time. That higher education abroad was an unfamiliar and isolating experience is highlighted in the story by Yesayian's description of the building where she lived. She says that workers and their families inhabited the first five floors while the sixth floor was divided into small rooms occupied by female foreign students. The young women are portrayed as separated from the inhabitants of the house by space, gender, occupation and social class. Isolated, Yesayian admired the manner in which the Russian girls bonded together and acted as family to each other far from their country.[479] She also admired their determination, but this is not unmixed. She describes the Russian students as:

> . . . sad, blonde girls, who with difficulty climbed the six flights of stairs. In their bloodless and depressed faces, however, their eyes shone calmly and unwavering with a vigorous and determined light.[480]

In the representation of sadness and determination, the author seems to be hinting at the psychological cost of the women's studies abroad. The frequent images of illness in this text accentuate this cost: there is the illness of Miss. Zavatska, the "bloodless" faces of the girls and the nauseating stench coming from the building and nearby factories. The emphasis on illness suggests anxiety around the roles and lifestyles of the women who live abroad alone and attend university.

The short story, *The Man*, added the new element of the experience of a single woman studying in a European university, to contemporary discussions of Armenian women's access to the public sphere. Nor was this an irrelevant topic, as the numbers of Armenian women going abroad appear to have been increasing in the early years of the twentieth century. Marie Beylerian mentions this phenomenon in *Artemis*, and several memoir sources mention some young Armenian women going to university or having been offered the opportunity to study abroad.[481] Interesting as this theme is, however, Yesayian only explored it in short pieces, instead she preferred to focus on empowering aspects of her life abroad, for although Yesayian felt anxiety about women's entry into the public sphere, she also characterized that period of her life as enjoyable and liberating.[482] *The Man* is about Yesayian's personal experience of exile, alienation and anxiety about entry in higher education.

## Motherhood and Migration: *In the Waiting Room*

Yesayian's first novel, *In the Waiting Room*, published in serial form in the journal *Tsaghik* in 1903, was Yesayian's earliest exploration of exile and alienation. To my knowledge this novel has never been reprinted in Armenian since it first appeared in the pages of *Tsaghik*.[483] This is a shame as the novel is an important part of Yesayian's oeuvre and deals with the theme of exile, a subject central to later Armenian literature. In addition, women's migration and exile is a vital historical and literary theme as the nineteenth and early twentieth centuries witnessed the beginning of the emigration of people of various nationalities to industrial Europe. Women's experience of migration to France is the theme of *In the Waiting Room*. As has been discussed throughout this volume, the value of motherhood was central to turn-of-the-century debates on Armenian women and society. Consequently, Zabel Yesayian's first novel examines exile from the perspective of a mother. The novel explores the economic conditions experienced by a foreign woman, her relations with the French, and the emotional and psychological affects of poverty and exile. She also investigated the areas in which French and foreign women's concerns and problems overlapped.

In the nineteenth century numerous novels written by Europeans appeared describing romance between Eastern women and Western men in "exotic" Eastern landscapes. One of the most famous and popular at the time of publication was a series of novels written by Pierre Loti (1850–1923). Loti's novels are characterized by a "formulaic" plot. Irene Szyliowicz argues that in each novel the European male hero visits a distant country and "fascinates, and in turn is enthralled by, an 'Oriental' woman."[484] In Loti's novels, not only is the landscape described as exotic, but so too are the women. The female characters in Loti's novels are all characterized by a "sameness," including lack of intelligence, submissive behaviour and great physical beauty.[485] In contrast to Loti's portrayal of the 'Orient,' a segment of the Armenian literary tradition was concerned with depicting Europe, which was represented as the locus of civilization, beauty and art. By 1900 visiting Paris or Rome was a literary pilgrimage for the Armenian intelligentsia.[486] The image of Europe in Armenian literature tended to be a romantic one in which the Armenian characters interact with wealthy, titled Europeans in Paris as in Dussap's novel *Mayta*, or talented, artistic Europeans in Rome as in *Siranush*. Yesayian's novel, while responding to these two different traditions, reflects a crucial deviation from these literary models, as her lovers leave the East for Paris and are confronted with the reality of life with little money in an industrial city. Her portrayal of the relationship between a Frenchman and an Algerian woman in the novel, *In the Waiting Room*, represents a departure from the contemporaneous literary models, European and Armenian, which Yesayian had read. The author rejected the misrepresentation of foreigners in both literary traditions, saying:

> What absurd ideas I've heard from foreigners about the French-woman. And likewise I've encountered Europeans, who have lived for years in the East, but understand Eastern people from the strange and wonderful stories written in travel books.[487]

*In the Waiting Room* is the story of a young Jewish woman from Algeria, Eva, who marries a French Catholic, André, and goes to Paris with him. In Paris, the couple lives with their baby daughter in poverty in the poor student district. Following the birth of her baby, Eva becomes ill with puerperal fever and cannot nurse the child. Therefore, each day she must go to a hospital for the poor to receive a ration of milk. Eva's husband is ill and unemployed; consequently, he and Eva have little money and food. The plot of the novel revolves around Eva's attempts to secure milk each day for her daughter from a hostile hospital administration. The story confronts women's powerlessness and vulnerability caused by factors such as the dehumanizing ways in which women give birth in the hospital, poverty, and the inability to express experience because of limitations in language.

The author describes the beginning of the relationship between Eva and André in terms similar to Loti's exotic novels. In Algeria, André met Eva through her brother and is said to have been drawn to "the sweet, young Eastern girl" who attracted his "European and artistic enthusiasm."[488] This image of the Eastern woman stimulating European male desire is a common representation, as Joanna De Groot has noted, in nineteenth-century art and literature women are "presented as the means for imagining or finding out about the Orient."[489] Yesayian's André is not portrayed as the all-powerful Frenchman of Loti's novels; instead his is a weak personality. The author informs the reader that André was sent to Paris by his family to study law, where he discovered that he did not have the "authoritative presence" required for the subject. He quit law school and joined a theatre group heading for Algeria. Loti's heroes use local women for sex and entry into the other culture and then invariably leave them at the end of his trip, in contrast, André is depicted as more honourable because he does not abandon Eva.[490] When he and Eva fall in love, they flee to Paris together and marry despite her family's objections.[491] Yesayian's removal of the pair from Algeria to Paris, and her depiction of their life there, enables the author to explore the reality of immigrant life stripped of the exoticism of Loti's novels and the upper-class milieu of Dussap's.

Yesayian's Paris of *In the Waiting Room* is not the city of freedom and enlightenment of other Armenian novels or even the city of wealthy characters like the Russian-born Mrs. Zanski who is a Parisian salon hostess briefly mentioned in *In the Waiting Room*. Rather Paris is the city in which Eva walks in rain and grey fog with a hungry baby. It is a grey, industrial city contrasted in the text with Eva's "sunny and beloved country."[492] Eva is represented by the author as unable to survive in the harsh city she encounters. She is described as a "delicate plant" which cannot blossom in the foggy city due to lack of sun.[493] This image of Paris as a place where the sun does not shine is found in several of Yesayian's texts and signifies yearning for the homeland, which is always portrayed as sunny and warm.[494] Paris is represented, in the text, as a place where foreigners are unwelcome, as the tirade of a woman who lives in Eva's building demonstrates:

> These penniless foreigners think we have to be their servants for the sake of their pretty eyes. Oh no, let them go to their own countries if they aren't satisfied among us. Isn't it strange that these indigent people come to Paris to die?[495]

At the end of the novel Eva tells her friend, Sadarof, that her life is spent in the waiting rooms of hospitals.[496] This final reference to the waiting room at the end of the story, alluding to the title of the novel, is part of the author's portrayal of Paris as a place where Eva merely waits, but does not in fact live. Yesayian showed that what made Eva vulnerable to this reality of Paris is her poverty. By placing her characters in an environment of poverty, Yesayian was able to explore the connections between poverty, social class, nationality and gender. The place where these categories meet in the novel is the charity hospital.

The hospital, described in the novel *In the Waiting Room*, is a maternity hospital for the poor and its patients are made up of French and foreign women.[497] In her essay, *How I Write or How I Would Like to Write* (1934), Yesayian stated that while in Paris she worked in a hospital to study first hand its inner workings in order to write about it.[498] *In the Waiting Room* is the result of that work and was published after a seven-year silence, during which Yesayian underwent a self-imposed apprenticeship of her craft.[499] Yesayian portrays the women who visit the hospital as made vulnerable by their reproductive function in a society, which does not value them or their children, as demonstrated by the hospital staff's indifference. Yesayian depicts all the women who enter the hospital to be vulnerable; in the novel working-class French women and foreign women share many of the same problems based on the social construction of gender and motherhood. Where Yesayian makes a distinction between the experiences of working-class French women and foreign women will be treated subsequently in the chapter. The helplessness of the women at the hospital is demonstrated by a scene Eva witnesses of a heavily pregnant woman who enters the hospital about to give birth and who is harassed by a nurse, who asks her a variety of questions, such as what her parents' names are, and demands to see her marriage certificate. The interrogation ends when the woman collapses on the floor and begins to give birth.[500] Eva watches as the doctors strip off the woman's clothes while she is unconscious. The scene fills her with disgust and shame.[501] The sense of disgust and shame that Eva experiences is indicative of her own feelings of helplessness. Like the unknown woman, she too is subject to humiliation when she attempts to secure milk for her child. Motherhood is represented, in this text, as making women subject to humiliation as victims of their bodies' reproductive capacity, and this is represented not as feminine weakness, nor an inevitable feature of childbirth, but rather the result of the administration's attitude and treatment of the women.

In Europe, the practice of giving birth in a hospital attended by male doctors was relatively recent in the nineteenth century while in the Ottoman Empire, childbirth was commonly assisted by midwives. In her autobiography Yesayian mentions that she was delivered at home by a midwife.[502] By the early twentieth century, some wealthy families had Western trained doctors at births with midwives in attendance as demonstrated by Alice Muggerditchian Shipley's story of her birth in early twentieth-century Diyarbekir.[503] Giving birth at home, however, was still standard. In pre-industrial Europe midwifery was practiced exclusively by women. In the eighteenth century male doctors attempted to enter the field of childbirth, but were hindered because the male doctor was denied access to the female patient's body on the basis of propriety.[504] The charity hospital facilitated male doctors' entry into obstetrics as it enabled them access to women's bodies because the conditions set in receiving charity, ensured patient compliance. Charity patients were required to obey the doctors and nurses and to follow rules regarding personal conduct or they would not be admitted to the hospital.[505] In the scene when Eva witnesses a pregnant woman being stripped of her clothing by a male doctor, in a large room with many people watching, Yesayian reveals how she viewed women's position in the relatively recent conception of childbirth as a medical, rather than a familial, concern. In the story the pregnant woman is depicted alone, passive and subject to male control over her body.

The subordinate status of the female patients at the charity hospital is established by Yesayian through the behaviour of the nurses who work there. The women who go to the hospital in order to receive milk for their babies are subject to the tyranny of the woman, Leontine, in charge of milk distribution. Yesayian portrays the character of Leontine as a cruel, vindictive woman who enjoys upsetting the poor women who must come to the hospital to receive free milk. She is deliberately late in entering the hall, she shouts at the women and calls them crude names.[506] The women do not dare protest, however, because they fear that if they do, they will not be allowed to receive milk for their babies, as eventually happens to Eva when she confronts Leontine about her rude behaviour.[507] The neglect and abuse by the nurses of the patients, in the novel, cause the women or the babies to become ill and even to die. During a visit to the hospital, Eva witnesses a scene in which a woman, who has given birth a few days earlier, finds that her child has died due to the nurses' neglect. The mother requested the nurses to summon a doctor because she thought the child was unwell, but the nurses ignored her and the child died. The episode ends with the doctor's anger and the nurse in charge being fired. The other nurses, however, do not think that the woman did anything wrong and are confident that she will find a job at another hospital with ease.[508]

The action of this novel occurs at a time when nursing in France was changing. The nurses depicted by Yesayian are untrained laywomen, who were replacing Roman Catholic nuns, as nurses. In a discussion in the text of the merits or lack thereof of lay nor religious nurses, Yesayian has the patrons and doctors state that both lay and religious nurses are detrimental to health care since neither lay or religious women are properly trained.[509] In part, *In the Waiting Room* can be read as the author's criticism of the structure of the contemporary medical profession, particularly in its administration of charity, which is bureaucratic, impersonal and indifferent to the women who are obliged to utilize its services, as demonstrated by the lack of quality nursing they receive while at the hospital.

The problems of humiliation and neglect, which Yesayian identified as being common to all women who enter the hospital, are compounded when the women are foreign. Yesayian states that when Eva gives birth to her daughter, she feels not only physical, but mental discomfort because she is foreign.[510] Eva is fortunate because she has a doctor who treats her well. The story of an unnamed Russian woman in the novel, *In the Waiting Room*, serves to illustrate the particular vulnerability that women experienced when they did not have familial support and were not conversant in French. The Russian woman enters the hospital in a weak state and recounts her story to a Russian man who translates her words into French for a doctor at the hospital. The story the woman tells is one of extreme abuse. She says that after giving birth to her child, in a private nursing home, the baby was taken away from her; consequently, she does not even know if the baby is female or male. She was left, unattended, in wet and dirty sheets. The nurses ignored her but kept her a virtual prisoner in the house because they received money for having patients. The woman finally escaped and went to the hospital to beg them to find her baby and return it to her. There is a strong implication in the story, which the listeners suspect, but not the mother does not, that the baby has already died.[511] The woman's powerlessness is highlighted, in the text, by her inability to convey her tale of suffering and loss to the doctor herself, because she cannot speak French, and instead she must wait until a translator can be found to explain her medical condition and inquire after her baby. The relationship between language, gender and power in this passage is illuminating when considered from the perspective of current feminist discussions in France about language. In a discussion of women's use of language, which is understood to have been created by and for male experience, Marie Cardinal, as Luce Irigaray and Hélène Cixous have done, questioned how women can convey female experience in masculine language:

> How can we say our sex, the experience of pregnancy, time,
> women's endurance? We must invent. Language will femi-
> nize itself, will open itself, will embellish itself, and will grow
> rich.[512]

Cardinal's identification of pregnancy as an experience not adequately represented in 'masculine' language highlights the problem experienced by the Russian woman in Yesayian's *In The Waiting Room*. In this text the Russian woman's giving birth and her experience of abuse, a consequence in part of her inability to speak French, must be filtered through a male translator to a male doctor, in a foreign language, which contributes to the woman's silence in the text and in the society. The translator and the doctor tend to her immediate, physical needs, but ignore the more pertinent issue to the mother: that of the fate of her baby. This woman does not have the chance to articulate her experience directly and therefore cannot begin to "feminize" language as Cardinal states must be done. As a consequence, her story disappears unresolved from the narrative and the reader is never informed what becomes of the woman or the fate of her baby. Eva's experience of the hospital is more positive than the Russian woman's because she speaks French and has access to the world of the hospital's benefactors who intercede on her behalf after her milk card has been taken away from her by Leontine. The image of the hospital system itself, however, emphasizes the helplessness of the women and their dependency on the institution and the people who run it.

It is clearly demonstrated, in the text, that the underlying cause of the women's horrible encounters in the hospital is their position in the hierarchy of French society. At the maternity hospital the women are made victims of their reproductive role. The French legal code, the Civil Code or Napoleonic Code of 1804, did not recognize women as citizens, gave a woman little power in marriage and almost no rights vis-à-vis her children. A married woman was not allowed to dispose of her own property without her husband's permission, a wife had to take on her husband's nationality, losing her own, and she was not permitted to live separately from him; if she left the home the husband could cut off support and the wife could legally be required to pay her husband an indemnity.[513] Fathers had great authority over their children and had the sole right to administer to the financial affairs of minor children. The father could forbid his child's marriage and even had the right to imprison his children for disobedience, called the "right to correction" in French law. The father retained this power even if he no longer lived with his family.[514] In the case of the death of the father, a French mother had rights to the guardianship of her children, but this was not unrestricted as paternal guardianship.[515]

Women's social and legal subordination in France is reflected in Yesayian's portrayal of their powerlessness in the hospital, which is a microcosm of the society, where male doctors and the upper classes govern and finance charity hospitals. The charity component meant that the women patients were drawn from the poor and were easily controlled. Yesayian's linking of poor Frenchwomen (and it is clearly indicated in the story that the Frenchwomen Eva encounters are unmarried, or very poor, or even prostitutes) with foreign women illustrates how the author understood the status of immigrant women in French society as relegated to the bottom of the social hierarchy. Her portrayal of camaraderie between the French and foreign women at the hospital, unlike the hostility which Eva sometimes experiences outside of the hospital, demonstrates Yesayian's sense that in the confines of the maternity hospital, differences between women are diminished by their subordinate, dependent status. Differences between the women at the hospital are reduced in the story because they are poor and vulnerable mothers who must care for babies in the absence of fathers. The care of children is portrayed as the women's responsibility despite the legal authority of fathers.[516] In this novel, Yesayian's portrait of motherhood is stripped of the romanticism of other novelistic portrayals. In this novel and her later novel, *Shirt of Flame* (1934), Yesayian portrays mothers as struggling to survive while caring for children, rather like many of the mothers in Shushanik Kurghinian's poetry, in contrast to the empowered and national image of motherhood in Dussap's, Sibyl's and Khatisian's works.

It is not accidental that Yesayian chose to portray in the novel, *In the Waiting Room*, the experience of migration and exile to Paris through the experience of a young Jewish woman, a member of a large community, historically dispersed from its homeland, and a community with which the Armenians shared several common features. She demonstrated in the two texts, *In the Waiting Room* and *The Man*, the combined effects of poverty, ethnicity and migration on women. But she was also careful to demonstrate how women, as a group, despite national divisions, experienced many of the same problems in society because of gender and because of motherhood, categories that were determined by the conceptualization of gender and the value placed upon women in the host society. Because Yesayian understood that these categories affected many women, not simply Armenian women in Paris, her texts describe Jewish, Russian, Armenian and French women, a feature not found in her other writings, which exclusively focus on Armenian society. She was particularly concerned to portray the problems of learning and speaking a foreign language and the sense of diminished power it bred in women who were not conversant in the host society's language. As a writer, she was also concerned with the psychological sense of loss of identity not speaking one's own tongue caused in women living abroad. Yesayian's *In the Waiting Room* (1903) and *The Man* (1905) represent the disintegration of identity, including loss of language, and status, as mothers, which occurred due to exile and emigration. These texts are forerunners of the literature of Diaspora that became prevalent following 1915.

## The Armenian Genocide in Zabel Yesayian's Writings

Marie Beylerian's foreshadowing of the problem of women and exile, in the pages of *Artemis* in 1902–1903, came to pass after the Cilician Massacres in 1909 and the Armenian Genocide in 1915. The deportations of the Armenians from their homes in the towns and villages of Western Armenia resulted in the death of over a million Armenians and forced the surviving population into exile in the Russian Empire, Iran, Syria, Europe and North America. Among the many consequences and affects of these events was the demise of Constantinople, as the centre of Armenian intellectual life, and with it the debates on modernity and society that had so occupied intellectuals in that city throughout the nineteenth century. As this book has focused on women's writing, especially the debates surrounding women's roles, this final chapter will examine the effects of the Armenian Genocide on the figure of the modern Armenian woman, through a reading of a selection of Zabel Yesayian's non-fiction articles and novels.

Yesayian's work portraying the Cilicia massacres in 1909, *Among the Ruins*, is one of the greatest works in Armenian literature. The excellence of *Among the Ruins* has led many to speculate on why Yesayian did not write a comparable text following 1915.[517] Although Yesayian did not write directly about the Armenian Genocide, in the same manner as she had written about the Cilician Massacre, her post-1915 writing is irrevocably altered by this event and nowhere is this more obvious than her treatment of the figure of the modern Armenian woman. As has been argued throughout this volume, women's writing of the nineteenth century had linked the modern Armenian nation's fate to that of the Armenian woman's development. The Genocide altered both how women and national development were perceived. In the remainder of this chapter, I will discuss two types of texts written by Zabel Yesayian after 1915; the first set of texts are the testimonials of the Armenian Genocide: *The Agony of A People* (1917) and *Le rôle de la femme arménienne pendant la guerre* (1922) and the second set of texts consists of Zabel Yesayian's *My Soul in Exile* (1922) and her autobiography, *Gardens of Silihtar* (1935).

### Agony of A People and The Role of Armenian Women during the War

The two texts, *The Agony of A People* (1917) and *Le rôle de la femme arménienne pendant la guerre* (1922), are non-fiction accounts of the deportations of the Armenians in 1915. *The Agony of A People* (1917) was published in the Baku-based journal *Gorts*

[Labour] and is the eyewitness account of the deportations and camps of Armenians along the Euphrates by one Haig Toroyan, but recorded and introduced by Zabel Yesayian. *The Role of Armenian Women during the War* (1922) was based on a speech given by Zabel Yesayian in 1920 and published in French in the *Revue des Études Arémeniennes* in 1922. What is immediately striking upon reading these two texts is Yesayian's sense of loss of legitimacy as a writer. Prior to 1915, Yesayian had been an authoritative author who wrote confidently on literature, education, women, and politics. In 1922, Yesayian displayed none of her former confidence in her right to write of the Armenian Genocide. In *Le rôle de la femme arménienne pendant la guerre*, Yesayian was careful to explain that she was able to write the article because she had witnessed the appalling conditions of the Armenian deportees:

> If I dare to speak of such a complex subject, it is not because I believe that I can adequately present the totality of the superhuman effort, the great tragedy, the sacrifice and faith that Armenians have shown and which surely deserve the passionate attention of all historians, beyond all political and moral considerations. Rather I affirm my right to speak on the sole basis of the fact that during this war I lived in Turkey, Russia and Iran and crossed into Iraq."[518]

In the above quoted passage, Yesayian hints at the other issue which hindered her ability to write, the feeling that the Genocide was simply too enormous to be adequately represented and could not be contained by language. In *Gender and Destiny: Women Writers and the Holocaust*, author Marlene Heinemann, notes that: "Survivors sometimes describe the death camps as beyond language."[519] In 1922, Yesayian expressed a similar sentiment:

> It would be possible to tell of some episodes in this great martyrology, but no human language could ever translate, in its entirety, this horrible thing: the attempt of extermination of a whole race.[520]

To overcome the problems of authority and the limitation of language, Yesayian's accounts of the Genocide rely on the use of other published narratives, a technique she did not employ in any other context.  In *The Agony of A People*, more than half the article is the testimony of a Mr. Haig Toroyan and is expressed in his voice. Although it was Yesayian who prepared the text for publication, she inserts no authorial voice, unlike in *Among the Ruins*, she never uses the first person narrative to refer to herself.[521] In *Le rôle de la femme arménienne pendant la guerre*, Yesayian employs the same technique by quoting from Haig Toroyan's testimony and from a published account by a Mrs. Captanian, whose narrative of her deportation, had already been published as *Memoires d'une Déportée arménienne* (1919).

Yesayian's use of published texts by different authors appears to have had two advantages to her, as eyewitness accounts, they enabled her to write in an authoritative voice of the fate of the Armenian people in 1915, and by using various texts, as well as her own observations, she was able to more fully represent a multitude of experiences of the Genocide. In 1922, she wrote:

> It is difficult to give names because the list would be so very long and I would be afraid of being unjust by omitting those who through oblivion or ignorance I would forget.[522]

The use of various accounts and testimonies appears to have assisted the act of remembering and not "omitting" anyone, a goal performed in order to counteract the dehumanizing effects of genocide.

Zabel Yesayian's writing career had begun through journal writing. She was a regular contributor to the women's pages in *Tsaghik* and *Arakatz* and, therefore, had an established practice of writing about Armenian women in the women's pages of major journals. In these articles, Yesayian had discussed modernity, the future of the Armenian woman and the nation. She had advocated Armenian women's participation in social and charitable work in order to improve the conditions of the Armenian people.[523] And she had stated outright that the declaration of the Ottoman Constitution in

1908, had not treated any of the problems facing the Armenian community, but that women had gallantly made efforts to provide charitable assistance to the needy in the Armenian provinces.[524] In the two articles, *Agony of a People* and *Le rôle de la femme arménienne pendant la guerre*, Yesayian emphasizes the fate of national development and the figure of the modern Armenian woman. In *The Role of Armenian Women during the War*, Yesayian composed a brief history of the establishment of female education by the Armenian women's associations of Constantinople and then abruptly contrasts this laudatory effort with the fate of the teachers and pupils of these schools:

> Two important ladies association, founded in Constantinople thirty years ago, provided for the instruction of young Armenian girls in the most distant provinces. Everywhere, in the most obscure villages, where Armenians, as a result of their small numbers could not provide for the expense of the schools, one of these associations organized the budget or procured money for the expense of the installation and the maintenance of schools, while the other associations trained, in its normal schools, teachers for the provinces. One could count the numbers of their pupils by the tens of thousands. At this moment, the pupils, as well as the teachers, and several members of these associations are dispersed, or were exterminated on the road of exile, dead of hunger and thirst, or were massacred, or imprisoned in Turkish harems.[525]

In *The Agony of A People* and *Le rôle de la femme arménienne pendant la guerre*, Yesayian gave a detailed description of one of these educated young women during deportation. The account is based on Haig Toroyan's testimony. Toroyan, who was working for a German officer as a translator, travelled along the Euphrates into Iraq in 1915, with the German officer's entourage, which included Turkish gendarmes. In this capacity, Toroyan witnessed the caravans of deported Armenians along the Euphrates. Although the German officer knew Toroyan was an Armenian, Toroyan and the officer claimed he was an Arab Christian. When the boats stopped for provisions, Toroyan often spoke with the deported Armenians, and where possible learned of their circumstances and sufferings and also made inquires about his aunt's family. On one such stop, he noticed a woman of about twenty-five years, who was pretty and wore fairly clean clothes, he noticed her moving about the groups of deported Armenians, talking, comforting, and being treated with respect by the deportees. Toroyan spoke with the young woman and learned that she was from Izmit and was a teacher. He asked her why she was walking through the crowds and she answered: "I have found my comfort in supporting and comforting the people."[526] They spoke Turkish to each other, but when Toroyan ascertained that she spoke French, they began to speak in that language. Toroyan remarked that the teacher did not complain about anything or speak against the government, instead she merely asked if it were possible for him to provide people with bread and medicine. During their conversation, the teacher fainted. People around them said she had fainted from hunger. Toroyan did procure some bread and medicine and when he returned, he discovered the teacher roused from her faint, but weak and ill. Toroyan distributed the bread and medicine and then returned to the German officer's boat.

That evening, the gendarmes, approached Toroyan, and invited him to come and have some "amusement with the Armenian women," saying, "God created them for us, so that we could find them here." The German officer ordered them not to leave the boats, but they did so in the middle of the night. When the boats left the next morning, Toroyan noticed a body in the water, and by distinguishing the clothes and face, recognized the teacher from Izmit. The gendarmes told him he was stupid to not have joined with them the night before. They had taken the teacher and raped her. She had argued with them, "like a lawyer," the gendarme said. After they had tortured her, she had run away and drowned herself in the river.[527]

In *The Agony of a People* there are many tragic accounts of deportation, degradation and death, yet it was the account of the schoolteacher from Izmit that Yesayian was compelled to retell in 1922 in *The Role of Armenian Women during the War*. This young woman appears to have embodied the ideal, modern Armenian woman discussed since the middle of the nineteenth century. She was educated, and at the same time devoted to her people, this is demonstrated not only by the fact that she had been a teacher but also by her behaviour during deportation, although starving, she tried to offer assistance to her fellow sufferers. As has been discussed the modern, Armenian woman was expected to use her education for the benefit of her people, as this young woman clearly tried to do. Her fate, however, deportation, rape and death, signals the end of this ideal role for women in Armenian women's writing.

After 1915, in place of the nineteenth-century, national female image, Yesayian looks farther back into history to provide models for contemporary women. As has been stated in chapter two, Armenian women writers of this period drew upon a genealogy of literary and activist foremothers in Armenian history to provide models of activism. The most compelling of such figures were the women of Vardan Mamikonian and his allies' families. In Zabel Yesayian's *The Role of Armenian Women during the War*, the author alludes to the women of that period, and as models of resistance, they become the model to represent contemporary Armenian women's resistance. Yesayian wrote:

> In everyday life, kept at home, the Armenian woman had not had the opportunity to brilliantly show her abilities and these qualities were ignored. But when the days of adversity arrived, despite the most difficult conditions, they showed themselves to be the true sisters of the Armenian ladies of the fifth century, whose admirable behaviour in the days of St. Vardan has been transmitted to us by the historian Élisée [Eghishe].[528]

Yesayian portrays two models of women's activism in 1915 and throughout the war period. There are those who engaged in non-combatant methods of resistance, such as supporting and assisting armed resistance, and those who took up arms to oppose deportation. In *The Agony of A People* and *Le rôle de la femme arménienne pendant la guerre* women generally act as supporters of armed resistance, although there are exceptions in which women act as fighters. For example, Yesayian depicted women who acted as actual combatants, stating that when the Turkish soldiers captured Edessa they discovered the corpses of Armenian girls who had been killed in battle, and whose chests "were adorned with rows of cartridges."[529] In general, however, Yesayian portrays women's traditional roles as care givers and nurturers as acts of resistance, similar to the women of Vardan Mamikonian's time. In Edessa and Shabine Karahisar, she says, women encouraged men in not complying with deportation orders and assisting in the building of defences.[530] During the resistance in Van, Yesayian writes of the women's activities in supplying food and medical care for male fighters:

> During the admirable defence of the city of Van, women and young
> girls contributed their invaluable cooperation. It was they who
> prepared and distributed food to the fighting combatants despite
> the uninterrupted fire of the enemy. They worked in the work-
> shops improvised to prepare ammunitions, they established a com-
> munication service, they nursed the invalids and the wounded and
> when the buildings, which sheltered the wounded, were shaken
> by the cannonade, they transported the wounded who were in their
> care through the streets or through tunnels.[531]

In Yesayian's writing, women's traditional roles, such as providers of food and nurses to the ill, are celebrated and become in the context of the Armenian Genocide, heroic acts of resistance, without which armed resistance could not be sustained. Yesayian's description of the privations the Armenian women, who worked with the refugees, experienced resembles Eghishe's account of the work of the Vardan Mamikonian women. The following passage by Eghishe, translated by Robert Thomson, is as follows:

> The delicate women of Armenia, who had been cosseted and pam-
> pered in their litters and sedan chairs, regularly attended the houses
> of prayer without shoes and on foot, begging with tireless entreat-
> ies that they might be able to endure their great tribulation. Those
> who from their childhood had been raised on the marrow of steers
> and the dainty parts of game, most joyfully ate grass, living like
> wild animals and not at all mindful of their accustomed luxury.

The skin of their bodies turned black in colour, for by day they were burned by the sun, and the whole night they lay on the ground.[532]

In *Le rôle de la femme arménienne pendant la guerre*, Yesayian portrayed Western and Eastern Armenian women's care for the wounded, and selfless dedication to the orphans, as follows:

One must recognize the simple dedication of educated women, most of whom abandoned a life of well-being and pleasure, and who did not hesitate to stay months and years in forsaken corners of the world, deprived of everything, sharing the misery of their charges and doing all of this with patience and cheerful simplicity. During these events of a very serious nature, Armenians, of all social classes, displayed unceasing dedication. Ladies Associations organized orphanages in Tiflis, Baku, Alexandropol and Yerevan and other locations and nursed and cared for tens of thousands of orphans. The community of Moscow, rich and influential, rendered great services by providing money, doctors and voluntary nurses. Many women doctors gave all their time and knowledge to care for the refugees and voluntary soldiers.[533]

The connecting of the Vardan Mamikonian women with contemporary Armenian women is a means of refashioning the present circumstances. By alluding to the Vardan Mamikonian women and fifth century Armenian history, Yesayian formed a model of survival. As the Armenians of the fifth century survived that early attempt at assimilation, her message is that so too will present day Armenians. In this context, the Vardan Mamikonian women provide a model of courage and hope. Yesayian's vision of the Vardan Mamikonian women differs from Sibyl's earlier speech and usage of the image of these fifth century women, in that Yesayian's portrait emphasizes women's resistance to the enemy rather than simply education and charitable work. It was through the care of orphans, the ill, and intercommunity cooperation, (and Yesayian lauds the activities of women and men, urban dwellers and peasants, Eastern and Western Armenians) that she saw the success of the continuation of the Armenian people. In fact,

Yesayian was committed to the rebuilding of Armenian society following the Armenian Genocide. For this reason, in the 1930s when she lived in Yerevan and was asked how she could stand the inconveniences there after living in Paris, she replied: "These inconveniences are meaningless in my eyes, because I take an active part in building the future of our country."[534]

### *My Soul in Exile* and *The Gardens of Silihtar*

The literary critic, Hagop Oshagan, called Yesayian a master of the psychological novel, the majority of which appeared after 1915. Critics, who have read Yesayian's post 1915 novels, have read them looking for a portrayal of the Armenian Genocide, a second *Among the Ruins*, and have been disappointed by what is seen as Yesayian's wilful lapse into the realm of women's psychology. Here I intend to discuss *My Soul in Exile*, from the perspective of Yesayian's continuum of women's writing, her pre-existing interest in the psychology of women and the figure of the modern Armenian woman. It is through comparison of Yesayian's pre-1915 and post-1915 writings that we can comprehend how the Armenian Genocide altered Yesayian's writing.

*My Soul in Exile* is not ostensibly "about" the Armenian Genocide, in that it does not describe massacre and deportation, but it bears the stamp of the Genocide in the author's treatment of the themes so central to previous women's writing, including love and motherhood, as well as adding into the Armenian women's tradition, the notion of homeland and exile, in a manner that exceeds Marie Beylerian's suggestions in 1902–1903, and even Yesayian's pre-1915 representations of emigration. Yesayian's post-1915 treatment of themes central to earlier women's writings (as well as her own early writing) suggests how discussions of women altered after 1915. As I have argued throughout this book, the literary focus on women's roles at the turn-of-the-century was closely connected to the creation of a modern, national identity, and changes in this construction and the figure of the Armenian woman, tell us something about the changes in conceptualizing the Armenian nation. The issues of power, love and motherhood, homeland and exile in this novel by Yesayian reveal the author's despair, and perhaps her belief that the nineteenth-century vision of national identity had failed the Armenians.

The novel, *My Soul in Exile*, published in 1922, continues Yesayian's exploration of alienation. In its subject matter it is unique among Yesayian's works, after the publication of this novel, her novels shifted focus to the Caucasus and when Yesayian did return to Constantinople, it would be to the past, the world of her childhood in her autobiography, *The Gardens of Silihtar* (1935), or the unfinished and posthumously published *Barba Khach'ik* (1966), which is a fictionalized account of her uncle's life.

*My Soul in Exile* portrays the post-1915 world of Constantinople (destined to be renamed Istanbul soon after the novel's publication), particularly the remaining artistic and intellectual community. At the opening of the novel, the principal character, Emma, has returned from Europe to her father's house in Constantinople. The opening paragraphs of the novel portray a world in which the past is more distinct than the present. In this world linear time does not exist because the reality of the present (which the reader learns at the end of the novel is actually a memory) is not in accord with the narrator's desire. She has come home to her paternal house in Constantinople, longing for her native city, but the present is devoid of life, as evinced by the opening lines of the novel:

> I returned to Constantinople today. It is Spring and the April evening, with its feverish and fragrant atmosphere, has agitated me with sweet turmoil. At my father's nearly empty house in Baghlar Bashi, I stood before an open window, looking out and thinking, for a long time.[535]

Emma's severe displacement in Constantinople is shown by the fluidity of time. Standing at the window, Emma hears the sounds of frogs croaking and it reminds her of other Springs and her longing for her homeland increases, so that she feels "as if I

was still far from Bolis and Scutari and from my father's house."[536]
The fluidity of time here is because the present has ceased to
exist and Emma is longing for the past as much as for her homeland.

Emma is a painter and through her relationship to her art and
loss of homeland, Yesayian explores how exile affected artistic
endeavour and identity. Emma has returned to Constantinople
where she will present her paintings. The majority of these paintings have been painted in Europe, away from Constantinople,
Emma's beloved, but "feverish" city. To Emma's eyes, the painting portray her alienation and homesickness when she was in
Europe:

> I stayed indoors the entire day and looked at my work, some-
> times with a critical eye, sometimes with a despairing eye and
> sometimes with wonder. I wanted to do something different and
> of course there was something else in my soul. In me there was
> light, joy and life, however, all my paintings are covered in fog.
> My homeland's brilliant sun doesn't appear in these paintings on
> display, but I feel that in my future works that fog will disappear
> and my sun will rise.
>
> It is difficult to explain those thoughts and how I came to such
> a conclusion. It's as if my desire and my yearning for my home-
> land had stamped that fog and sadness upon my paintings. I con-
> tinue to search for myself and I suffer through searching and my
> psychological twisting and turnings are visible in the lines of my
> paintings.[537]

Later Emma realizes that the fog that covers her paintings is
the result of her "sadness, desire and homesickness," and that it
has prevented her from knowing herself.[538] Because the fog, which
is exile and sadness, has obscured her work, Emma has been unable
to discover her identity. As already stated, loss of language in *The
Man* (1905) caused identity fragmentation. In *My Soul in Exile* it
is not language, but loss of homeland, which obscures identity. In
order to recover herself, Emma searches for her identity through
art. She states:

I still cannot successfully express and fix upon my soul's music, my inner storms and inner peace. Will I ever succeed in removing the mysterious veil to one corner? Will I ever succeed in sinking to the bottom and coming out self-aware, radiant and victorious?

I am interested in myself. I can say, with certainty, that what people see in my work is that veil and not what lies behind it. That fog prevented me from knowing myself and that fog is the sadness, which first came from my yearning, homesickness and incompetence.[539]

Emma believes that by returning to Constantinople her work will lose its fogginess and she will reconnect to her homeland. The description of Emma's self-portrait, however, foreshadows that reconnection will be impossible. The reader sees the painting through Emma's eyes:

The greenish blue folds of my clothes, whose colour shades repeat on the eyes, gives my paintings the appearance of a Byzantine princess, especially as she was painted after an illness and that emaciated face, wide pupils, high, thin, arched eyebrows emphasized that impression. But the lips don't have the weak expression seen in the older paintings and on them lingers yearning and a sort of desire, the desirable and surprised face of a woman at the start of a hectic day.[540]

The description of this face as emaciated and ill hints at the blight affecting the Armenian community, and one wonders if it does not hint at the emaciated and starved faces of the deported Armenians, a reality Yesayian had seen and was well aware of, when this novel was written. The reference to a Byzantine princess is also suggestive, when contemplating the fact that the Byzantines lost Constantinople to the Turks. The portrait evokes the devastated state of the Armenians and highlights the demise of Constantinople as the centre of Western Armenian intellectual and artistic life.

The sense of loss of homeland and people is heightened by Emma's interaction with the remnants of the Constantinople Armenian intellectual and artistic community. Emma is welcomed back to the Armenian community, but that community is an altered one. The artistic and intellectual community in *My Soul in Exile* is cut off from the Armenian people and sunk into despair. When Emma is introduced into the Armenian artistic and intellectual community, she encounters Siranush Tanielian, a well-known poet, who is described as keeping her best poems, unrevealed, within her.[541] The name of this character is suggestive as it appears to be a mix of the title of Dussap's novel, *Siranush*, and the last name resembles Sibyl's first married name "Tonelian." The silencing of this poet, in the novel, seems to imply the silencing of the past and the intellectual debates that went along with it. This image of the silenced poet is an indicator of what is going to happen to Emma upon returning to Constantinople. For Emma, Constantinople is her birthplace and home, but as the character Siranush Tanielian tells her, it is now possible to be in exile in one's birthplace:

> "It's as if we are exiles in a foreign and distant land. We are exiles in our birthplace, because we are deprived of that atmosphere which our people with their communal life, should create around us . . . only with fragile and tenuous ties are we connected to our native land . . . " After a pause she continues, "But at least we artists can become friends in exile."[542]

Emma, newly returned from Europe, and full of happiness at her return, wants to reject Tanielian's words. Following this speech, she thinks, "I will pursue my dreams along every path and my soul must get its freedom. I want to spread it everywhere. I want to say not that we are friends in exile but friends in the struggle." But at the same time as she thinks this, Emma begins to comprehend Tanielian's predicament and feels empathy for her: "Suddenly, I felt that not only was I like her, but that I was the same, that we were two sister souls, friends in exile."[543]

In this novel, exile, and specifically being cut off from the Armenian people, is the death of art. After a good reception of her work, Emma becomes increasingly paralysed and by the last page of the novel, Emma experiences difficulty when painting:

But today I again hesitate over my brush . . . I feel that I am returning to my inner prison, which is only adorned anymore with memories and desires.

It would be better to leave everything and go to Mme. Tanielian's house where I can meet Hrant Cherkezian . . . Perhaps his severe and accusing glance will soften when in my eyes he sees yearning for new Springs, yearning for life, in which light and grief raise in confused waves around me . . . Maybe he will feel that despite my presumptuous separateness, and despite that faith with which I take my flight of freedom and takes me away from them, we are always friends in exile, we are prisoners in our man-made inner prisons and strict jailers of each other.[544]

Emma is reduced to living only through memories, in fact the story is recounted as her remembering her return to Constantinople, her hopes and desires at that time, her brief abortive love for an Armenian man, Diran Bey, who is one of the few that understands her paintings. As stated in chapter two, at the turn-of-the-century, marriage based on romantic love was connected to a political perspective, which advocated "modern" social practices and democratic and patriotic political forms in contrast to the older system of arranged marriage and the amira and other elite governance of the Armenian millet. Implicit in Armenian modernist novels is the construction of romantic love as potentially able to break down, social, if not political, authority. Romantic love is therefore a transformative force in modern Armenian novels. This is true of Srpuhi Dussap's novels in particular, and Zabel Yesayian concurred to a certain extent to this vision in some novels, particularly, as we have seen in chapter three, in *The Last Cup* (1917), where Yesayian portrayed romantic love as personally transforming for the protagonist, Atriné, of the novel. *The Last Cup*, like *My Soul in Exile*, was written after 1915 and represents the demise of the turn-of-the century social transformation projects. In *The Last Cup*, romantic love is still important, although doomed, in *My Soul in Exile*, romantic love never really signifies anything at all. Emma and Diran Bey are attracted to each other, but nothing comes of it, not even the unhappy parting of Atriné and Arshak in *The Last Cup*. Some have viewed Yesayian's post-1915 "psychological" novels as frivolous, however, if one situates these novels in the modern Armenian literary tradition, and women's writing in particular, the demise of romantic love, signifies the demise of the idea that society can be transformed for the better. *My Soul in Exile* is the beginning of a post-Genocide trend in which the figure of the Armenian passes through life, alone and alienated from the world. *My Soul in Exile* (1922) portrays the breakdown of the fictional representation of love and intimacy among urban Armenians. In these novels, the isolation of the characters are indicative of a world in which human emotions have been damaged, due to oppression, genocide and exile. In the post-1915 period, Yesayian can no longer imagine any kind of sustainable relationship between a woman and a man, all such relationships are doomed to fail, in part because, each person is trapped in their own "man-made inner prison." The ending of the novel confirms this sense of isolation and alienation, when Emma decides not to visit Siranush Tanielian's house and thinks:

> It is better to remain alone listening to my soul's whispers. I will go into the garden and stand under the blossoming cherry trees, whose white petals rained down upon us in beautiful times.[545]

The ending reinforces the sense of the non-existence of the present, with its reference to the vanished past, and Emma's isolation and depression.

The post-1915 novels by Zabel Yesayian represent the beginning of a literature in exile and a literature concerned with the consequences and psychological repercussions of the Armenian Genocide. Zabel Yesayian's autobiographical account, *The Gardens of Silihtar*, was published in Yerevan in 1935, although its publication date makes it outside the timeframe of this study, it would be remiss not to at least mention this text in this chapter on Yesayian's life and works. *The Gardens of Silihtar* portrays Yesayian's childhood in Constantinople to roughly 1893. This book has the distinction of being the only one of Yesayian's novels translated in its entirety in French, and partially in English.[546] The book has been well liked in the Diaspora as it portrays the life of a well-known writer and the pre-1915 world of Armenian Constantinople. Here, however, I want to look at the novel from the perspective of a post-Genocide book. Like *My Soul in Exile*, this work is not about the Armenian Genocide. *The Gardens of Silihtar* ends long before 1915, and before Yesayian's journeys to Europe and Transcaucasia. Yesayian had plans to continue her autobiography in several volumes, but her arrest in 1937, ended such plans. Although *The Gardens of Silihtar* ends before 1915, the volume published in 1935, is in part a response to the Armenian Genocide. As Rachel Feldhay Brenner suggests, in her study of women writers of the Holocaust, "life narratives affirm individuality and personhood" when the author is confronted by the dehumanizing genocidal process.[547] Brenner's emphasis on "life narratives" as resistance is illuminating when we examine Yesayian's *The Gardens of Silihtar.* Yesayian's autobiography of her childhood appeared close in time to Vahan Totovents' account of his childhood, *Keank'ë Hin Hrovmeakan Chanaparhi Vra* [Life on the Roman Road] (1930). Both authors describe their childhoods before 1915. Totovents, more than Yesayian, refers to what will happen to his family, friends and acquaintances in 1915 through references such as "the turquoise of the sky crumbled on her head."[548] The act of recreating this world of childhood is an act of literary resistance, by affirming the existence of family and friends and Armenian life, Yesayian and Totovents affirm the existence of those destroyed communities. By the 1930s, when both Yesayian and Totovents wrote their childhood memoirs, the Armenian communities of their childhoods had disappeared and the denial of the existence of Armenian life in Anatolia and the very fact of the Armenian Genocide as having occurred, had already begun. Thus writing of the existence of these worlds was an act, by both Yesayian and Totovents, to resist such deliberate "forgetting." Yesayian's autobiographical account of her childhood and, in particular, the inducement to write of the pre-1915 Armenian life and community in Constantinople, was part of the development of a new literary form in Armenian literature—that of the memoir. The basic goal of which is to preserve Armenian culture and history, and to resist the genocidal process, through memory.

# Legacies and Directions

## Diaspora and Soviet Armenia

The Armenian women writers of the late nineteenth and early twentieth century fashioned a distinct tradition of women's writing. This pioneering generation not only witnessed the advent of women into education, and philanthropic and political organization, they pushed the boundaries of what was acceptable, to introduce women's voices and perspectives into Armenian literary and intellectual circles. The reception of these women writers was mixed. On the one hand, they were welcomed as indicators of modernity and progress and among some intellectuals there existed genuine support for a new role for women. On the other hand, some members of the literary establishment made it clear that topics, such as overt criticisms of patriarchal structures of Armenian society and family structure, were not acceptable. The difficulties women experienced entering the public and literary spheres is also hinted at by the frequent accusations that women who wrote were immoral. This was demonstrated by persistent and unsubstantiated rumours that Srpuhi Dussap and her teacher of Armenian, the poet Mkrdich Beshiktashlian, were in love, or that Sibyl had an affair with her second husband, while the first was still alive, or that Yesayian, had lived an "immoral" life in Paris, and that she was divorced from her husband.[549]

The greatest textual legacy that these women writers left was their constructions of new visions of women's roles. Equally significant was their legacy of Armenian women's participation in the formation of the discursive public sphere. As the proceeding chapters have demonstrated, the development of a sense of self is crucial to the authors' discussions of education, employment, romantic love and marriage. This new vision of the Armenian woman was essentially a modern phenomenon. In an article published in 1903, Yesayian stated that the Armenian woman of that period was significantly different from her mother and grandmother in terms of "emotions, customs and progress." The customs she identified as having been altered were the prohibition against the expression of romantic love and the notion of arranged marriage as the only possible form of marriage. Yesayian attributed the change between generations of women as the result of the modern age, the spirit of which facilitated acceptance of female learning and emergence into the public sphere, a phenomenon she saw as a direct result of the learning and worldview of the intellectuals of the *Zartonk*.[550] Yesayian's aligning of the altered status of women with progress or modernity reflects the Armenian intellectual concern with participating in the modern through literature and ideology. The conscious break with past customs was one of the goals of the *Zartonk* and by extension Armenian women's writing. These authors were essentially modern in orientation both in terms of their literary form and content. The first appearances of the novel, the short story and drama appear in Western Armenian letters between 1850 and 1875.[551] What is not widely acknowledged in histories of Armenian literature, however, is that the novel in Armenian was still experimental by the time Srbuhi Dussap published *Mayta* in 1883. Vahe Oshagan states that *Mayta* was particularly unique as it is epistolary in form, a style not widely employed in Armenian literature.[552] Dussap's innovation, both in adopting the epistolary style and in experimenting with the novel, marks her as a modern author and one of the founders of the modern Armenian novel.

The novel and print culture had radical implications for women by facilitating women's entry into the public, intellectual sphere. The novel enabled women to have a voice in public space and stimulated activism in many of the authors. Sally Ledger observes in the English context that there was a close association in New Woman's fiction between novel writing and feminist activism as the very act of writing became a liberatory activity.[553] Jane Eldridge

Miller in *Rebel Women: Feminism, Modernism and the Edwardian Novel* takes this concept even further suggesting that:

> . . . in revealing the constructed nature of society's essential concepts of gender, the feminist novel also reveals not only the provisionality of its own procedures and assumptions but also the provisionality of social organization, the family and, ultimately, essential concepts of identity and self.[554]

In Armenian fiction too, the act of writing is often portrayed as a liberating activity, subverting social conventions, especially traditional notions of femininity. In Sibyl's play *The Daughter-in-Law*, the heroine writes novels, an activity, which asserts her sense of self, and enables her to escape the restrictions of conventional feminine behaviour. In Zabel Yesayian's *The Last Cup*, the main character's writing about her life is presented as an emancipatory act, which enables her to further explore her subjectivity in oppressive social and political conditions.

The content of these novels, particularly the rewriting of Armenian notions of femininity, distinguishes the novels as modernist. As Jane Eldridge Miller states:

> . . . modernism constitutes a break with tradition; it involves the questioning of the most basic certainties which provide the foundation for social organization, morality, and concepts of self, among other things. . . . to challenge ideals of femininity and maternity, to depict women as active participants in the public sphere, to write about women's desires for power and autonomy, entailed a radical break with social and cultural traditions.[555]

Armenian women's writing challenged social constructs of femininity through a process of examination, rejection and reinterpretation of traditional customs. The protagonists of women novelists of this period are not content with traditional gender constructions, they are educated and want to work and participate in social reform. The authors saw Armenian society as being atrophied by rigid gender conventions, which did not allow members to know themselves or each other. Therefore the authors' works tend to collapse the boundaries between the feminine and masculine. In their texts the Armenian woman is given qualities customarily attributed to the masculine: she is portrayed as rational, able to grasp sciences, mathematics and business matters and can participate in the public sphere through education, employment and intellectual activities such as writing and other forms of artistic endeavour. The Armenian man is given qualities, which are traditionally associated with the feminine: he is emotional, artistic and sensitive. The qualities of emotion and sensitivity are shown in the texts by the desired male character's ability to understand his female counterpart and through his creativity. Artistic and creative are primary attributes of both the Armenian woman and man in literature of this period.

This is not to say that the authors rejected all constructions of femininity and masculinity. The women writers accepted some gender distinctions; for example, the concept of maternal feeling is invested with a semi-sacred reverence and is seen as exclusively characteristic of women, while fatherhood is not represented in the same sacred and innate terms in these texts. When the authors' subversion of conventional constructions of femininity and masculinity occurs, it is designed to facilitate women's participation in societal development, in engagement with the modern world, in the intellectual realm, and in the Armenian national movement. And on a more individual level, the construct of the Armenian woman was designed to encourage women to enter schools, find employment and function as full equal partners with their spouses.

The question is often asked as to how "realistic" were these novels and the female characters. The answer to this question is complicated because of the absence of historical studies on the Armenian woman of the late nineteenth and early twentieth century. There are no scholarly works to give us statistical evidence on how many Armenian women went to school, how many were employed outside of the home, how many children, on average, women gave birth to and other such issues, which would help us in determining what conditions effected women's lives and what was changing in this period. Nevertheless, we have some clues as to the conditions of Armenian women's lives in this period through oral records, family stories and memoir literature written by survivors of the Armenian Genocide. In discussing Armenian women's history and experiences, we also need to take into account differences in women's lives based on social class and regional location. There was not a monolithic "Armenian Woman." The authors of family histories and memoirs frequently supply information about their families, customs and social institutions prior to 1915 and are therefore an invaluable source of information about Armenian women. Despite the accepted popular belief today that Armenian women's lives were somehow static and unchanging, the memoir literature portrays Armenian women in a variety of roles: for example Serpoohi Jafferian's portrayal of her youngest aunt's opening a shop in the early part of the twentieth century, by herself, and her eventual migration to Egypt, independent of her family. The memoir literature also expresses rebellious feelings towards social customs such as arranged marriage, as in Diruhi Highgas' portrayal of her aunt's marriage and separation from her husband in pre-1915, in the town of Konya.[556] There are also indications that the numbers of Armenian women studying abroad had increased considerably by 1915. In the absence of full studies of women of the period, it is difficult to know exactly the structure of women's lives and the changes occurring, but that change was occurring is hinted at by family stories in memoirs.

In this volume I chose to end my discussion of Armenian women's writing in 1922, because the Armenian Genocide and the loss of independence of the first Armenian Republic altered how women were discussed in literature and national development, as well as effecting literary production in profound ways, a fact so obvious it seems almost redundant to state it. Here I would like to suggest the ways in which the early period of Armenian women's writing left legacies and the new directions Armenian women's writing took after 1922 through the 1930s and up to the 1950s, after the 1950s changes are discernible again in Armenian writing, but this period is outside of the scope of this study.

In the early period of the 1920s and 1930s, the city of Constantinople, as the most common birthplace of women writers,
was still true. Thematically, however, the Constantinople born
writers began to represent new themes of Diaspora and fears of
loss of Armenian culture and identity and problems of assimilation. Constantinople born, Zaruhi Bahri (1880–1958) began writing only after having moved to France, and losing her son in World
War II. Although there was some early mention of Bahri in the
early twentieth century journals, her novels were written after her
migration to France and display a concern with the experience of
exile and Diaspora, only begun in Zabel Yesayian's 1903 novel,
*Spasman Srahin Mej*. Bahri wrote two sets of trilogies about Armenian life before and after the Armenian Genocide. One series
was entitled, *Vospori Aperoun Vray* [On the Shores of the
Bosphorus], and depicts, in three volumes, Armenian life in the
Ottoman Empire. The second trilogy, called *Seni Aperoun Vray*
[On the Shores of the Seine], covers the emigration of an Armenian
family to France, and portrays the family's life there from 1922 to
1945. The volumes of the latter series appeared in Armenian journals and were never published in book form. One of Bahri's most
interesting novels is *Chambaneroun Yerkaynk'in/Par'andzem*,
published in Paris in 1946, which traces the history of an Armenian woman and her family from 1872 Arabkir to 1942 Paris.
The story portrays the family's tribulations during the massacres
in Cilicia in 1909, the Armenian Genocide, and finally their emigration to France. Bahri's novels explore the psychological and
material difficulties experienced by Armenians following the
Armenian Genocide and the creation of a Diaspora life in foreign
lands. Her novels also pay particular attention to women's experience of dispersion and emigration. The novel, *Louisette*,
published in the Paris based journal, *Azat Khosk* from 1949–1951,
tackled the question of mixed marriages, a question of increasing
significance in the Armenian Diaspora.

Like Zaruhi Bahri, Seza (1903–1973), penname of Siran
Zarifian-Kupelian, was born in Constantinople. After pursuing
graduate studies at New York's Columbia University, she returned

to Beirut where she established the journal, *Yeritasard Hayuhi* [The Young Armenian Woman], in 1932. *Yeritasard Hayuhi* began publication in October, 1932 and ran for two years, ceased publication for thirteen years, ran from 1947 to 1957, but ceased publication from 1957 to 1961, when it resumed publication until December 1968. The journal focused on issues such as women's education, women's philanthropic organizations, women's rights, motherhood and Armenian identity, themes found in Beylerian's *Artemis* and Haykanush Marrk's journal *Hay Kin* [Armenian Woman]. The latter journal ran from 1919 to 1932 in Istanbul, until its forced closure by the Turkish authorities in 1932, the year Seza began *Yeritasard Hayuhi* in Beirut. In her first editorial in 1932, Seza stated that the objective of the journal was to bring together Armenian women, despite age, education, religious denomination, and class differences, in order to assist their efforts to "enlighten, uplift, and ennoble themselves and their nation."[557] Seza's statement sounds remarkably like Zabel Yesayian's statement in an article, which appeared in *Tsaghik* in 1904:

> What we desire of our women, whatever social class they belong to, and whatever the level of their progress, is that every one of them must do her share in educational and charitable work. Women's place alongside men is necessary and valuable. [558]

By the 1950s, however, Seza's editorials discussed Armenian women's issues from the perspective of Diaspora and fear of assimilation to non-Armenian culture, a subject not found in the early twentieth-century women's journals. For example, although Marie Beylerian described political exile in *Artemis*, there is no suggestion of fears of assimilation or loss of cultural identity. In terms of political theory, Seza's editorials advocated a greater role for Armenian women in the governance of the internal community affairs, beyond administering the charitable organizations. She also encouraged Armenian women to vote in the Lebanese parliamentary elections and to make connections with Lebanese women to improve women's circumstances.[559]

The question of Diaspora and identity continued to be explored in the two-volume novel by Louisa Aslanian (1906–1945), penname Las. The novel, *Harts'akani Ughinerov* [The Paths of Doubt], published in Paris in 1936, explores the decisions and destinies of four young Armenians born in Tabriz, Iran. The two male characters study in Moscow, one marries a Russian woman and eventually immigrates to Paris, while the other supports an independent Armenia and goes mad at the fall of Kars. The two female characters go to Paris to study in the early 1920s, but one of the girls is persuaded to go to Soviet Armenia to participate in the rebuilding of the country there. Literary critic, Krikor Beledian has argued convincingly that the novel is about the conflicts of modernity: western civilization, colonialism and the destructive character of technology are positioned in opposition to the "Orient," especially the traditional life in Tabriz. Beledian posits that the new in the form of Soviet Armenia is finally chosen as the better road.[560] The book achieved fame in Soviet Armenia and was reprinted in Yerevan in 1959, where Las's membership in the French Communist party was emphasized. The novel is an exploration of the politics and decisions facing Armenians in the 1920s, following the Armenian Genocide and the end of the independent republic of Armenia.

In terms of genre, one of the new categories of Armenian women's writing, was the memoir. Two types of memoir appeared, one was written by women who had been active in Armenian intellectual circles and wrote about the early twentieth century literary milieu and the other was the surviving memoir. The former memoirs include: Anayis' *Hushers* [My Memoirs] (Paris, 1949), Zaruhi Galémk'earian's *Keank'is Chambén* [My Life's Path] (Ant'ilias, 1952), and Haykanush Marrk's *Keank'n u Gortsë* [Life and Works] (Istanbul, 1954). Each of these memoirs provide insight into the intellectual community of Constantinople at the turn of the century and typically include brief descriptions of the authors' schooling and work in education or literary journals as well as describing meetings with famous male and female Armenian intellectual figures, the debates of the turn of the century, and the institutions that promoted Armenian literary life. In Haykanush

Marrk's *Keank'n u Gortsë* [Life and Works], a selection of her editorials from the journal, *Hay Kin*, are included. In Eastern Armenia, memoirs were also written by women to describe the intellectual milieu of the late nineteenth and early twentieth centuries. For example, Mariam Toumanian (1870–1945), who supported and aided the writer Hovhaness Toumanian (1869–1923) (despite their shared surname the two were not related), wrote a memoir of her life and activities in 1943, this manuscript, however, remains unpublished.

The second type of memoir that tragically makes its appearance, as a result of the Armenian Genocide, is the survivor memoir. These memoirs make a departure from the earlier tradition of Armenian women's writing. They are typically written by women who were not living in Constantinople and describe the deportations, starvation, rape and killings, which constitute the Genocide of the Armenians living in the Ottoman Empire. As has already been discussed, in the chapter on Zabel Yesayian, eyewitness accounts of the Armenian Genocide appeared as early as 1916 and 1917. Armenian women survivors began to write of this experience soon after 1915. The earliest survivor memoir by an Armenian woman that I am aware of (and this does not preclude the existence of earlier ones) is Mrs. Captanian's *Mémoires d'une Déportée arménienne*, published in 1919. The survivor memoir usually centres on the deportation and experiences of the individual writer, her family, and village or town in 1915. Some memoirs also describe the pre-Genocide Armenian life, including information about towns and villages, family histories and local customs, and some are extended chronologically to include the author and her family's struggle to adjust to life in a foreign country and the diasporic experience. The survivor memoir departs from the objectives of early Armenian women's writing, because of the horror it describes and its function in Armenian society and identity formation. Lorne Shirinian describes the function of the survivor memoir as follows:

> There is the felt need underlying the survivor's narrative to resolve issues and to formulate ideas that will withstand time and thereby

give meaning to what the survivor lived through. These survivor memoirs are key texts of Armenian identity. Through their reading, they force individuals to re evaluate their commitment to their identity and their community.[561]

Therefore the survivor memoir is a significant genre in twentieth-century Armenian writing and is important for the understanding of contemporary Armenian identity and history.

The creation of Soviet Armenia in 1921 meant that Armenian women's writing there developed under very different social and political contexts than that of the Armenian Diaspora. The ideological restrictions and the arrests of Armenian intellectuals, who did not conform to Soviet ideological directions, particularly during the Stalinist period, are well known.[562] Women writers, like their male counterparts, were censored; and as we have seen in the case of Zabel Yesayian, actually imprisoned and killed. State control hindered the development of an independent literary movement. In addition, because Soviet policy restricted discussion of the Armenian Genocide and whatever was defined as "nationalistic," writers were prevented from exploring the psychological, social, cultural and political repercussions of recent history.

When examining the direction of Armenian women's writing in Soviet Armenia after 1922, two trends are discernible, one is that poetry predominates and second, is the creation of writing in Armenian for children, a genre primarily written by women. Those writers, who did not challenge the regime, were facilitated by the creation of a cultural infrastructure, Armenian was proclaimed the state language, a policy to promote national literacy was implemented in 1921, and elementary schooling was made mandatory in 1930. The state theatre, the national public library, and the state museum were founded in 1922.[563] Such institutions encouraged the development of women's writing by uniformly providing education for children and especially by opening up opportunities for women's entry into higher education. In her study of Armenian women writers, Zvart Ghukasian lists the names of several women writers who predominated in the 1920s and 1930s, these include Varsenik Aghasian, Araks, Anush, Maro, Flora and Aghavni, of these women writers several wrote for children. For example, Araks (1903–1978), penname of Araks Avetisian, born in Vanadzor, Armenia, was educated at the Mariamian-Hovnanian school for women in Tiflis, and graduated from Yerevan State University in 1930, before attending a course on journalism in Moscow in 1933. Araks worked primarily as a journalist, but also wrote for children. The writing for children, primarily produced by women, is suggestive of a carry-over of women's maternal role into the public sphere, characteristic of the nineteenth and early twentieth century constructions of women's public roles. The trend of Armenian women as the primary producers of fiction for children has continued to the present-day.

A brief survey of these early Soviet women writer's educational backgrounds reveals that the educational and charitable educational movement of the late nineteenth and early twentieth centuries was bearing fruit. Varsenik Aghasian (1898–1974), who was born in Jahri, Nakhijevan, moved with her family to Tiflis in 1905, where she attended the school run by the *Tiflis Hayuhyats' Baregortsakan Ënkerut'iun* [Tiflis Armenian Women's Philanthropic Association].[564] As the state education system was established, however, education would be provided in state schools. In addition, unlike the six writers discussed in this study, of whom only one, Zabel Yesayian, had attended university, the vast majority of women writers in the 1930s and 1940s were graduates of Yerevan State University and various institutes.

The poetic tradition was carried on by several women writers born immediately prior to the establishment of Soviet Armenia, these include the poets, Maro Markarian (1915–1999) and Silva Kaputikian (b.1919–). Markarian was born in Shahumian, Georgia and attended local schools. In 1933 she studied at the Academy of Painting in Tiflis, but transferred to the faculty of Philology at Yerevan State University, where she graduated in 1938. She attended a post-graduate course in Armenian folklore but gave up scholarly studies to pursue writing. Her first book of poems was published in 1940. Her poetry displays a coming of age in Armenian women's poetry, free from the classicism of Sibyl's poetry, and the rough-hewn quality of Shushanik Kurghinian. Makarian's poetry uses deceptively simple language and images to represent the human condition and emotion.

Silva Kaputikian is the most famous of the Soviet Armenian women poets. She was born in Yerevan, where she completed her studies in Armenian literature and language, graduating from Yerevan State University in 1941. She also studied at the Gorky Institute for literature in 1949–1950. She won the USSR literary prize in 1952. In keeping with the practice of producing literature for children, Kaputikian's early works included poetry for children. She is primarily a poet, although she has written travel books. Many of the themes of Kaputikian's poems are connected to early twentieth-century women's writing, especially early in her career, when she wrote of women, love, the Armenian homeland and motherhood from a patriotic perspective. One of her most famous poems, *Words to my Son* [Khosk' im Vordun], is narrated by a mother, admonishing her son to never forget the Armenian language. The persona of the mother is suggestive of the nineteenth century mother-educator whose objective was held to be to teach her children to be patriotic Armenians.

In Armenian women's writing, immediately following 1915–1921, new themes such as fears of assimilation, intermarriage alienation and psychological trauma as a consequence of the Armenian Genocide appeared, while thematic concerns such as the role of the mother remained important in both the Armenian Diaspora and Soviet Armenia.

# APPENDIX

# BIOGRAPHIES

The following section is intended to provide information on the biographies and principal texts of the pioneering Armenian women writers of the late nineteenth and early twentieth centuries. The list is not exhaustive; I have omitted those writers whose oeuvre consists of only a few poems or short stories or whose biographical details are obscure.

### Aganoor, Vittoria

Poet and letter writer. She was born in 1855 in Padua and died in 1910 in Rome, Italy. She was of Armenian origin. Although she lived in Italy and wrote in Italian, she was known in Western Armenian intellectual circles, where her poems were translated into Armenian. Armenian writers were aware of her works and considered her a model of an early Armenian woman writer. She published her first volume of poetry in 1900. In 1901 she married Guido Pompilj, a well-known deputy and man of letters.

### Anayis

Penname of Yevp'imé Avetisian. She was born in 1872 in Constantinople and died on August 5, 1950 in Paris. Anayis received her primary school education at Peshikt'ashi Mak'ruhian School and later attended a French school. She was a cousin of

Arshak Chobanian (1872–1954), editor of the journal *Anahit*. Her first short story, *Khrch'it'i më mej* [In a Hovel], appeared in *Masis* in 1885–1886. After her forced marriage to a uneducated man, twenty-four years her senior, Anayis did not write for several years, believing that it was inappropriate for a wife and a mother to write. She contributed to the journals *Hay Kin* and *Arevmutk*.

Principal Works

*Ayg u Verjaluys* [Dawn and Sunset] (Paris, 1942); a volume of verse and poems set to music.
*Houshers* [My Memoirs] (Paris, 1949).


### Bahri, Zaruhi

Novelist. She was born in Constantinople in 1880, died in Paris in 1958. Bahri immigrated with her husband and children to France in the 1920s. She lost a son during World War II.

Principal Works

*Tagrë* [The Brother-in-Law]. (Paris, 1942); novel.
*P'arrandzem* [P'arrandzem]. (Paris, 1946); novel.
*Tayean Gévorg Péy* [Dayian Kevork Bey]. (Paris, 1952); novel.


### Berberian, Mannig

Poet and translator. She was born in 1883, the daughter of the poet and teacher Retteos Berberian (1851–1907) and died in 1960.

Principal Works

*Ardzak Yerger* [Prose Poems]. (Constantinople, 1911); poetry.
*Arevot Chamban* [The Sunny Path]. (Paris, 1931); poetry.

*Het'anos Tghay* [The Pagan Youth]. (Alexandria, 1946);
poetry.


## Beylerian, Marie

Editor, short story writer, journalist and teacher. Beylerian was
born in 1880 in Constantinople and died, during the Armenian
Genocide, in 1915. Beylerian received her education at Constantinople's Yesayan School, where she later returned as a teacher.
Beylerian participated in the Bab Ali demonstrations in 1895 and
fled to Alexandria, Egypt in 1896 in order to avoid arrest by the
Ottoman authorities. In Alexandria, she taught at that city's Armenian school.  In Egypt, she founded and edited the journal,
*Artemis*, from 1900–1903. The journal concentrated on Armenian women's rights and educational and charitable activities. After
the declaration of the Ottoman Constitution in 1908, Beylerian
returned to Turkey, where she taught at Smyrna's Central School
and later at the Armenian School in Tokat.

Principal Works

Té Inch'u Ays T'ert'n Al [Why this Journal?], *Artemis* (Janu-
     ary, 1902); editorial.
Zavakë[The Child ], *Artemis* (February, 1902); editorial.
Aknark më Hay Knoj Ants'ealin Vray" [A Glance at the
     Armenian Woman's Past], *Artemis* (March 1902); editorial.
Kesurë (Gavarrakan Keank'é)[The Mother-in-Law: A Tale
     from Provincial Life], *Artemis*, (March 1902); short story.
Dprotsë [The School], *Artemis* (April, 1902); editorial.
Ashkhatelu Pétk'ë Knoj Hamar [Work is Necessary for
     Women], *Artemis* (May/June, 1902); editorial.
Yerku Khosk'Mej Lav Ch'ëmbrrnoghnerun [A few words to
     those who misunderstand us], *Artemis* (July/August 1902);
     editorial.
Ëntérts'anut'iunë Hay Kanants' Mej [Reading Among Arme-
     nian Women], *Artemis* (October/November, 1903); editorial.

Hay Knoj Harts' Masnavrapes t'é "Feminizmi" Pehanj [The
Armenian Woman Question or the Demands of "Feminism"],
*Artemis*, (December 1903); editorial.


### Dussap, Srpuhi

Novelist, philanthropist and salon hostess. She was born in
1841 and died on January 16, 1901 in Constantinople. Dussap
was the first female novelist in Armenian letters. She was the
daughter of Nazli Vahan, who was an active supporter of education and a philanthropist. Following her marriage in 1869 or 1870
to the French musician, Paul Dussap, Srpuhi ran a salon with her
husband where she entertained Armenian and French intellectuals, who discussed literary and social matters. In the 1870s, Dussap
had two children, Dorine and Edgar, whose education she supervised. In 1879, she became an ardent member and, eventually,
head of the *School-Loving Ladies' Association* [Dbrots'aser
Tiknants' Ënkerut'iun]. The Association's objective was to train
Armenian women as teachers for Armenian girls' schools outside
of Constantinople. After the appearance of her final novel, *Araksia
or The Governess*, in 1887, Dussap continued her activities in
benevolent organizations, particularly those devoted to education.
In 1889, she travelled to Paris with her daughter, Dorine, for medical treatment. Upon their return to Constantinople in 1891, Dorine
died at eighteen years. Following her daughter's death, Dussap
published no new works, although she did continue to keep a journal and hold literary salons at her house in Constantinople, until
her death in 1901.

Principal Works

Kanants' Dastiarakut'unë [Women's Education] in *Masis* (April
1880); article.
Kanants' Ashkhatut'ian Skzbunk'ë [The Principle of Women's
Employment] in *Arevelian Mamul* (December, 1881);
article.

K'ani më khosk' kanants' angortsutian masin [A Few Words on
Women's Unemployment] in *T'erchemanë Efk'iar* and
*Meghu Hayastani* (February 21, 1882); article.
*Mayta* (Constantinople, 1883); novel.
*Siranush* (Constantinople, 1884); novel.
*Arak'sia kam Varzhuhin* [Araksia or the Governess]. (Constan-
tinople, 1887); novel.

### Galémk'earian, Zaruhi

Poet, prose writer, and memoirist. She was born Zaruhi Seferian
on July 18, 1874 in Constantinople and died on July 20, 1971,
New York. She received her primary school education at Constantinople's Aramian school. She published under the pseudonyms,
Yevterpe, and after her marriage, G. Zaruhi. She published poetry and essays in the Armenian press in Constantinople and later
the United States. She settled in New York in 1921 where she was
involved in Armenian charitable associations.

Principal Works

*Zartonk* [The Awakening] (1893); poetry.
*T'orrnikis Girkë* [My Grandchild's Book] (1936); travel book.
*Keank'is Chambén* [My Life's Path] (1952); memoir.
*Orer ev Demk'er* [Days and Faces] (1965).

### Khatisian, Mariam

Novelist and philanthropist. She was born Mariam Marisian in
1845 and died on February 9, 1914, in Tiflis. Mariam Khatisian
served as president of the Caucasus (or Tiflis) Armenian Women's
Benevolent Association (T'iflisi Hayuhyats' Baregortzakan
Ënkerut'iun) from 1882 until 1907. Her novels concentrate on
Armenian women's emancipation and social issues.

Principal Works

*Heghine* (1890); novel.
*P'esay Vorsoghner*[The Husband Hunters] (Tiflis, 1894); novel.
*Nor Chanaparhi Vray* [On a New Path] (St. Petersburg, 1894); novel.
*Dzhbakht Kin* [The Unfortunate Wife] (Tiflis, 1899); novel.

## Kurghinian, Shushanik

Poet and short story writer. She was born Shushanik Poboldjian in 1876, in Alexandropol, present-day Gyumri, and she died on November 24, 1927 in Yerevan. She attended the Alexandropol Arghut'ian Girls' School. In 1893, she joined the Hnchak party, and with other young women, organized the first Hnchakian young women's group. Her first poem was published in *Taraz* in 1899 and her first short story in *Aghbyur* in 1900. She was in Russia at the time of the 1905 revolution and was sympathetic to the workers' demands and the attempt to overthrow the tsar. With the assistance of Aleksandr Myasnikian, a member of the Bolshevik party and, later, first president of Soviet Armenia, Kurghinian published her first volume of poetry, *The Ringing of the Dawn*, in 1907.

Principal Works

*Arshaluysi Ghoghanjner* [The Ringing of the Dawn]. (Nor Nakhichevan, 1907); poetry.
*Yerkeri Zhoghovatsu* [Collected Works]. (Yerevan, 1947); poetry.

Selected Criticism

Hovhannes Ghazarian, *Shushanik Kurghinian.* (Yerevan, 1955).
Zvart Ghukasyan, *Hay Kin Groghner.* (Yerevan, 1978).

Translations

The Eagle's Love. Translated by Alice Stone Blackwell. In *Armenian Poems*. (Boston, Massachusetts, 1917), pp. 247–248.
The Workers. Translated by Yedvard Gulbekian. *Ararat* (Winter, 1990):52.
Let Us Unite. Translated by Diana Der-Hovanessian. *Ararat* (Autumn, 2001):22.

## *Las*

Penname of Louisa Aslanian. Novelist and short story writer. She was born in 1906 in Tavriz, Iran. Las attended primary school in Tavriz, and later attended the Russian Gymnasium in Tiflis. She left for Paris to study literature at the Sorbonne in 1923. She participated in the work of the Armenian-French writer's society. She joined the French communist party in 1936. During the Second World War she participated in the Resistance. She was eventually arrested and died in a Nazi concentration camp in 1945. Her stories, poems and fables were published in the Parisian and Diaspora presses.

Principal Works

*Khane* [The Khan] (1928); short stories.
*Harts'akani Ughinerov* [The Paths of Doubt] (1936); novel.

Selected Criticism

Krikor Beledian. *Cinquante Ans de Littérature Arménienne en France*. Paris: CNRS Editions, 2001.

## Marrk Haykanush

Writer, teacher, editor and journalist. She was born in 1883 in Constantinople, and died there in 1966. She founded the feminist periodical, *Tsaghik Kanants*,' published between 1905–1907. She lived in Smyrna following her marriage to editor, Vahan Toshigian, in 1907. She edited the women's page of Toshigian's journal, *Arshaluys*, but in 1919, started her own journal *Hay Kin*, which was published from 1919 to 1932. Most of her writing is to be found in the aforementioned journals.

Principal Works

*Tsaghik Kanants'*, (1905–1907); editorials.
*Hay Kin*, (1919–1932); editorials.
*Tzulutean Paheres* [From My Idle Moments] (Constantinople, 1921); poetry.
*Keank'n u Gortsë* [Life and Works] (Istanbul, 1954); an account of her life and reprints some of her editorials from *Hay Kin*.

## Seza

Penname of Siran Zarifian-Kupelian. Prose writer and editor. She was born in 1903 in Constantinople and died on September 8, 1973, Beirut, Lebanon. She was editor of the journal, *Yeritasard Hayuhi* [The Young Armenian Woman], published in Beirut intermittently from 1932–1968. Seza studied literature and journalism at Columbia University, New York, before permanently settling in Beirut in 1932.

Principal Works

*Yeritasard Hayuhi* [The Young Armenian Woman] (1932–1968); journal.
*Badneshe* [The Rampart] (Beirut, 1959); novel.
*Meghavoruhin* [The Sinner] (Beirut, 1960); short stories.

## Sibyl

The penname of Zabel Khandjian, who was born in Constantinople in 1863. Sibyl attended a French language school, then the Armenian language Holy Cross school, and, finally, Scutari College from 1873 until 1879. At a young age Sibyl became interested in the issue of female education. In 1879, with eight girlfriends from Scutari College, she founded the *Patriotic Armenian Women's Association* [Azganvér Hayuhyats' Ënkerut'iun]. The goal of this association was to establish schools for rural Armenian girls. The Association continued its activities for twenty-two years, despite its forced closure by the Ottoman government during the Hamidian massacres of Armenians in 1894–1896. The Association ceased its activities until 1908, when it was re-established, and continued to assist the development of education among Armenian girls until 1915. In 1882, Sibyl married a lawyer named Garapet Tonelian. Following her marriage, Sibyl lived in the provincial towns of Biledjik, Bursa and Ankara. During this period she was busy teaching, writing articles about children's education and literature for Armenian papers published in Constantinople, and raising her daughter Atriné. In 1889, Sibyl returned to Constantinople and became involved in literary and educational work in the capital. In 1901, after the death of her first husband, Sibyl married Hrant Asatur (1862–1928), who was a co-editor with Krikor Zohrab (1861–1915), of the prestigious journal *Masis*. Sibyl published a series of Armenian grammar books for use in schools. In this period Sibyl had another daughter, Emma. An extremely gifted teacher Sibyl taught at the most distinguished schools in Constantinople including the Armenian language Yesayian and Central lycées, and the English language "High School" and Mme. Deveau's (French) higher educational institution. Hrant Asatur died in 1928 and Sibyl died in Constantinople in 1934. Sibyl's literary output consists of essays, poems, short stories, plays and a novel.

Principal Works

*Aghjkan më Sirtë* [The Heart of a Girl]. (Constantinople, 1891); novel.
Sibyl and Alp'asan. *Magnis* [The Magnet]. (Constantinople, 1909); play.
*Knoj Hoginer* [Women's Souls]. (Constantinople, 1925); short stories.
*Harse* [The Daughter-in-Law]. (Boston, 1938); play.

Translation

The Bride. [Harse] Translated by Nishan Parlakian. (New York: Griffon House, 1987).

### Teodik, Arshakuhi

Prose writer. She was born Arshakuhi Chezvechian in 1875 in Constantinople, and died on January 2, 1922 in Lusanne, Switzerland. She attended university in England. She married the author, Teodik Labjinjian (1873–1928). She was a member of *Patriotic Armenian Women's Association* [Azganvér Hayuhyats' Ënkerut'iun] and travelled to Adana in 1909 to assist in relief effort, following the Cilician massacres in 1909.

Principal Works

*Amis Më i Kilikia* [A Month in Cilicia]. (Constantinople, 1910); report on the aftermath of the Cilician massacres in 1909; and the efforts of the Armenian community to care for the children orphaned during the massacre.
Temoignages inédits sur les atrocites turques comises en *Arménie* (Paris, 1920); about the Armenian Genocide.

### Yesayian, Zabel

Novelist, short story writer and essayist. She was born Zabel
Hovhannisian on February 4, 1878, in the district of Silihtar, in
Constantinople. She graduated from the Armenian primary school,
Holy Cross, in Scutari, in 1892. In 1895, she went to Paris to
study literature and philosophy at the Sorbonne. In 1900, Zabel
married Armenian painter, Dikran Yesayian (1874–1921). They
had two children, Sophie and Hrant. Yesayian returned to Constantinople in 1902, where she continued her writing career. In 1909,
Yesayian was a member of a delegation sent to Cilicia to investigate the aftermath of the massacres of the Armenian population
there. Her report, *Among the Ruins*, which contains her interviews
with survivors, and her impressions and response to the massacres, was published in Constantinople in 1911. In 1915, after avoid-
ing arrest, she escaped from Constantinople to Bulgaria. In 1933,
at the invitation of the Soviet Armenian government, Yesayian
settled in Yerevan where she lectured on French literature at
Yerevan State University. In 1937, during the Stalinist arrests of
Armenian intellectuals, Yesayian was arrested and imprisoned.
She is believed to have died in prison in 1942/3.

Principal Works

*Spasman Srahin Mej* [In the Waiting Room]. (1903–1904); novel.
*Averaknerun Mej* [Among the Ruins]. (Constantinople, 1911);
   account of Cilician massacres.
*Yerb Aylevs Chen Sirer* [When They Are No Longer In Love].
   (1914); novel.
*Zhoghovurdi më Hogevark'ë* [Agony of a People]. (1917); testi-
   mony on the Armenian Genocide.
*Verjin Bazhakë* [The Last Cup]. (Constantinople, 1917); novel.
*Le rôle de la femme arménienne pendant la guerre* [The Role
   of the Armenian Woman during the War] (Paris, 1922);
   essay.
*Hogis Ak'sorial* [My Soul in Exile]. (1922); novel.
*Nahanjogh Uzher* [Retreating Forces]. (1926); novel.

*Méliha Nuri Hanëm* [Melihan Nuri Hanim]. (Paris, 1928); novel.
*Promet'éos Azatagrvats* [Prometheus Unchained]. (Marseille,
1928); travelogue.
*Kraké Shapikë* [Shirt of Flame]. (Yerevan, 1934); novella.
*Silihtari Partéznerë* [The Gardens of Silihtar]. (Yerevan, 1935);
autobiography.

Selected Criticism

Dasnabédian, Chouchik. *Zabel Essayan ou l'univers lumineux
de la literature*. Antélias, Lebanon: Armenian Catholicosate
of Cilicia, 1988.
Nichanian, Marc. *Writers of Disaster*. Princeton and London:
Gomidas Institute, 2002.
Oshagan, Hagop. *Hamapatker Arevmtahay Grakanutyan*
[Panorama of Western Armenian Literature]. Vol.6. Beirut:
Hamazgayini Hratarakch'ut'iun,1968.
Peroomian, Rubina. *Literary Responses to Catastrophe*.
Atlanta, Georgia: Scholars Press, 1993.

Translations

Gardens of Silihdar and Other Writings. Translated by Ara
Baliozian. New York: Ashod Press, 1982.
Les Jardins de Silidhar. Translated by Pierre Ter-Sarkissian.
Paris: Albin Michel, Paris: Albin Michel, 1994.

# NOTES

¹ This is true of Hagop Oshagan's *Hamapatker Arevmtahay Grakanutyan* [Panorama of Western Armenian Literature]. Vol.6. Beirut: Hamazgayini Hratarakch'ut'iun, 1968. And the multi volume: *Hay Nor Grakanutian Patmutiun*. Yerevan: Haykakan SSR Gitutiunneri Akademiayi Hratarakch'ut'iun, 1964.

² Vahe Oshagan, "Cultural and Literary Awakening of Western Armenians, 1789–1915," *Armenian Review* 36 (Autumn 1983):61.

³ James Etmekjian, *The French Influence on the Western Armenian Renaissance 1843–1915*, (New York: Twayne Publishers), 1964, p.160.

⁴ Ibid., p.160.

⁵ The work of these novelists in language creation is demonstrated by the fact that a dictionary published in 1969 in Yerevan quotes various authors' word usage to demonstrate word meaning and usage; Yesayian is one of the few women writer's whose word usage is included in the list of authors quoted in this dictionary. *Jamanakakits Hayots' Lezvi Batsatrakan Bararan*. (Yerevan: Haykakan SSH Gitutiunneri Akademia), 1969.

⁶ Kevork Bardakjian, *A Reference Guide to Modern Armenian Literature 1500–1920*, (Detroit: Wayne State University Press, 2000), p.102, 108.

⁷ Vahe Oshagan, "A Brief Survey of Literature," *Review of National Literatures*: Armenia 13, (1984):33; Etmekjian, *The French Influence,* p. 214.

⁸ Etmekjian, *The French Influence,* p. 214.

⁹ Vahe Oshagan, "A Brief Survey of Literature," p. 31.

¹⁰ Vahe Oshagan, *The English Influence on West Armenian Literature in the Nineteenth Century*, (Cleveland, Ohio: Caravan Books, 1990), p. 35.

¹¹Etmekjian, *The French Influence,* p. 196.

¹² Lilian R. Furst, *Romanticism*, (London: Methuen and Co., 1969), pp. 4–5.

¹³ Ibid., p. 60.

[14] Boghos Zekiyan, "Personal Tragedy and Cultural Backgrounds in the Poetry of Bedros Tourian," *Review of National Literatures: Armenia*, Vol 13, (1984):122.

[15] Lilian R. Furst, *Romanticism*, p. 31.

[16] The controversy surrounding *Mayta* is discussed in great detail in A. Sharuryan, *Srpuhi Dussap*, Yerevan: Yerevan Betakan Hamalsarani Hratarakch'utiun, 1963. pp. 128–50.

[17] Ibid., p.135.

[18] Sibyl, "Tikin Dussap Ir Srahin Mej" [Mrs. Dussap in her Salon], in *Yerker*, (Yerevan: Hayastan Hratarakch'ut'iun, 1965), p. 179.

[19] Etmekjian, *The French Influence*, p. 216.

[20] Hiranth Thorossian, *Historie de la littérature Arménienne*, (Paris: Araxes, 1951), p. 290.

[21] Quoted in Etmekjian, *The French Influence,* p. 223.

[22] Lilian Furst and Peter Skrine, *Naturalism*, (London: Methuen and Co., 1971), p. 21.

[23] Etmekjian, *The French Influence,* pp. 232–3.

[24] Yesayian, Hrant, "Im Mayrikë." *Sovetakan Grakanut'iun* 3 (1978):93.

[25] Lilian Furst and Peter Skrine, *Naturalism*, p. 8.

[26] Ibid., pp. 12, 42.

[27] Hagop Oshagan, *Hamapatker Arevmtahay Grakanutyan*, p. 243; Sevak Arzumanyan, *Zabel Yesayian: Keank'e ev Gortsë,* (Yerevan: Haykakan SSR Gitutiunneri Akademiayi Hratarakch'ut'iun, 1965), p.190; Vahe Oshagan, "A Brief Survey of Literature," p. 40.

[28] Jayawardena, *Feminism and Nationalism in the Third World*, 12.

[29] Boghos Levon Zekiyan, "Modern Armenian Culture," in *Armenian Perspectives*, ed. Nicholas Awde, (Richmond, Surrey: Curzon Press, 1997), p. 352.

[30] A brief description of Khosrovidoukht Koghtnatsi and Sahakdoukht Siunetsi, as well as samples of each author's poetry, has appeared in English translation in *Anthology of Armenian Poetry*, translated and edited by Diana Der Hovanessian and Marzbed Margossian, (New York: Columbia University Press, 1978), pp. 43–5.

[31] Sibyl, "Azganver Hayuhik" in *Yerker* (Yerevan, 1965), p. 160.

[32] Ghukasyan, Zvart, *Hay Kin Groghner*, (Yerevan: Haykakan SSH "Gidelik" Ënkerut'iun, 1978), p. 5.

[33] Virginia Woolf, *A Room of One's Own*, cited in *Feminist Literary Theory,* 2d ed., ed. Mary Eagleton, 9–10, (Oxford: Blackwell Publishers, 1996), p. 74.

[34] Carol Ohmann, "Emily Brontë in the Hands of Male Critics," in *Feminist Literary Theory,* ed. Mary Eagleton, p. 106.

[35] Charlotte Rosenthal, Women Prose Writers, 1885–1917, p. 13.

[36] Rosemary Betterton, "Women Artists, Modernity and Suffrage Cultures in Britain and Germany 1890–1920," in *Women Artists and Modernism*, Katy Deepwell ed., (Manchester: Manchester University Press, 1998), p. 19.

[37] Boghos Levon Zekiyan, *Armenian Perspectives*, p. 345.

[38] George Bournoutian, "A History of the Armenian People," Vol.II. (Costa Mesa, California: Mazda Publishers, 1994), p. 116.

[39] Zabel Yesayian, "Ink'nakensagrut'iun," *Sovetakan Grakanut'iun* (1979):74.

[40] Rosemary Betterton, "Women Artists, Modernity," p. 19.

[41] Zabel Yesayian, "Mer Kinerë." *Tsaghik* (April 26, 1903):150.

[42] Pamela Young, "Knowledge, Nation and the Curriculum: Ottoman Armenian Education (1853–1915)." Ph.D. diss., University of Michigan, 2001. p. 78.

[43] Ibid., p. 79.

[44] A.S. Sharuryan, *Srpuhi Dussap*, pp. 9–11.

[45] Ibid., p. 17.

[46] Barbara Merguerian, "The Beginnings of Secondary Education for Armenian Women: The Armenian Female Seminary in Constantinople," *Journal of the Society for Armenian Studies* 5 (1990–1991):108.

[47] Ibid., pp. 121, 116.

[48] Sibyl, *Dzrinere* [Charity Cases] in *Yerker*, p. 150.

[49] Ibid., p. 150.

[50] Ibid., p. 151.

[51] Pamela Young, "Knowledge, Nation," p. 93.

[52] A.S. Sharuryan, *Srpuhi Dussap*, pp. 41-3.

[53] Ibid., p. 43.

[54] Zabel Yesayian, "Ink'nakensagrut'iun," p. 53.

[55] Ibid., p. 56.

[56] Zabel Yesayian, "Ink'nakensagrut'iun," p. 57.

[57] Ronald Grigor Suny, *Looking Toward Ararat*, (Bloomington, Indiana: Indiana University Press, 1993), p. 58.

[58] Ibid., p. 69.

[59] Ghazarian, Hovhannes, *Shushanik Kurghinian*, (Yerevan: Haykakan SSR GA Hratarakch'ut'iun, 1955), pp. 9–10.

[60] Zabel Yesayian's letters to her husband make clear the lack of trust and liking between Sibyl and Yesayian, but they did work together in

philanthropic work when necessary. Zabel Yesayian, *Namakner* (Yerevan: Yerevani Betakan Hamalsarani Hratarakch'ut'iun, 1977), pp. 70–3.

[61] Sebouh Hovanessian, "Introduction," in *Armenian Women of the Stage*, by Alice Navasargian, (California: 1999), p. 47.

[62] See for example *Tsaghik* (1903–1904) and *Arakatz* (1911).

[63] In France and in Armenian circles in Constantinople the salon was presided over by a hostess, who was responsible for ensuring the success of the salon meetings. See James F. Macmillan, *France and women 1789–1914* (London: Routledge, 2000), p. 8.

[64] Anayis, *Houshers* [My Memoirs], (Paris, 1949), p. 13.

[65] *Hay Nor Grakanutian Patmutiun*, Vol.3. (Yerevan: Haykakan SSR Gitutiunneri Akademiayi Hratarakch'ut'iun, 1964), p. 535.

[66] Zaruhi Galémk'earian, *Keank'is Chamben*, (Antilias, 1952), p. 332.

[67] Ibid., p. 108.

[68] Ibid., pp. 109–110.

[69] Nishan Parlakian and Peter Cowe, eds. *Modern Armenian Drama*, (New York: Columbia University Press, 2001), p. ix.

[70] Galémk'earian, p. 331.

[71] Alice Navasargian, *Armenian Women of the Stage*, p. 66.

[72] Sebouh Hovanessian, "Introduction," in *Armenian Women of the Stage*, p. 37.

[73] Bardakjian, *A Reference Guide*, p. 104.

[74] Cited in *Gardens of Silihdar and Other Writings*, translated by Ara Baliozian, (New York: Ashod Press, 1982), p. 21.

[75] Sharuryan, *Srpuhi Dussap*, p. 11.

[76] Sibyl, "Dzrinere," in *Yerker*, p. 151.

[77] Yesayian, *Silihtari Partéznerë* [The Gardens of Silihtar], in *Yerker* (Yerevan: Haypethrat, 1959), p. 490.

[78] Sharuryan, *Srpuhi Dussap*, p. 16.

[79] Ghazarian, *Shushanik Kurghinian*, p. 13.

[80] Zabel Yesayian, "Ink'nakensagrut'iun," p. 57.

[81] Ghazarian, *Shushanik Kurghinian*, p. 11.

[82] Charlotte Rosenthal, "Women Prose Writers, 1885–1917", p. 133.

[83] Galémk'earian, p. 336–7; Anayis, *Houshers*, p. 73.

[84] Dussap, *Mayta*, in *Yerker* (Yerevan: Sovetakan Grogh Hratarakch'ut'iun, 1981), p. 13.

[85] Yesayian, *Silihtari Partéznerë* [The Gardens of Silihtar], in *Yerker*, p. 412.

[86] Ibid., p. 422.

[87] Ibid., p. 411.

[88] Ibid., p. 394.

[89] Agop J. Hacikyan, ed. *Heritage of Armenian Literature*, p. 25.

[90] Arpik Minasyan, *Sipil*, (Yerevan: Yerevani Hamalsarani Hratarakch'ut'iun, 1980), pp. 8–9.

[91] Zabel Yesayian, "Ink'nakensagrut'iun," pp. 60–1.

[92] Virginia Woolf, "Professions for Women," in *Death of the Moth* (1942), included in *Feminist Literary Theory*, 2nd ed., ed. Mary Eagleton, p. 79.

[93] Sibyl, *Harse* [The Daughter-in-Law], (Boston: Hayrenik Press, 1938), pp. 7–8.

[94] Boghos Levon Zekiyan, "Modern Armenian Culture," in *Armenian Perspectives*, p. 352.

[95] In 1852 the Dedeyan brothers established a printing press in Smyrna, hired a team of translators and began to sell European novels. By 1880 approximately 200 volumes had been printed by the Dedeyan Press. Translations of Moliere, Dumas, Hugo, Sue, Racine, Goldini, Lamartine, Voltaire, Prevost, Sand and Musset were thus made available to western Armenian readers. Vahe Oshagan, "A Brief Survey of Literature," p. 31.

[96] Elishe, *History of Vardan and the Armenian War*, translation and commentary by Robert W. Thomson, (Cambridge, Mass.: Harvard University Press, 1982), p. 51.

[97] Pamela Young, "Knowledge, Nation," p. 210.

[98] Elishe, *History of Vardan and the Armenian War*, p. 9.

[99] Sibyl, "Azganver Hayuhik" in *Yerker*, pp. 156–7.

[100] Zabel Yesayian, *Le rôle de la femme arménienne pendant la guerre*, Revue des Études Arméniennes, (Tome II, 1922):133.

[101] One of the most visible examples of Armenian women's casting off of immediate custom was their abandonment of wearing the veil. In contrast to the pages of paper filled in Arabic, Persian and Turkish on the issue of women's clothing, very little discussion of the rapid change of clothing styles for Armenian women occurred. In his account of Ottoman social life Krikor Basmajian states that when he was a boy in the 1850s in the city of Adrianople Armenian women wore the veil, but by the time of his writing, 1890, Armenian women wore European dress. Krikor H. Basmajian, *Social and religious Life in the Orient*, (New York: American Tract Society, 1890), p. 166. Zabel Yesayian's account of her youth in Constantinople confirms Basmajian's observation. Yesayian states that while her grandmother's generation had worn the veil her generation wore European clothes. Zabel Yesayian, "Silihtari Partéznerë" in *Yerker*, p. 399. It appears that the abandonment of the veil among

urban Armenian women was not problematic as this style of dress was associated with Islamic not Armenian custom.

[102] *Hay Nor Grakanutian Patmutiun,* Vol.3, p. 535.

[103] A.S. Sharuryan, *Srpuhi Dussap,* pp. 32, 45.

[104] Significantly, since the collapse of the Soviet Union and the foundation of the Republic of Armenia in 1991, women in Armenia, especially those involved in the non-governmental organizations, are claiming Srpuhi Dussap as a foremother. Dussap and her contemporaries serve as an inspirational model in women's work in rebuilding Armenia and Armenian society at present. See for example Marietta Sahakian, "Armenian Women in Politics," in *Women with University Education* (June 1999):8–10; Anahit Harutiunian, "Hay Kanants Sharzhoume 19-rd daroum ev 20-rd dari skzbin" [The Armenian Women's Movement in the nineteenth and early twentieth Centuries] in *Feminizmi Tesut'iun ev Patmut'iun,* ed. Jemma Hasrat'ian. Yerevan: The Association of Women with University Education, 1999.

[105] Sharuryan, *Srpuhi Dussap,* pp. 141–50.

[106] Cited in Vahe  Oshagan, "Cultural and Literary Awakening of Western Armenians, 1789–1915," *Armenian Review* 36 (Autumn 1983): 60.

[107] Cited in Arpik Minasyan, *Sibyl,* p. 81.

[108] Hayk Ghazarian, *Arevmtahayeri Sotsial-Tntesakan ev Kaghakakan Katsutiune 1800–1870* [The Western Armenian Socioeconomic and Cultural Situation 1800–1870], (Yerevan: Haykakan SSR Gitutiunneri Akademiayi Hratarakch'ut'iun, 1967), p. 392.

[109] Zabel Yesayian, "Silihtari Partéznerë" in *Yerker,* p. 525.

[110] Zaruhi Galémk'earian, *Keank'is Chambén,* p. 333.

[111] Sibyl, "Tikin Srpuhi Dussap Ir Srahin Mej" [Mrs. Srpuhi Dussap in her Salon], in *Yerker,* p. 179.

[112] See Appendix for information on the life and career of Arshakuhi Teodik.

[113] Zabel Yesayian, "Silihtari Partéznerë" in *Yerker,* pp. 526–7.

[114] Z. "Tikin Srpuhi Dussapi Mahvan Tarelitsin Artiv," [On the Occasion of the First Year Anniversary of Mrs. Srpuhi Dussap's Demise], *Artemis* 1 (January 1902):26.

[115] Joanna Russ, *How To Suppress Women's Writing,* (London: Women's Press, 1983), p. 87.

[116] Lila Abu-Lughod, ed. *Remaking Women: Feminism and Modernity in the Middle* East, (Princeton, New Jersey: Princeton University Press, 1998), p. 8.

[117] Minasyan, *Sibyl,* p. 76.

[118] Abu-Lughod, ed. *Remaking Women*, p. 8.

[119] Raffi, *Parskakan Patkerner* [Persian Images] (Vienna, 1913): pp. 454–6, quoted in and translated by Houri Berberian, "Armenian Women in Turn-of-the-Century Iran: Education and Activism," in *Iran and Beyond*, ed. Rudi Mathee and Beth Baron (Costa Mesa: Mazda Publishers, 2000), p. 82.

[120] Raffi, *Khent'ë*, (Beirut: Hamazgayin Tparan, 1981), pp. 396–414.

[121] Abu-Lughod, ed. *Remaking Women*, p. 17.

[122] Joanna de Groot, "Coexisting and Conflicting Identities: Women and Nationalisms in Twentieth Century Iran," in *Nation, Empire, Colony*, ed. Ruth Roach Pierson and Nupur Chaudhuri, (Bloomington: Indiana University Press, 1998), p. 143.

[123] Sibyl, "Azganver Hayuhik'" in *Yerker*, p. 161.

[124] See Diruhi Kouymjian Highgas, *Refugee Girl*, (Watertown, Mass.: Baikar Publications, 1985), p. 163 and Elise Hagopian Taft, *Rebirth*, (Plandome, New York: New Age Publishers, 1981), p. 13. These authors, born at the beginning of the twentieth century, were from medium sized towns and described the practice of arranged marriage as commonplace in their towns.

[125] Susie Hoogasian Villa, and Mary Kilbourne Matosian, *Armenian Village Life Before 1914*, (Detroit: Wayne State University Press, 1982), p. 72.

[126] Ibid., p. 74. For example Villa's informants state that a boy could sometimes influence his family to select the girl he preferred. In some families girls had the right of refusal. In 1900 the American missionary Theresa Huntington described the situation whereby an Armenian woman's parents accepted her refusals of all suitors until she was twenty-four years old, at that time, however, they insisted on arranging her marriage to a suitor she did not like. In Theresa Huntington Ziegler, *Great Need Over the Water*, ed. Stina Katchadourian, (Ann Arbor, Michigan: Gomidas Institute, 1999), p. 170.

[127] Villa, *Armenian Village Life Before 1914*, p. 80.

[128] Zabel Yesayian, "Silihtari Partéznerë" in *Yerker*, p. 405.

[129] Dussap's commitment to modernity is also evident in her writing style. Vahe Oshagan noted that in her three novels Dussap made "a genuine effort, in form and content, to revitalize and modernize the genre." The epistolary form she used in *Mayta*, although experimented with by Mamurian, was relatively new in Armenian literature. Vahe Oshagan, "Modernization in Western Armenian Literature," *Armenian Review* 36 (Spring, 1983):68.

[130] Susan Hendrick and Clyde Hendrick, *Romantic Love* (Newbury Park, California: Sage Publications, 1992), pp. 34–5.

[131] The amira usually acted as bankers or moneylenders in the Ottoman taxation system. They were permitted to wear clothes reserved for Ottoman officials and ride horses, privileges denied to non-Muslims in the Ottoman Empire. Due to their power at court the amiras had a great deal of power in the Armenian community, including the election of the patriarch. See Hagop Barsoumian, "The Dual Role of the Armenian Amira Class within the Ottoman Government and the Armenian Millet (1750–1850)," in *Christians and Jews in the Ottoman Empire*, Vol.1. ed. Benjamin Braude and Bernard Lewis, (New York: Holmes and Meier Publishers, 1982), p. 171.

[132] Srpuhi Dussap, "Siranush" in *Yerker* (Yerevan: Sovetakan Grogh Hratarakch'ut'iun, 1981), p. 155. All subsequent references to *Siranush* are based on this edition.

[133] Ibid., p.155.

[134] Hagop Barsoumian, "The Dual Role of the Armenian Amira," pp. 179, 181.

[135] George Bournoutian, *A History of the Armenian People*, pp. 22–3.

[136] Dussap, *Siranush*, p. 155.

[137] Ibid., p. 178.

[138] Ibid., p. 180.

[139] Ibid., p. 180.

[140] Ibid., p. 247.

[141] Ibid., p. 279.

[142] Ibid., p. 281.

[143] Ibid., p. 146.

[144] Ibid., p. 172.

[145] Ibid., p. 156.

[146] Ibid., pp. 168–9.

[147] Ibid., p. 147.

[148] Ibid., pp. 146–7.

[149] Zabel Yesayian, "Silihtari Partéznerë" in *Yerker*, p. 527.

[150] Dussap, *Siranush*, p. 293.

[151] Ibid., p. 295.

[152] For this reason Zaruhi is accused of compromising her husband's honour by working for money, which suggested he could not support his family through his own endeavours. Dussap, *Siranush*, 169. In rural areas proof of virginity at the time of marriage was demonstrated by displaying bloodied sheets from the marriage bed. The presentation of a

bloodied sheet at this time was said to have brought honour to the girl and her family. Villa, *Armenian Village Life Before 1914*, p. 85.

[153] Dussap, *Siranush*, p. 304.

[154] Ibid., p. 297.

[155] Dussap, *Araksia or the Governess*, in *Yerker* (Yerevan: Sovetakan Grogh Hratarakch'ut'iun, 1981), p. 363. All subsequent references are based on this edition.

[156] Ibid., pp. 363–4.

[157] Ibid., p. 368.

[158] Hagop Oshagan, *Hamapatker Arevmtahay Grakanutyan*, p. 252.

[159] Zabel Yesayian, "Silihtari Partéznerë" in *Yerker*, pp. 523, 525.

[160] Yesayian, "Mer Kinerë." *Tsaghik* (April 26, 1903):151.

[161] Yesayian, Zabel, *Verjin Bazhakë* [The Last Cup], (Constantinople, 1924), p. 10. All subsequent references to *Verjin Bazhakë* are based on this edition.

[162] Ibid., p. 13.

[163] Ibid., p. 12.

[164] Ibid., p. 19.

[165] Ibid., p. 25.

[166] Ibid., p. 6.

[167] Ibid., p. 38.

[168] Ibid., p. 27.

[169] Ibid., pp. 27–8.

[170] Ibid., p. 28.

[171] Eliz Sanasarian, "Gender Distinction in the Genocidial Process: A Preliminary Study of the Armenian Case," *Holocaust and Genocide Studies*. vol.4. n.s.4. (1989):453.

[172] Yesayian, Zabel, *Verjin Bazhakë* [The Last Cup], p. 30.

[173] Ibid., p. 29.

[174] Ibid., p. 30.

[175] Rev. Matthias Bedrossian, *New Dictionary Armenian-English*. (reprint, Lebanon: Libraire du Liban, 1985), p. 687.

[176] Yesayian, Zabel, *Verjin Bazhakë* [The Last Cup], p. 32.

[177] Ibid., p. 43.

[178] Ibid., p. 63.

[179] Ibid., p. 87.

[180] Ibid., p. 60.

[181] "Srpuhi Dussap" in *Hay Nor Grakanutian Patmutiun*. Vol.3. (Yerevan: Haykakan SSR Gitutiunneri Akademiayi Hratarakch'ut'iun, 1964), p. 545.

[182] Kumari Jayawardena, *Feminism and Nationalism in the Third World,* pp. 11–2.

[183] Pamela Young, "Knowledge, Nation," p. 79.

[184] Tikranuhi Apkariants, "The Education of Women in Nor Jugha," *Artemis* 2–3, (February/March, 1903):55.

[185] Pamela Young, "Knowledge, Nation," pp.234–5.

[186] Afsaneh Najmabadi, "Crafting an Educated Housewife in Iran," in *Remaking Women*, ed. Abu-Lughod, pp. 113–4.

[187] Anne K. Mellor, Mothers of the Nation, pp. 3–4.

[188] For a description of each organization see A.S. Sharuryan, *Srpuhi Dussap* and Arpik Minasyan, *Sibyl.*

[189] Minasyan, *Sibyl*, p. 9.

[190] Ibid., p.11.

[191] Ibid., p. 9.

[192] Sibyl, "Azganver Hayuhik" in *Yerker*, p. 157.

[193] Ibid., p. 157.

[194] Ibid., p. 157.

[195] Lucy Bland, Banishing the Beast: English Feminism And Sexual Morality 1885–1914, (London: Penguin Books, 1995), p. 51.

[196] Minasyan, *Sibyl*, p. 13.

[197] Arshakuhi Teodik, *Amis Më i Kilikia* [A Month in Cilicia], (Constantinople: V and H Der Nersesian, 1910), p. 77.

[198] Pamela Young, "Knowledge, Nation," pp. 211–212.

[199] Minasyan, *Sibyl*, p. 8.

[200] Cited in Pamela Young, "Knowledge, Nation," p. 216.

[201] Quoted from a letter from Atriné Tonelian to Arpik Minasyan in *Sibyl*, p. 13.

[202] Sibyl, Azganver Hayuhi, in *Yerker*, p.161.

[203] Ibid., p. 161.

[204] Yesayian, along with other intellectuals, routinely referred to European countries as "kaghakirt" (civilized). See for example Zabel Yesayian, "Nor Kin." *Tsaghik* (April, 1903):141.

[205] Sibyl, *Azganver Hayuhi*, in *Yerker*, p. 160.

[206] Jayawardena, *Feminism and Nationalism in the Third World*, p. 14.

[207] Gerard Libaridian, "The Changing Armenian Self-Image in the Ottoman Empire: Rayahs and Revolutionaries," in *The Armenian Image in History and Literature*, ed. Richard G. Hovannisian (Malibu, California: Undena Publications, 1981), p. 162.

[208] Ronald Suny, Looking Toward Ararat, pp. 57–8.

[209] Ibid., p. 58.

[210] Anahit Harutiunian, "Hay Kanants' Sharzhumë 19[rd] darum ev 20[rd] dari skzbin" in *Feminizmi Tesut'iun ev Patmut'iun*, ed. Jemma Hasrat'ian, (Yerevan: The Association of Women with University Education, 1999), p. 379.

[211] Ibid., p. 379.

[212] For a description of the activities and women's organizations in Iran see Berberian, "Armenian Women in Turn-of-the-Century Iran: Education and Activism," pp. 77–92.

[213] Jasmin Rostam-Kolayi, "Foreign Education, the Women's Press, and the Discourse of Scientific Domesticity in Early Twentieth-Century Iran," in eds. Nikki Keddie and Rudi Mathee, *Iran and the Surrounding World: Interactions in Culture and Cultural Politics*, (Seattle: University of Washington Press, 2002), pp. 182–202. Rostam-Kolayi notes that the teaching of health and hygiene were taken over by government ministries in the Reza Shah period. The connection between women's organizations and government ministries are even clearer in the case of Argentina where a voluntary association, Sociedad de Beneficencia, through its work with public health and social policy, used the concept of "maternalism" to influence governmental policy and was eventually made a part of the ministry of the interior. See Karen Mead, "Beneficent Maternalism: Argentine Motherhood in Comparative Perspective, 1880–1920" in *Journal of Women's History* (Autumn 2000):pp. 120–145.

[214] Villa, Armenian Village Life Before 1914, p. 92.

[215] Zabel Yesayian, "Ink'nakensagrut'iun," p. 61.

[216] Sibyl, *Aghjkan më Sirtë* [A Girl's Heart], in *Yerker*, p. 414. All subsequent references to this novel come from this edition.

[217] Grigor Hakobian, ed. *Zapel ev Hrant Asaturner: Sirayin Namakner* [The Love Letters of Zabel and Hrant Asatur], (Yerevan: State Museum of Literature and Art, 2001), p. 75.

[218] Sibyl, *Aghjkan më Sirtë* [A Girl's Heart], in *Yerker*, p. 200.

[219] Ibid., p. 205.

[220] Ibid., p. 215.

[221] Ibid., p. 216.

[222] Ibid., p. 216.

[223] Ibid., p. 217.

[224] Ibid., p. 217.

[225] Ibid., p. 241–2.

[226] Ibid., p. 300.

[227] Ibid., p. 246–7.

[228] Ibid., p. 297–8.

[229] Joanna de Groot, "Coexisting and Conflicting Identities: Women and Nationalisms in Twentieth Century Iran," in *Nation, Empire, Colony*, p. 143.

[230] Sibyl, *Aghjkan më Sirtë* [A Girl's Heart], in *Yerker*, p. 195.

[231] Ibid., p. 307.

[232] Ibid., p. 200.

[233] Tess Cosslett, *Woman to Woman: Female Friendship in Victorian Fiction*, (Brighton: Harvester Press, 1988), p. 12.

[234] Sibyl, *Aghjkan më Sirtë* [A Girl's Heart], in *Yerker*, p. 448.

[235] Ibid., p. 198.

[236] Ibid., p. 208.

[237] Ibid., p. 199.

[238] Ibid., p. 200.

[239] Ibid., p. 203.

[240] Highgas, "Refugee Girl," p. 20.

[241] Sibyl, *Aghjkan më Sirtë* [A Girl's Heart], in *Yerker*, p. 326.

[242] Pamela Young, "Knowledge, Nation," p. 156.

[243] Sibyl, *Aghjkan më Sirtë* [A Girl's Heart], in *Yerker*, p. 332.

[244] Sibyl, *Dardzeal Feminizm* [Feminism Once Again], *Tsaghik* 16 (1904):122–3.

[245] Louise Nalbandian, *The Armenian Revolutionary Movement*, (Berkeley, University of California Press, 1963), p. 50.

[246] Zabel Yesayian, "Feminizmi Artiv" [On the Subject of Feminism], *Tsaghik* (April 17, 1904):8.

[247] Sibyl, *Aghjkan më Sirtë* [A Girl's Heart], in *Yerker*, p. 335.

[248] Ibid., p. 337.

[249] Ibid., p. 339.

[250] Ibid., p. 448.

[251] Ibid., p. 404.

[252] This is most evident in Krikor Zohrab's hostility to Dussap's novel, *Mayta*, in 1883, as detrimental to the Armenian family. Outward expressions of feminism were condemned in the Armenian press, as in Yenovk Armen's series of articles about women writers in 1911 in the pages of the New York based journal *Arakatz*.

[253] Zaruhi Galémk'earian, *Keank'is Chambén,* p. 336.

[254] Sibyl and Alpasan, *Magnis* [Magnet], (Constantinople, 1909), pp. 26–7.

[255] Tess Cosslett, *Woman to Woman*, p. 2.

[256] Mariam Khatisian, *Nor Chanaparhi Vray* [On a New Road], (St. Petersburg: I.N. Skorokhodovi Tparan, 1894), p. 13. All further references are to this edition.

[257] Suny, *Looking towards Ararat*, p. 57.

[258] Khatisian, *Nor Chanaparhi Vray* [On a New Road], p. 14.

[259] Ibid., pp. 16–17.

[260] Ibid., p. 18.

[261] For an in-depth discussion of the influence of Chernyshevsky's novel on Russian radical thought see Richard Stites, *The Women's Liberation Movement in Russia*, (Princeton, Princeton University Press, 1978), pp. 89–114.

[262] Mariam Khatisian, *Nor Chanaparhi Vray* [On a New Road], p. 20.

[263] Raffi, "Hay Kinë," [The Armenian Woman], *Yerkeri Zhoghovatsu* (Yerevan: Nairi, 1991), p. 142.

[264] Mariam Khatisian, *Nor Chanaparhi Vray* [On a New Road], p. 38.

[265] Ibid., p. 15.

[266] Ibid., p. 54.

[267] Ibid., p. 164.

[268] Bournoutian, *A History of the Armenian People, Vol.II*. pp. 113–116.

[269] Mariam Khatisian, *Nor Chanaparhi Vray* [On a New Road], p. 43.

[270] Ibid., p. 84.

[271] Zabel Yesayian, "Mer Kinerun" [To Our Women], *Tsaghik* (January 10, 1904):27.

[272] Suny, *Looking Toward Ararat*, pp. 64–6.

[273] Mariam Khatisian, *Nor Chanaparhi Vray* [On a New Road], p. 9.

[274] Ibid., p. 123.

[275] Suny states that this movement among Caucasian Armenians was influenced by Russian populism and its programme of "going to the people." Suny, p. 67.

[276] Mariam Khatisian, *Nor Chanaparhi Vray* [On a New Road], p. 255.

[277] Ibid., p. 29.

[278] Ibid., p. 72.

[279] Ibid., p. 88.

[280] Ibid., p. 89.

[281] Ibid., p. 96.

[282] Ibid., p. 257.

[283] Ibid., p. 10.

[284] Ibid., p. 44.

[285] Ibid., p. 164–5.

[286] Ibid., p. 161.

[287] Ibid., p. 173.

[288] Ibid., p. 176.

[289] Ibid., p. 176.

[290] Pamela Young, "Knowledge, Nation," p. 225.

[291] Mariam Khatisian, *Nor Chanaparhi Vray* [On a New Road], p. 178.

[292] Anahit Harutiunian, "Hay Kanants' Sharzhumë 19-rd darum ev 20-rd dari skzbin" in *Feminizmi Tesut'iun ev Patmut'iun*, p. 380.

[293] Mariam Khatisian, *Nor Chanaparhi Vray* [On a New Road], p. 179.

[294] Pamela Young notes that textbook publication in the Ottoman Empire increased in the late 1880s and 1890s. Young, "Knowledge, Nation," p. 206. Khatisian's novel, although printed in 1894, is set earlier, and therefore Liza's lament may be placed in the context of a newly developing publishing industry.

[295] Mariam Khatisian, *Nor Chanaparhi Vray* [On a New Road], p. 205. In fact, one of Khatisian's novels, *Dzhbakht Kin* [The Unfortunate Wife] (1899), was published through funding of a publication society, *Tiflisi Hayots' Hratarakch'akan Ënkerut'iun* [The Tiflis Armenian Publication Association].

[296] Mariam Khatisian, *Nor Chanaparhi Vray* [On a New Road], p. 207.

[297] Ibid., 208.

[298] A. Najmabadi, 'Crafting an Educated Housewife in Iran.' In *Remaking Women,* pp. 102–3.

[299] Mariam Khatisian, *Nor Chanaparhi Vray* [On a New Road], p. 181.

[300] Ibid., p. 222.

[301] Richard Stites, *The Women's Liberation Movement in Russia*, p.93.

[302] Mariam Khatisian, *Nor Chanaparhi Vray* [On a New Road], p. 245–6.

[303] Ibid., p. 246.

[304] Ibid., p. 262.

[305] Ibid., p. 263.

[306] Ibid., p. 97.

[307] Ibid., p. 225.

[308] Ibid., p. 230.

[309] Ibid., p. 263.

[310] For example, Zabel Yesayian wrote articles about Armenian women in journals published in Constantinople, Paris and New York, thereby reaching Armenian communities geographically distant from each other.

[311] Anahit Harutiunian, "Hay Kanants' Sharzhumë 19-rd darum ev 20-rd dari skzbin" in *Feminizmi Tesut'iun ev Patmut'iun*, p. 388.

[312] Ibid., p. 388.

[313] Haykanush Marrk viewed the journals she edited as part of this women's journal and editing movement. Haykanush Marrk, *Keank'n u Gortsë* [Life and Work], (Istanbul, 1954), pp. 40–41.

[314] Sona Zeitlian, "Pioneers of Women's Journalism in the Western Armenian Media, 1862–1968, in *Voices of Armenian Women*, ed. Barbara Mergeurian and Joy Renjilian-Burgy, (Belmont, Mass.: AIWA Press, 2000), pp. 124–5. See also Appendix for a biographical entry on Seza.

[315] Zaruhi Galémk'earian, p. 337. See Appendix for information on Galémk'earian.

[316] Zabel Yesayian, "Mer Kinerun" [To Our Women], *Tsaghik* (January 10, 1904):27.

[317] For biographical details of Beylerian's life see Appendix.

[318] Marie Beylerian, *Té Inch'u Ays T'ert'n Al* [Why this Journal?], *Artemis* (January, 1902):1.

[319] Valerie Abrahamsen, *Women and Worship at Philippi*, (Portland, Maine: Astarte Shell Press, 1995), p. 46.

[320] Ibid., p. 47.

[321] Kumari Jayawardena, *Nationalism and Feminism in the Third World*, p. 2.

[322] Nancy Cott, "Feminist Theory and Feminist Movements: The Past Before Us," in *What is Feminism?*, ed. Juliet Mitchell and Ann Oakley, (Oxford: Blackwell Press, 1986), p. 50.

[323] Beth Baron, *The Women's Awakening in Egypt*, (New Haven: Yale University Press, 1994), p. 103.

[324] Nancy Cott, "Feminist Theory and Feminist Movements: The Past Before Us," p. 60.

[325] Marie Beylerian, *Hay Knoj Harts' Masnavrapes t'é "Feminizmi" Pehanj* [The Armenian Woman Question or the Demands of "Feminism], *Artemis* (December 1903):305.

[326] See for example Karen Offen's discussion of historical feminisms as politics not philosophy or "paradoxes." Karen Offen, *European Feminisms, 1700–1950: A Political History*, (Stanford: Stanford University Press, 2000).

[327] Marie Beylerian, "Hay Knoj Harts' Masnavrapes t'é "Feminizmi" Pehanj," p. 306.

[328] Ibid., p. 307.

[329] James McMillan, *France and Women*, (London: Routledge Press, 2000), pp. 16–18.

[330] Marie Beylerian, "Aknark më Hay Knoj Ants'ealin Vray" [A Glance at the Armenian Woman's Past], *Artemis* (March 1902):66.

[331] Ibid., pp. 66–7.

[332] Ibid., p. 67.

[333] Ibid., p. 68.

[334] Villa, *Armenian Village Life Before 1914*, p. 92.

[335] Marie Beylerian, *Zavakë* [The Child], *Artemis* (February, 1902): 36–7.

[336] Elise Hagopian Taft, *Rebirth*, (Plandome, N.Y.: New Age Publishers, 1981), p. 4.

[337] A. Najmabadi, "Crafting an Educated Housewife in Iran" in *Remaking Women*, p.102.

[338] Christine Srpuhi Jafferian, *Winds of Destiny: An Immigrant Girl's Odyssey*, (Belmont, Mass.: Armenian Heritage Press, 1993), p. 159. Jafferian's mother-in-law from Kharpert always bathed her grandchildren, according to Kharpert custom.

[339] Beylerian, *Kesurë* (*Gavarrakan Keank'é*) [The Mother-in-Law: A Tale from Provincial Life], *Artemis* (March 1902):88–96.

[340] Ibid., p. 92.

[341] Ibid., p. 91.

[342] Nancy Cott, *Public Vows*, (Cambridge, Mass.: Harvard University Press, 2000), p. 10.

[343] Mohamad Tavakoli-Targhi, *Refashioning Iran: Orientalism, Occidentalism and Historiography*, (Basingstoke, Hampshire: Palgrave, 2001), pp. 64–5.

[344] Villa, *Armenian Village Life Before 1914*, pp. 23–6.

[345] Ibid., p. 29.

[346] Lucy Garnett, *The Women of Turkey And Their Folklore*, (London: David Nutt, 1893), p. 197.

[347] A. Najmabadi, "Crafting an Educated Housewife in Iran" in *Remaking Women*, pp. 102–3.

[348] Barbara Mergeurian, "The Beginnings of Secondary Education for Armenian Women, p. 104.

[349] Mazian, Florence. "The Patriarchal Armenian Family System: 1914." *Armenian Review* 36 (Winter1983):20.

[350] Sibyl, *Harse* [The Daughter-in-Law], (Boston: Hayrenik Press, 1938), p. 10.

[351] Ibid., p. 33.

[352] Anahit Harutiunian, "Hay Kanants' Sharzhumë 19-rd darum ev 20-rd dari skzbin" in *Feminizmi Tesut'iun ev Patmut'iun*, p. 369.

[353] Beylerian, *Zavakë*, p. 35.

[354] Ibid., p. 35.

[355] Ibid., p. 36.

[356] Marie Beylerian, *Té Inch'u Ays T'ert'n Al*, pp.2-3.

[357] Ibid., p. 3.

[358] A. Najmabadi, "Crafting an Educated Housewife in Iran" in *Remaking Women*, p. 113.

[359] Beylerian, *Zavakë*, p. 37.

[360] Beylerian, *Kesurë (Gavarrakan Keank'é)*, p.92.

[361] Matteos Mamurian, "Hrrip'simé Krt'aser Ënkerut'iun," *Arevelian Mamul* (May 1881):182.

[362] Villa, *Armenian Village Life Before 1914*, p. 71.

[363] Beylerian, "Aknark më Hay Knoj Ants'ealin Vray," p. 68.

[364] Beylerian, *Dprotsë* [The School], *Artemis* (April, 1902):98.

[365] Ibid., p. 98.

[366] See for example Kerop Bedoukian's account of his family following deportation in 1915, when the knowledge of how to weave cloth by handloom by a female cousin, assisted in the family's survival. It also had a positive psychological affect on the woman who possessed the skills. Bedoukian says: "Elizabeth, (my father's sister's daughter) was about twenty-five, with her husband's whereabouts unknown, and her child dead on the road, she was apathetic and did not care what happened next. When she realized that through her trade all of us could be saved she suddenly came alive." Kerop Bedoukian, *The Urchin*, (London: John Murray, 1978), p. 55.

[367] Beylerian, *Dprotsë* [The School], p. 97.

[368] Zabel Yesayian, "Mer Kinerun." *Tsaghik* (January 10, 1904):26.

[369] Jan Wellington, "Blurring the Borders of Nation and Gender: Mary Wollstonecraft's Character (R)evolution," in Rebellious Hearts: British Women Writers and the French Revolution, ed. Adriana Craciun and Kari E. Lokke, (Albany, New York: SUNY, 2001), p. 46.

[370] Beylerian, *Dprotsë* [The School], p. 98.

[371] Ibid., p. 100.

[372] Dussap, *Mayta*, p. 27.

[373] Anahit Harutiunian, "Hay Kanants' Sharzhumë 19-rd darum ev 20-rd dari skzbin" in *Feminizmi Tesut'iun ev Patmut'iun*, p. 380.

[374] Sibyl, "Azkanver Hayuhik" in *Yerker*, p. 161.

[375] Naomi Topalian, Dust to Destiny, (Watertown, MA: Baikar Publications, 1986), pp. 9,19.

[376] Beylerian, *Dprotsë* [The School], p. 99.

[377] Ibid., p. 99.

[378] Ibid., p. 100.

[379] A. Najmabadi, "Crafting an Educated Housewife in Iran" in *Remaking Women*, p. 102.

[380] Pamela Young, "Knowledge, Nation," p. 234.

[381] Najmabadi, "Crafting an Educated Housewife in Iran" in *Remaking Women*, p. 114.

[382] Anahit Harutiunian, "Hay Kanants' Sharzhumë 19-rd darum ev 20-rd dari skzbin," p. 376.

[383] Pamela Young, "Knowledge, Nation," p. 106.

[384] Beylerian, *Dprotsë* [The School], p. 100.

[385] Pamela Young, "Knowledge, Nation," p. 149.

[386] Beylerian, *Dprotsë* [The School], p. 100.

[387] Beylerian, *Ëntérts'anut'iunë Hay Kanants' Mej* [Reading Among Armenian Women], *Artemis,* (October/November, 1903):259.

[388] Marie Beylerian, *Ashkhatelu Pétk'ë Knoj Hamar* [Work is Necessary for Women], *Artemis* (May/June, 1902):130.

[389] Ibid., p. 131.

[390] Ibid., p. 132.

[391] Ibid., p. 132.

[392] Villa, *Armenian Village Life Before 1914,* pp. 71, 48.

[393] Yesayian, "Silihtari Partéznerë," in *Yerker*, p. 432.

[394] Beylerian, *Yerku Khosk'Mej Lav Ch'ëmbrrnoghnerun* [A few words to those who misunderstand us] *Artemis* (July/August 1902):196.

[395] Dussap, "Arak'sia kam Varzhuhin" in *Yerker*, p. 375.

[396] Sibyl, *Aghjkan më Sirtë*, p. 375.

[397] Krikor Zohrab, "Postal" [Whore] *Yerkeri Zoghovatsu*, Vol.1. (Yerevan: Haypethrat, 1962), 3–19.

[398] Beylerian, *Yerku Khosk'Mej Lav Ch'ëmbrrnoghnerun* [A few words to those who misunderstand us], p. 195.

[399] Ibid., p. 196.

[400] Quoted in Barbara Mergeurian, "The Beginnings of Secondary Education for Armenian Women," p. 113.

[401] Ibid., p. 113.

[402] Pamela Young, "Knowledge, Nation," p. 93.

[403] Mary Patrick, *A Bosporus Adventure*, (California: Stanford University Press, 1934), p. 233.

[404] Beth Baron, *The Women's Awakening in Egypt*, p. 155.

[405] Beylerian, *Yerku Khosk'Mej Lav Ch'ëmbrrnoghnerun* [A few words to those who misunderstand us], p. 197.

[406] Ronald Suny, *Looking Toward Ararat*, p. 65.

[407] George Bournoutian, *A History of the Armenian People*. Vol.2., p. 120.

[408] Kevork Bardakjian, *A Reference Guide to Modern Armenian Literature 1500–1920*, p. 180.

[409] Suny, *Looking Toward Ararat*, p. 10.

[410] Siamanto, *Prayer to Anahid on the Feast of Navasart*, translated in *Anthology of Armenian Poetry*, eds. Der Hovanessian, Diana and Marzbed Margossian, (New York: Columbia University Press, 1978), pp. 138–140.

[411] Shushanik Kurghinian, *Het Tar k'o Khach'ë* [Begone with your cross] in *Yerkeri Zhoghovatsu*, (Yerevan: Haypethrat, 1947), pp. 161–4.

[412] Suny, *Looking Toward Ararat*, p. 69.

[413] Hovhannes Ghazarian, *Shushanik Kurghinian*, pp. 9–10.

[414] Details of Shushanik Kurghinian's life in the absence of any other source come from her Soviet biographer, Hovhannes Ghazarian's *Shushanik Kurghinian*, (Yerevan: Haykakan SSR GA Hratarakch'ut'iun, 1955), p. 13.

[415] Suny, *Looking Toward Ararat*, pp. 72–3.

[416] Ibid., p. 74.

[417] Suny notes the youthfulness of many of the Caucasian Armenian intelligentsia. *Looking Toward Ararat*, pp. 65–67. In addition, as we have seen, Sibyl was only seventeen, when she founded *Azganvér Hayuhyats' Ënkerut'iun* in the Ottoman Empire, with eight female classmates.

[418] Sheila Fitzpatrick, *The Russian Revolution 1917—1932*, (Oxford: Oxford University Press, 1982), p. 11.

[419] Ibid., pp. 27—29.

[420] Kurghinian, *Hangst'rek' Jaherë* [Extinguish the Lamps], in *Yerkeri Zhoghovatsu*, pp. 111—12.

[421] Ghazarian, *Shushanik Kurghinian*, p. 20.

[422] Ghazarian, "Shushanik Kurghinian" in *Hay Nor Grakanutian Patmutiun*, Vol.5. (Yerevan: Haykakan SSR Gitutiunneri Akademiayi Hratarakch'ut'iun, 1979), p. 939.

[423] Ghazarian, *Shushanik Kurghinian*, p. 26.

[424] Kurghinian, *Geghjkuhu Mormuk'ë* [The village Girl's Lament], in *Yerkeri Zhoghovatsu*, p. 97.

[425] Bardakjian, *A Reference Guide to Modern Armenian Literature 1500–1920* p. 181.

[426] Hovhannes Toumanian, "Maron" [Maro] in *Entir Yerker*, (Yerevan: Sovetakan Grogh Hratarakch'ut'iun, 1978), pp. 144–9.

[427] Dussap, *Siranush* in *Yerker*, p. 198.

[428] Kurghinian, *Artsvi Serë* [Eagle's Love], in *Yerkeri Zhoghovatsu*, p. 250.

[429] Srbouhi Hairpetian, *A History of Armenian Literature: From Ancient Times to the Nineteenth Century*, (Delmar, New York: Caravan Books, 1995), p. 357.

[430] Marie Beylerian, "Aknark më Hay Knoj Ants'ealin Vray," p. 67.

[431] Kurghinian, Menk'él Mianank' [Let's Unite], in *Yerkeri Zhoghovatsu*, p. 242.

[432] Sheila Fitzpatrick, *The Russian Revolution 1917–1932*, p. 21.

[433] Parlakian and Cowe, *Modern Armenian Drama*, p. 130.

[434] Kurghinian, *Banvorner* [The Workers], in *Yerkeri Zhoghovatsu*, pp. 175–6.

[435] Suny, *Looking Toward Ararat*, p. 82.

[436] Richard Stites, *The Women's Liberation Movement in Russia,* pp. 250–7.

[437] See Anayis, *Houshers*; Zaruhi Galémk'earian, *Keank'is Chambén*.

[438] Kurghinian, *Aghjikë* [The Girl], in *Yerkeri Zhoghovatsu*, pp. 404–5.

[439] Kurghinian, *Banvoruhin* [The Female Worker], in *Yerkeri Zhoghovatsu*, pp. 265–6.

[440] Kurghinian, *Banvoruhin* [The Female Worker], in *Yerkeri Zhoghovatsu*, p. 361.

[441] Sona Zeitlian, *Hay Knoj Dere Hay Heghapokhakan Sharzhman Mej* [Armenian Women's Role in the Armenian Revolutionary Movement], (Los Angeles: Hraztan Sarkis Zeitlian Publications, 1992) pp. 147–9.

[442] Yesayian, *Le rôle de la femme arménienne pendant la guerre*, Revue des Études Arméniennes, (Tome II, 1922):134.

[443] Suny, *Looking Toward Ararat*, p. 126.

[444] Bournoutian, *History of the Armenian People*, Vol.2., p. 135.

[445] Kurghinian, *Gaght'akan Kin* [The Refugee Woman], in *Yerkeri Zhoghovatsu*, p. 529.

[446] Kurghinian, *Gaght'akan Ëntanik'ë* [The Refugee Family], in *Yerkeri Zhoghovatsu*, p. 531.

[447] Yesayian, *Silihtari Partéznerë* [Gardens of Silihtar], in *Yerker*, p. 528.

[448] Zabel Yesayian, "Ink'nakensagrut'iun," p. 74.

[449] James Etmekjian, *The French Influence*, p. 94.

[450] By subjectivity I mean the development of selfhood, which is independent of the roles, such as mother and wife, which a women may play.

[451] Chouchik Dasnabédian, *Zabel Yesayian ou l'univers lumineux de la littérature*, (Antelias, Lebanon: Catholicossat Arménien de Cilicie, 1988), p. 16.

[452] Yesayian, Hrant, "Im Mayrikë." *Sovetakan Grakanut'iun* 3 (1978):86–90.

[453] From the Zabel Yesayian archive, Museum of Literature and Art, Yerevan, document no.10.

[454] Yesayian, "Ink'nakensagrut'iun," p. 60.

[455] Yesayian, *Inchpes em grum kam inchpes em uzum grel* [How I Write or How I would Like to Write], *Grakan Serund* (Yerevan, No. 6–7, 1934):42.

[456] Ibid., p. 43.

[457] Yesayian, Hrant, "Im Mayrikë," p. 91.

[458] Sevak Arzumanyan, *Zabel Yesayian: Keank'ë ev Gortsë*, p. 26.

[459] Hagop Oshagan, *Hamapatker Arevmtahay Grakanutyan* p. 245.

[460] Yesayian, "Ink'nakensagrut'iun," pp. 67, 74.

[461] Yesayian, Silihtari Partéznerë [Gardens of Silihtar], in *Yerker*, p. 527.

[462] For example, Serpouhi Christine Jafferian writes that her sister who was a good student in Smyrna before 1915, was offered a scholarship to go to France to continue her studies. The girl's father, however, fearful of what might befall her in France, refused permission for her to study abroad. Serpouhi Christine Jafferian, *Winds of Destiny*, p. 28.

[463] Zabel Yesayian, "Mardë" [The Man], *Masis*, (March 26, 1905): 68.

[464] Ibid., p. 68.

[465] Ibid., p. 69.

[466] Ibid., p. 69.

[467] Marceline J. Hutton, *Russian and West European Women, 1860–1939*, (Lanham, Maryland: Rowman and Littlefield, 2001), p. 5.

[468] Yesayian, "Knoj Tiparner: Rus Usanoghuhin Parizi Mej." *Tsaghik* (June 14, 1903):234.

[469] Richard Stites, *The Women's Liberation Movement in Russia*, pp. 131–2.

[470] Yesayian, "Mardë"[The Man], p. 69.

[471] Ibid., p. 70.

[472] Ibid., p. 72.

[473] Ibid., p. 73.

[474] Ibid., p. 69. Yesayian read Poe's works in French, the translation of which had been done by Baudelaire, whose poetry Yesayian also mentioned reading in this period.

[475] Cora Sandel, *Alberta and Freedom*. Translated by Elizabeth Rokkan, (London: Peter Owen Ltd., 1963), p. 18.

[476] Ibid., p. 11.

[477] Mary Maynard, "Privilege and Patriarchy: Feminist Thought in the Nineteenth Century," in *Sexuality and Subordination*, ed. Susan Mendus and Jane Rendall, (London: Routledge, 1989), p. 232.

[478] Yesayian, "Mardë" [The Man], p. 69.

[479] Yesayian gave this information about the Russian students she lived next to in a separate article: "Knoj Tiparner: Rus Usanoghuhin Parizi Mej." *Tsaghik* (June 14, 1903):234.

[480] Yesayian, "Mardë" [The Man], p. 68.

[481] Marie Beylerian, *Artemis* (July–August 1902 No.7–8):196. Although Beylerian was critical of sending female students to Paris, which she viewed as a sinful city, she advocated sending Armenian girls to Belgium or Switzerland. Serpoohi Christine Jafferian mentions that her sister was offered a scholarship to study in Paris, but was forbidden to go by her father. Jafferian, *Winds of Destiny*, p. 28. Peter Balakian mentions that his grandmother, born in 1889, graduated from the American Women's College in Constantinople, before doing graduate work in Chartes. Peter Balakian, *Black Dog of Fate* (New York: Broadway Books, 1997), p. 86.

[482] Yesayian, *Silihtari Partéznerë* [Gardens of Silihtar], in *Yerker*, p. 527.

[483] *Spasman Srahin Mej* [In the Waiting Room] appeared in serial form weekly over four months in 1903 in the journal *Tsaghik*. It has never been reprinted and all subsequent page references refer to the issues of *Tsaghik*.

[484] Irene Szyliowicz, *Pierre Loti and the Oriental Woman,* (Basingstoke, Hampshire: Macmillan Press, 1988), p. 15.

[485] Ibid., p. 52.

[486] Vahe Oshagan, "Cosmopolitanism in West Armenian Literature," *Review of National Literatures* 13 (1984):199.

[487] Yesayian, "Nor Kin." *Tsaghik* (April, 1903):141.

[488] Yesayian, "In the Waiting Room," *Tsaghik* (October 2, 1903):391.

[489] Joanna De Groot, "'Sex' and 'Race' The Construction of Language and Image in the Nineteenth Century," in *Sexuality and Subordination*, ed. Susan Mendus and Jane Rendall, (London: Routledge, 1989), p. 105.

[490] Szyliowicz, *Pierre Loti and the Oriental Woman*, p. 55.

[491] Yesayian, "In the Waiting Room," *Tsaghik* (October 2, 1903):391.

[492] Ibid., 391

[493] Yesayian, "In the Waiting Room," *Tsaghik* ( December 20,1903):500.

[494] See Yesayian, *Hogis Ak'sorial*, in *Yerker* (Yerevan: Haypethrat, 1959), p. 133. And *Mardë*, p. 68.

[495] Yesayian, "In the Waiting Room," *Tsaghik* (November 28, 1903):475.

[496] Yesayian, "In the Waiting Room," *Tsaghik* (December 20, 1903):501.

[497] Yesayian, "In the Waiting Room," *Tsaghik* (September 25, 1903):381.

[498] Yesayian, *Inchpes em grum kam inchpes em uzum grel*, p. 43. As is evident from the title of this essay, it was written in Eastern Armenian; following Yesayian's settling in Yerevan in 1933, she began to experiment with writing in Eastern rather than her native Western Armenian.

[499] Ibid., p. 43.

[500] Yesayian, "In the Waiting Room," *Tsaghik* (October 16, 1903):420.

[501] Yesayian, "In the Waiting Room," *Tsaghik* (October 24, 1903):434.

[502] Yesayian, Silihtari Partéznerë [Gardens of Silihtar], in *Yerker*, p. 393.

[503] Alice Muggerditchian Shipley, *We Walked Then Ran*, (Phoenix, Arizona: By the author, 1983), p. 11–12.

[504] Margaret Connor Versluysen, "Midwives, medical men, and 'poor women labouring of child:' lying-in hospitals in 18th century London," in *Women, Health and Reproduction,* ed. Helen Roberts, (London: Routledge and Kegan Paul, 1981), p. 23.

[505] Ibid., p. 40.

[506] Yesayian, "In the Waiting Room," *Tsaghik* (September 25, 1903):383.

[507] Ibid., p. 383.

[508] Yesayian, "In the Waiting Room," *Tsaghik* (October 24, 1903):434.

[509] Yesayian, "In the Waiting Room," *Tsaghik* (November 21, 1903):467.

[510] Yesayian, "In the Waiting Room," *Tsaghik* (October 16,1903):419.

[511] Yesayian, "In the Waiting Room," *Tsaghik* (December 5, 1903):484–5.

[512] Cited in Susan Sellers, *Language and Sexual Difference,* (Basingstoke, Hampshire: Macmillan Press, 1991), p. 27.

[513] Claire Goldberg Moses, *French Feminism in the Nineteenth Century*, (Albany N.Y.: State University of New York Press, 1984), p. 19.

[514] Ibid., p. 19.

[515] Ibid., p. 18.

[516] Women's responsibility for children's care, especially the care of illegitimate children, is portrayed in a number of novels by French women in the same period Yesayian wrote *In the Waiting Room*. Jennifer Waelti-Walters, *Feminist, Novelists of the Belle Époque,* (Bloomington and Indianapolis: Indiana University Press, 1990), p. 54.

[517] See for example, Rubina Peroomian, *Literary Responses to Catastrophe* (Atlanta, Georgia: Scholars Press, 1993), pp. 89–116. Marc Nichanian, *Writers of Disaster* (Princeton and London: Gomidas Institute, 2002), pp. 188-242.

[518] Zabel Yesayian, *Le rôle de la femme arménienne pendant la guerre,* p. 121.

[519] Marlene Heinemann, *Gender and Destiny: Women Writers and the Holocaust,* (New York: Greenwood Press, 1986), p. 2.

[520] Yesayian, *Le rôle de la femme arménienne pendant la guerre,* p. 125.

[521] This discussion on "Zhoghovurdi më Hogevark'ë" [Agony of a People] is based on a paper I presented at the MESA conference 1998.

[522] Yesayian, *Le rôle de la femme arménienne pendant la guerre,* p. 134.

[523] Yesayian, [To Our Women], *Tsaghik* (January 10, 1904):27.

[524] Yesayian, "Hay Kinë Sahmanadrut'enén Yetk'ë." [The Armenian Woman After the Constitution], *Arakatz* (July 6, 1911):99–100.

[525] Yesayian, *Le rôle de la femme arménienne pendant la guerre,* p. 124.

[526] Yesayian, "Zhoghovurdi më Hogevark'ë." *Gorts.* (1917):p. 68.

[527] Ibid., pp. 69–70.

[528] Yesayian, *Le rôle de la femme arménienne pendant la guerre,* p. 133.

[529] Yesayian, "Zhoghovurdi më Hogevark'ë" [The Agony of A People], p. 59.

[530] Yesayian, "Zhoghovurdi më Hogevark'ë" [The Agony of A People], p. 55 and *Le rôle de la femme arménienne pendant la guerre,* p.132.

[531] Yesayian, *Le rôle de la femme arménienne pendant la guerre,* p. 132.

[532] Elishe, *History of Vardan and the Armenian War*, translated by Robert Thomson, p. 246.

[533] Yesayian, *Le rôle de la femme arménienne pendant la guerre,* pp. 134–35.

[534] This encounter was recounted by Rouben Zarian. Cited in Zabel Yessayan, *The Gardens of Silihtar and Other Writings,* p.20.

[535] Yesayian, *Hogis Ak'sorial* [My Soul in Exile] in *Yerker,* p. 131.

[536] Ibid., p. 132.

[537] Yesayian, *Hogis Ak'sorial* [My Soul in Exile] in *Yerker,* p. 133.

[538] Ibid., pp. 134–5.

[539] Ibid., p. 134–5.

[540] Ibid., p. 154.

[541] Ibid., p. 143.

[542] Ibid., p. 146.

[543] Ibid., pp. 146–7.

[544] Ibid., p. 170.

[545] Ibid., p. 171.

[546] See Appendix for translations of Zabel Yesayian's works.

[547] Rachel Feldhay Brenner, *Writing as Resistance: Four Women Writers Confronting the Holocaust,* Pennsylvania State University Press, 1996, p. 5.

[548] Vahan Totovents, *Scenes from an Armenian Childhood,* translated by Misha Kudian (London: Oxford University Press, 1962). This phrase is repeated several times, see p. 136.

[549] To this day it is difficult to determine if Zabel and Dikran Yesayian were divorced. It is claimed that they were, but as late as 1978, their son, Hrant denied this. Hrant Yessayian, "Im Mayrikë."

[550] Zabel Yesayian, *Mer Kinerë* [Our Women ], *Tsaghik* (April 26, 1903):150.

[551] Vahe Oshagan, "Modernization in Western Armenian Literature," p. 67.

[552] Ibid., p. 68.

[553] Sally Ledger, *The New Woman: Fiction and feminism at the fin de siècle,* (Manchester: Manchester University Press, 1997), p. 27.

[554] Jane Eldridge Miller, *Rebel Women: Feminism, Modernism and the Edwardian Novel,* (London: Virago Press, 1994), p. 8.

[555] Ibid., p. 7.

[556] Serpoohi Christine Jafferian, *Winds of Destiny: An Immigrant Girl's Odyssey,* pp. 7–8 and Dirouhi Kouymjian Highgas, *Refugee Girl,* pp. 20–2.

[557] Cited in Sona Zeitlian, "Pioneers of Women's Journalism in the Western Armenian Media, 1862–1968," p. 126.

[558] Zabel Yesayian, "Mer Kinnerun," p. 27

[559] Cited in Sona Zeitlian, "Pioneers of Women's Journalism in the Western Armenian Media, 1862–1968", pp. 126–7.

[560] Krikor Beledian, *Cinquante Ans de Littérature Arménienne en France*, (Paris: CNRS Editions, 2001), pp. 252–4.

[561] Lorne Shirinian, *Survivor Memoirs of the Armenian Genocide*, (Reading, England: Taderon Press, 1999), pp. 11–12.

[562] The best account of the Stalinist destruction of Armenian literary leaders is Marc Nichanian's *Writers of Disaster*, (Gomidas Institute, 2002).

[563] Kevork Bardakjian, *A Reference Guide to Modern Armenian Literature 1500–1920*, p. 202.

[564] Biographical details about Varsenik Aghasian are found in Hayk Khach'atryan, *Hayuhiner*, (Yerevan: Zangak, 2001), p. 18.

# BIBLIOGRAPHY

**Primary Texts**

Anayis, *Hushers*. Paris, 1949.

Abgariants', Tigranuhi. "Nor Jughayi Kananats' Krt'ut'iunë." *Artemis* 2–3, (February/March 1903).

Armen, Yenovk. "Hay Kin Groghner." *Arakatz* (1911).

Beylerian, Marie. "Té Inch'u Ays T'ert'n Al." *Artemis* (January 1902).

_____. "Zavakë." *Artemis* (February 1902).

_____. "Aknark më Hay Knoj Ants'ealin Vray." *Artemis* (March 1902).

_____. "Kesurë (Gavarrakan Keank'é)." *Artemis* (March 1902).

_____. "Dprotsë." *Artemis* (April 1902).

_____. "Ashkhatelu Pétk'ë Knoj Hamar." *Artemis* (May/June 1902).

_____. "Yerku Khosk'Mej Lav Ch'ëmbrrnoghnerun." *Artemis* (July/August 1902).

_____. "Ëntérts'anut'iunë Hay Kanants' Mej." *Artemis* (October/November 1903).

_____. "Hay Knoj Harts' Masnavrapes t'é "Feminizmi" Pehanj." *Artemis* (December 1903).

Dussap, Srpuhi. *Yerker*. Yerevan: Sovetakan Grogh Hratarakch'ut'iun, 1981.

Galémk'earian, Zarouhi. *Keank'is Chambén*. Ant'ilias, 1952.

Kirishchian, Levon. "Hay Gragituhin Fransakan Grakanut'ian Mej." *Masis* 17 (June 18, 1905).

Khatisian, Mariam. *Nor Chanaparhi Vray*. St. Petersburg: I.N. Skorokhodovi Tparan, 1894.

_____. *P'esay Vorsoghner*. Tiflis, Tparan M.D. Rrotineants', 1894.

_____. *Dzhbakht Kin*. Tiflis, Tparan M.D. Rrotineants', 1899.

Kurghinian, Shushanik. *Yerkeri Zhoghovatsu*. Yerevan: Haypethrat, 1947.

Hakobian, Grigor, ed. *Zapel ev Hrant Asaturner: Sirayin Namakner*. Yerevan: State Musuem of Literature and Art, 2001.

Marrk, Haykanush. *Keank'n u Gortsë*. Istanbul, 1954.

"Mer Kin Groghnerë." *Masis* 30 (October 1, 1905).

Raffi, "Hay Kinë. In Raffi: *Yerkeri Zhoghovatsu*. Yerevan: Nairi, 1991.

_____. *Khent'ë*. Beirut: Hamazgayin Tparan, 1981.

Sibyl. "Dardzeal Feminizm." *Tsaghik* (March 1904).

Sibyl and Alp'asan. *Magnis*. Constantinople, 1909.

_____. *Yerker*. Yerevan: Hayastan Hratarakch'ut'iun. 1965.

_____. *Harse*. Boston: Hayrenik Press, 1938.

Teodik, Arshakuhi. *Amis Më i Kilikia*. Constantinople: V and H Der Nersesian, 1910.

"Tikin Srpuhi Dussapi Mahvan Tarelitsin Artiv." *Artemis* 1 (January 1902):24–26.

Yesayian, Hrant. "Im Mayrikë." *Sovetakan Grakanut'iun* 3 (1978):84–95.

Yesayian, Zabel. "Nor Kin." *Tsaghik* (April 1903).

_____. "Mer Kinerë." *Tsaghik* (April 26, 1903).

_____. "Knoj Tiparner: Rus Usanoghuhin Parizi Mej." *Tsaghik* (June 14, 1903).

_____. "Spasman Srahin Mej." *Tsaghik* (1903–1904).

_____. "Mer Kinerun." *Tsaghik* (January 10, 1904).

_____. "Feminizmi Artiv." *Tsaghik* (April 17, 1904).

_____. "Mardë." *Masis* (March 26, 1905).

_____. "Knoj Datin Noragoyn Yerevoyt'nerë." *Arakatz* (May 25, 1911).

_____. "Hay Kinë Sahmanadrut'enén Yetk'ë." *Arakatz* (July 6, 1911).

_____. "Zhoghovurdi më Hogevark'ë." *Gorts* (1917).

_____. "Le rôle de la femme arménienne pendant la guerre." *Revue des Études Arméniennes* (Tome II, 1922).

_____. *Verjin Bazhakë*. Constantinople, 1924.

_____. Inchpes em grum kam inchpes em uzum grel. *Grakan*

*Serund* (Yerevan, No. 6–7, 1934).

_____. *Yerker*. Yerevan: Haypethrat, 1959.

_____. *Yerb Aylevs Chen Sirer*. Beirut: Chirag, 1972.

_____. "Ink'nakensagrut'iun." *Sovetakan Grakanut'iun* (1979).

_____. *Namakner*. Yerevan: Yerevani Betakan Hamalsarani Hratarakch'ut'iun, 1977.


**General Works**


Abrahamsen, Valerie. *Women and Worship at Philippi*. Portland, Maine: Astarte Shell Press, 1995.

Abu-Lughod, Lila, ed. *Remaking Women: Feminism and Modernity in the Middle East*. Princeton, New Jersey: Princeton University Press, 1998.

Arzumanyan, Sevak. *Zabel Yesayian: Keank'e ev Gortsë*. Yerevan: Haykakan SSR Gitutiunneri Akademiayi Hratarakch'ut'iun, 1965.

Balakian, Peter. *Black Dog of Fate*. New York: Broadway Books, 1997.

Bardakjian, Kevork. *A Reference Guide to Modern Armenian Literature 1500–1920*. Detroit: Wayne State University Press, 2000.

Baron, Beth. *The Women's Awakening in Egypt*. New Haven: Yale University Press, 1994.

Barsoumian, Hagop. "The Dual Role of the Armenian Amira Class within the Ottoman Government andthe Armenian Millet (1750–1850)." In *Christians & Jews in the Ottoman Empire*. Vol.1., ed. Benjamin Braude and Bernard Lewis, 171–184. New York: Holmes and Meier Publishers, 1982.

Basmajian, Krikor H. *Social and Religious Life in the Orient*. New York: American Tract Society, 1890.

Bedoukian, Kerop. *The Urchin*. London: John Murray, 1978.

Bedrossian, Rev. Matthias. *New Dictionary Armenian-English*. Lebanon: Libraire du Liban, reprint, 1985.

Beledian, Krikor. *Cinquante Ans de Littérature Arménienne en France*. Paris: CNRS Editions, 2001.

Berberian, Houri. "Armenian Women in Turn-of-the-Century Iran: Education and Activism." In *Iran and Beyond*, ed. Rudi Mathee and Beth Baron. Costa Mesa, California: Mazda Publishers, 2000.

Betterton, Rosemary. "Women Artists, Modernity and Suffrage Cultures in Britain and Germany 1890–1920." In *Women Artists and Modernism*, ed. Katy Deepwell. Manchester: Manchester University Press, 1998.

Bland, Lucy. *Banishing the Beast: English Feminism And Sexual Morality 1885–1914*. London: Penguin Books, 1995.

Bournoutian, George. *A History of the Armenian People*. Vol.2. Costa Mesa, California: Mazda Publishers, 1994.

Brenner, Rachel Feldhay. *Writing as Resistance: Four Women Writers Confronting the Holocaust*. Pennslyvania State University Press, 1997.

Cosslett, Tess. *Woman to Woman: Female Friendship in Victorian Fiction*. Brighton: Harvester Press,1988.

Cott, Nancy. "Feminist Theory and Feminist Movements: The Past Before Us." In *What is Feminism?*, ed. Juliet Mitchell and Ann Oakley, 49-62. Oxford: Blackwell Press, 1986.

_____. *Public Vows*, Cambridge, Mass.: Harvard University Press, 2000.

Dasnabédian, Chouchik. *Zabel Essayan ou l'univers lumineux de la littérature*. Antelias, Lebanon: Catholicossat Arménien de Cilicie, 1988.

De Groot, Joanna. "'Sex' and 'Race': The Construction of Language and Image in the Nineteenth Century." In *Sexuality and Subordination*, ed. Susan Mendus and Jane Rendall, 89–128. London: Routledge, 1989.

_____. "Coexisting and Conflicting Identities: Women and Nationalisms in Twentieth Century Iran." In *Nation, Empire, Colony*, ed. Ruth Roach Pierson and Nupur Chaudhuri. Bloomington: Indiana University Press, 1998.

Der Hovanessian, Diana and Marzbed Margossian, eds. *Anthology of Armenian Poetry*. New York: Columbia University Press, 1978.

Elishe. *History of Vardan and the Armenian War*. Translation and

Park, California: Sage Publications, 1992.

Highgas, Dirouhi Kouymjian. *Refugee Girl*. Watertown, Mass.: Baikar Publications, 1985.

Hovanessian, Sebouh. Introduction. In *Armenian Women of the Stage*, by Alice Navasargian. California, 1999.

Hovannisian, Richard G. "The Armenian Question in the Ottoman Empire, 1876–1914." In *The Armenian People from Ancient to Modern Times*. Vol.1. ed. Richard Hovannisian, 203–238. New York: St. Martin's Press, 1997.

_____. "The Historical Dimensions of the Armenian Question, 1878–1923," in *The Armenian Genocide in Perspective*, ed. Richard G. Hovannisian, 19–41. New Brunswick, N.J.: Transaction Books, 1986.

Hutton, Marcelline J. *Russian and West European Women, 1860–1939*. Lanham, Maryland: Rowman and Littlefield, 2001.

Jafferian, Serpoohi Christine. *Winds of Destiny: An Immigrant Girl's Odyssey*. Belmont, Mass.: Armenian Heritage Press, 1993.

*Jamanakakits Hayots Lezvi Batsatrakan Bararan*. Yerevan: Haykakan SSH Gitutiunneri Akademia, 1969.

Jayawardena, Kumari. *Feminism and Nationalism in the Third World*. London: Zed Books, 1986.

Kalajian, Hannah. *Hannah's Story: Escape from Genocide in Turkey to Success in America*. Belmont,Mass.: Armenian Heritage Press, 1990.

Kapoian, Seta. "On the Threshold," *Ararat* (Winter, 1979):14-17.

Khach'atryan, Hayk. *Hayuhiner*. Yerevan: Zangak, 2001.

Ledger, Sally. *The New Woman: Fiction and feminism at the fin de siècle*. Manchester: Manchester University Press, 1997.

Libaridian, Gerard. "The Changing Armenian Self-Image in the Ottoman Empire: Rayahs andRevolutionaries." In *The Armenian Image in History and Literature*, ed. Richard G. Hovannisian, 155–169. Malibu, California: Undena Publications, 1981.

Macmillan, James F. *France and women 1789–1914*. London: Routledge, 2000.

Mamurian, Matteos. "Hrrip'simé Krt'aser Ënkerut'iun." *Arevelian Mamul* (May 1881):182.

Maynard, Mary. "Privilege and Patriarchy: Feminist Thought in the Nineteenth Century." In *Sexuality and Subordination*, ed. Susan Mendus and Jane Rendall, 221–247. London: Routledge, 1989.

Mazian, Florence. "The Patriarchal Armenian Family System:1914." *Armenian Review* 36 (Winter 1983):14–26.

Mead, Karen. "Beneficient Maternalism: Agrentine Motherhood in Comparative Perspective, 1880–1920." *Journal of Women's History* (Autumn 2000):120–145.

Mellor, Anne K. *Mothers of the Nation*. Bloomington & Indianapolis: Indiana University Press, 2000.

Merguerian, Barbara. "The Beginnings of Secondary Education for Armenian Women: The Armenian Female Seminary in Constantinople," *Journal of the Society for Armenian Studies* 5 (1990–1991):103–123.

Miller, Jane Eldridge. *Rebel Women: Feminism, Modernism and the Edwardian Novel*. London: Virago Press, 1994.

Minasyan, Arpik. *Sipil*. Yerevan: Yerevani Hamalsarani Hratarakch'ut'iun, 1980.

Moses, Claire Goldberg. *French Feminism in the Nineteenth Century*. Albany N.Y.: State University of New York Press, 1984.

Najmabadi, Afsaneh. "Crafting an Educated Housewife in Iran." In *Remaking Women: Feminism and Modernity in the Middle East*, ed. Lila Abu-Lughod, Princeton, New Jersey: Princeton University Press, 1998.

Nalbandian, Louise. *The Armenian Revolutionary Movement*. Berkely, California: University of California Press, 1963.

Nichanian, Marc. *Writers of Disaster*. Princeton and London: Gomidas Institute, 2002.

Offen, Karen. *European Feminisms, 1700–1950: A Political History*. Stanford: Stanford University Press, 2000.

Ohmann, Carol. "Emily Brontë in the Hands of Male Critics." In *Feminist Literary Theory,* ed. Mary Eagleton, 105–109. Oxford: Blackwell Publishers, 1996.

Oshagan, Hagop. *Hamapatker Arevmtahay Grakanutyan.* Vol.6. Beirut: Hamazgayini Hratarakch'ut'iun, 1968.

Oshagan,Vahe. "Cultural and Literary Awakening of Western Armenians, 1789–1915." *Armenian Review* 36 (Autumn 1983):57–70.

———. "Modernization in Western Armenian Literature." *Armenian Review* 36 (Spring1983):62–75.

———. "A Brief Survey of Literature." *Review of National Literatures*: Armenia 13, (1984):28-44.

———. "Cosmopolitanism in West Armenian Literature." *Review of National Literatures: Armenia* 13 (1984): 194–213.

———. *The English Influence on West Armenian Literature in the Nineteenth Century.* Cleveland, Ohio: Caravan Books, 1990.

Parlakian, Nishan and Peter Cowe, eds. *Modern Armenian Drama.* New York: Columbia University Press, 2001.

Patrick, Mary. *A Bosporus Adventure.* California: Stanford University Press, 1934.

Peroomian, Rubina. *Literary Responses to Catastrophe.* Atlanta, Georgia: Scholars Press, 1993.

Rosenthal, Charlotte. "Women Prose Writers, 1885–1917." In *Gender and Russian Literature*, ed. Rosalind Marsh. Cambridge: Cambridge University Press, 1996.

Rostam-Kolayi, Jasmin. "Foreign Education, the Women's Press, and the Discourse of Scientific Domesticity in Early Twentieth-Century Iran." In *Iran and the Surrounding World: Interactions in Culture and Cultural Politics*, ed. Nikki Keddie and Rudi Mathee, 182–202. Seattle: University of Washington Press, 2002

Russ, Joanna. *How To Suppress Women's Writing.* London: Women's Press, 1983.

Sahakian, Marietta. "Armenian Women in Politics." In *Women with University Education Bulletin* (June 1999):8–10.

Sanasarian, Eliz. "Gender Distinction in the Genocidial Process: A Preliminary Study of the Armenian Case." *Holocaust and Genocide Studies.* vol.4. (1989): 449–461.

Sandel, Cora. *Alberta and Freedom*. Translated by Elizabeth Rokkan. London: Peter Owen Ltd., 1963.

Scarce, Jennifer. *Women's Costume of the Near and Middle East*. London: Unwin Hyman, 1987.

Sellers, Susan. *Language and Sexual Difference*. Basingstoke, Hampshire: Macmillan Press, 1991.

Sharuryan, A.S. *Srpuhi Dussap*. Yerevan: Yerevani Betakan Hamalsarani Hratarakch'ut'iun, 1963.

Shipley, Alice Muggerditchian. *We Walked Then Ran*. Phoenix, Arizona: By the author, 1983.

Shirinian, Lorne. *Survivor Memoirs of the Armenian Genocide*. Reading, England: Taderon Press, 1999.

Spender, Dale, ed. *Feminist Theorists: Three Centuries of Women's Intellectual Traditions*. London: Women's Press, 1983.

Stites, Richard. *The Women's Liberation Movement in Russia*. Princeton, Princeton University Press, 1978.

Suny, Ronald Grigor. *Looking Toward Ararat*. Bloomington, Indiana: Indiana University Press, 1993.

Szyliowicz, Irene. *Pierre Loti and the Oriental Woman*. Basingstoke, Hampshire: Macmillan Press, 1988.

Taft, Elise Hagopian. *Rebirth*. Plandome, N.Y.: New Age Publishers, 1981.

Tavakoli-Targhi, Mohamad. *Refashioning Iran: Orientalism, Occidentalism and Historiography*. Basingstoke, Hampshire: Palgrave, 2001.

Thorossian, Hiranth. *Historie de la littérature Arménienne*. Paris: Araxes, 1951.

Tololyan, Khachig. "The Representation of Woman's Desire in Zabel Esayian's  Verchin Pazhag'eh." *Ararat* (Autumn, 1988):81–85.

Topalian, Naomi. *Dust to Destiny*. Watertown, MA: Baikar Publications, 1986.

Vahan Totovents. *Scenes from an Armenian Childhood*. Translated by Misha Kudian. London: Oxford University Press, 1962.

Toumanian, Hovhannes. "Maron" [Maro]. In *Entir Yerker*. Yerevan: Sovetakan Grogh Hratarakch'ut'iun, 1978.

Versluysen, Margaret Connor. "Midwives, medical men, and 'poor women labouring of child': lying-in hospitals in 18th century London." In *Women, Health and Reproduction*, ed. Helen Roberts. London: Routledge and Kegan Paul, 1981.

Villa, Susie Hoogasian and Mary Kilbourne Matosian. *Armenian Village Life Before 1914*. Detroit: Wayne State University Press, 1982.

Waelti-Walters, Jennifer. *Feminist Novelists of the Belle Époque*. Bloomington and Indianapolis: Indiana University Press, 1990.

Wellington, Jan. "Blurring the Borders of Nation and Gender: MaryWollstonecraft's Character (R)evolution," in *Rebellious Hearts: British Women Writers and the French Revolution*, ed. Adriana Craciun and Kari E. Lokke. Albany, New York: SUNY, 2001.

Woolf, Virginia. *A Room of One's Own*, cited in *Feminist Literary Theory,* 2nd ed., ed. Mary Eagleton, 9–10. Oxford: Blackwell Publishers, 1996.

_____. "Professions for Women," in *Death of the Moth* (1942), cited in *Feminist Literary Theory*, 2d ed. ed., Mary Eagleton, 78–80. Oxford: Blackwell Publishers, 1996.

Yessayan, Zabel. Gardens of Silihdar and Other Writings. Translated by Ara Baliozian. New York: Ashod Press, 1982.

Young, Pamela. "Knowledge, Nation and the Curriculum: Ottoman Armenian Education (1853–1915)." Ph.D. diss., University of Michigan, 2001.

Zeitlian, Sona. *Hay Knoj Dere Hay Heghapokhakan Sharzhman Mej.* Los Angeles: Hraztan Sarkis Zeitlian Publications, 1992.

_____. "Pioneers of Women's Journalism in the Western Armenian Media, 1862–1968." In *Voices of Armenian Women*, ed. Barbara Mergeurian and Joy Renjilian Burgy, 119–141. Belmont, Mass.: AIWA Press, 2000.

Zekiyan, Boghos Levon. "Personal Tragedy and Cultural Backgrounds in the Poetry of Bedros Tourian." *Review of National Literatures: Armenia*, Vol 13. (1984): 121–149.

_____. "Modern Armenian Culture." In *Armenian Perspectives*, ed. Nicholas Awde. Richmond, Surrey: Curzon Press, 1997.

Ziegler, Theresa Huntington. *Great Need Over the Water*. Edited by Stina Katchadourian. Ann Arbor, Michigan: Gomidas Institute, 1999.

Zohrab, Krikor. *Yerkeri Zoghovatsu*. Vol.1. Yerevan: Haypethrat, 1962.

# INDEX